ECOLOGY AND DEMOCRACY

Ecology and Democracy

edited by

Freya Mathews

FRANK CASS
LONDON • PORTLAND, OR

First published in 1996 in Great Britain by
FRANK CASS & CO. LTD.
Crown House, 47 Chase Side
Southgate, London N14 5BP

and in the United States of America by
FRANK CASS
c/o ISBS
5824 N.E. Hassalo Street
Portland, Oregon 97213-3644

Copyright © 1996 Frank Cass & Co. Ltd.

Reprinted 2002

British Library Cataloguing in Publication Data

A catalogue record for this book is available
from the British Library

ISBN 0-7146-4252-5 (paperback)

Library of Congress Cataloging in Publication Data

Ecology and Democracy / edited by Freya Mathews.
        p.   cm.
    Originally published in 1995 as v. 4, no. 4 of Environmental Politics.
    Includes bibliographical references.
    ISBN 0-7146-4252-5 (pbk)
    1. Ecology–Political aspects. 2. Environmentalism. 3. Green
    movement. 4. Democracy.   I. Mathews, Freya, 1949–
JA75.8.E28   1996   96-14009
322.4'4–dc20   CIP

Website: www.frankcass.com

This group of studies first appeared in a Special Issue:
'Ecology and Democracy' of *Environmental Politics*, Vol.4, No.4,
published by Frank Cass & Co. Ltd.

Typeset by Frank Cass & Co. Ltd.

Printed and bound by Antony Rowe Ltd, Eastbourne

Contents

Introduction

FREYA MATHEWS

This collection originated in a research project based in Australia which involved a group of scholars meeting and corresponding over a two-year period. This explains why the collection has an Australian flavour, and why there is a certain amount of 'conversation' and cross-referencing amongst the pieces. The focus of our discussion was the question whether liberal democracies are, even in principle, capable of responding adequately to the environmental challenge in its regional and global dimensions: are they capable of sustaining the degree of environmental reform demanded by the ecological crisis? If not, is there any form of democracy better equipped to meet this challenge, or is there ultimately just an irreconcilable tension between the ideals of democracy and contemporary environmental imperatives? Most of the members of the research group agreed that democracy in some form was indeed our best hope for true environmental sustainability. What we disagreed upon was which form of democracy could best deliver environmental reform and whether the degree of reform it could be expected to deliver would be enough.

Of course, no-one at present knows what degree of reform *would* be 'enough': estimates of the degree of reform required to meet the global ecological crisis will vary according to our assumptions about what should be preserved. From a strictly anthropocentric perspective, only those aspects or components of the biosphere which have utility for human beings need to be conserved or preserved; from a biocentric or ecocentric perspective, the entire biosphere is entitled to our moral consideration, and should not be damaged or utilised beyond the point necessary for the satisfaction of basic (or vital [*Naess, 1989*]) human needs. (Since a large enough human presence on the planet would monopolise the resources of the biosphere even if human individuals satisfied only their basic needs, an

Freya Mathews teaches in the School of Philosophy, La Trobe University, Australia. The editor would like to give very special thanks to Robyn Eckersley, and also to Robert Young and Janna Thompson, for their patient and unstinting help and advice throughout this rather protracted project. Thanks, too, to all the participants in the *Ecology and Democracy* research group. Tony Coady and the Centre for Philosophy and Public Issues at the University of Melbourne made the project possible, and provided ongoing support. Thanks to Rachel Sommerville for administrative assistance and to Marilyn Richmond for extensive and arcane word processing. Parts of this Introduction were originally published in the *Legal Services Bulletin*, Vol.16, No.4 (1991).

ecocentric regime would also entail management of human population.)

It is worth noting here that opting for either the anthropocentric or the ecocentric perspective in this connection does not in itself immediately resolve the indeterminacy surrounding this question of the degree of reform required effectively to address the ecological crisis. For if an anthropocentric approach is adopted, there will be an unavoidable tendency to err on the side of saving too little rather than too much, since every part of the natural environment which is spared will be perceived as a *loss* to humanity – the energy such spared portions of nature use or embody could generally, in principle, be converted into other forms of energy which *would* be utilisable by humanity. So, leaving wetlands for the birds, for instance, would be seen, from an anthropocentric perspective, as effectively a waste, or even a *theft* against humanity, since either the biological reserves of the wetlands, or the land itself, could be turned over to human use.[1] Anthropocentrism thus generates a certain pressure to harness more rather than less of the biosphere to direct human use, and in the absence of a thorough understanding of global ecology, the potential encroachment into vital systems this implies constitutes a threat to the viability of the biosphere.

Ecocentrism in contrast offers a clearer goal for reform: from an ecocentric point of view we are called upon simply to *minimise* absolutely our impact on the natural world – as far as possible simply to let things be. An appeal to the 'precautionary principle', in a broadly prudential sense thereof, might at this point suggest that the potential of any political system to effect environmental reform should, in the first instance at any rate, be tested against an ecocentric rather than an anthropocentric standard. A capacity to ensure the viability of the biosphere is the minimal requirement for any standard of reform, and since we know that ecocentric reform has this capacity but do not know whether anthropocentric reform has it, it would seem that, in order to be on the safe side, we should, at least initially, test political systems against ecocentric standards.

In framing the agenda for the *Ecology and Democracy* research project, then, it was clearly important that, regardless of where individual participants stood on the anthropocentrism/ecocentrism issue, the project should keep in view the question of whether or to what extent liberal and other forms of democracy are capable of protecting nature for its own sake, as well as for the sake of humankind. An ecocentric yardstick of reform is accordingly at least in the background, and occasionally in the foreground, of most of the contributions.

In the original discussion paper for the project [*Mathews, 1991*], three questions were posed as problem areas for the project to address. These questions, with subsequent elaborations, were as follows:

(i) Can a democratic system respond adequately to crisis when the crisis is not directly 'visible'– that is, when it is identifiable to experts and to persons specially briefed, but not to ordinary citizens?

(ii) What is the relation of ethics to democracy? Are democratic systems based on moral values or on self-interest? If they rest ultimately on self-interest, can they guarantee adequate protection of the natural world?

(iii) What in fact constitutes the best political scenario for environmental reform? Would such reform best be facilitated by the devolution of power away from the state into local communities, or by the centralisation of power into federal and international agencies?

The first question raises the issue of whether, in a parliamentary democracy, a government would be hypothetically justified in, and capable of, over-riding the will of its citizens for the sake of a long-term good not fully recognised by them. One immediate response to this question might be to insist that since democracy hinges on the social awareness of its citizens, its citizens must be educated so as to be capable of appreciating and therefore demanding important goods. However, this response overlooks the fact that even though education is fundamental to the viability of democracy, the members of a given democratic system may not recognise this, and may thus refuse to support adequate education programmes in their own communities. In other words, education may itself be one of the vital goods that citizens fail to appreciate and consequently fail to mandate governments to provide. Moreover, even if citizens were fully cognisant of the ecological crisis and apprised of the need for environmental reform, they might still be reluctant to subordinate their immediate interests to such a long-term and seemingly abstract good.

Indeed, in the Western world in the late 1980s we experienced a great popular awakening to environmental concern. The extreme gravity and urgency of the global ecological crisis were conveyed to the public by sustained media exposure of the problem. The public became alarmed, and individuals began, in small ways, to modify their consumption patterns – giving preference, for instance, to 'environment-friendly' products. They appeared to be anxious that governments should act. At the same time, however, there was a sense that, having switched to benign products and signalled their concern to governments, ordinary citizens were absolved from any further responsibility, and could simply hand the problem over to the authorities. It may be, however, that the lifestyle changes that the ecological crisis demands are broader and deeper than the public is willing to acknowledge, and that the social and economic costs of these changes would be higher than the public would be prepared to accept. (That this may be so is evidenced by the general reluctance of electorates in parliamentary democracies to vote green parties into office.) Lacking a popular mandate for vital environmental reforms then, a democratic government would appear to have little power to implement them, and even if it had the power, its justification for doing so would be questionable.

The answer we give to the first question depends to a certain extent on our answer to the second, for the issue of whether or not a government should pursue a significant good without a mandate from its people depends partly on whether the good in question is a good of the people themselves or another kind of good. If it is their own collective interest that the people fail to appreciate, then the government may be justified in (though probably not capable of) pursuing that interest in a unilateral fashion. But if it is a moral good of another kind – for instance, the good of other species or life forms – that the people fail to appreciate, then it is even more questionable that a democratic government would be justified in pursuing it without the support of its people.

This brings us to the second question. Should policy in democratic systems have moral or purely pragmatic foundations? Although Western democracies were built, with much trumpeting, on the liberal values of freedom and equality, their moral rhetoric is currently sustained by appeals to self-interest. In liberal philosophy the moral values of freedom and equality are in fact rationally 'justified' in terms of such self-interest. This 'rational' attitude to morality presupposes a basically contractual and instrumental model of society. From the viewpoint of this model, individuals are assumed to support society and the state to the extent that they perceive it as being in their own long-term interest to do so. (Such a self-interested rationale for society does not necessarily preclude a willingness to extend protection to minorities and disadvantaged groups, since a given individual can never be entirely certain that she or he will not some day become a member of such a group: a minimal level of humaneness is, in most circumstances at any rate, in the interests of all.) Competing politicians accordingly waste little time appealing to the moral conscience of voters, and such appeals are currently generally regarded as outside the proper sphere of politics in any case. Politics is seen as the art of balancing the conflicting demands of self-interested groups.

Such a conception of politics relieves politicians of any responsibility for considering the interests of those who are not even potentially party to the social contract – for example, non-human beings. In so far as the protection of the natural world serves the long-term interests of the parties to the social contract, those parties can be expected to require of the state that it provide such protection. But to the extent that the (human) benefits of exploiting the natural world outweigh the (human) benefits of protecting it, the state will be justified in such exploitation. Without any fundamental commitment to altruism or to the protection of life as an end in itself, the liberal state has no obligation to defend the interests of those who cannot even potentially represent their interests in the political arena. This might cause us to consider whether the project of environmental reform involves revising the contractarian and instrumentalist presuppositions of the contemporary liberal state, and envisaging a new role for ethics in public life.

It is worth expanding on this question a little more,[2] because what is at issue here is whether liberalism, as it stands, does indeed have the ideological resources to protect the natural environment. Liberalism as it stands is, of course, anthropocentric in its outlook: it takes human interest as the measure of all value. This anthropocentrism stems from its dualistic conception of human nature: human beings enjoy metaphysical equality on account of their essential human-ness, where human-ness is taken to be constituted by reason, a faculty which is supposedly unique to our species, setting us above the rest of nature.[3] In the context of this anthropocentrism – this view that moral consideration is the exclusive prerogative of human beings – liberalism seeks to deal with the problem of environmental protection by treating nature as a set of resources for human use, resources which must be distributed and conserved in accordance with liberal principles of justice. Liberal philosophers seek to limit the destructive use that individuals and corporations make of the environment basically by appeal to the 'harm principle': the freedom of one group to use a particular resource has to be offset not only against alternative uses that other groups might wish to make of it, but against the harm that such use might occasion for non-interested parties. The main ideological innovation that liberal philosophers introduce into their arguments in addressing the problem of environmental degradation or resource exhaustion is the idea that the harm principle applies not only to present individuals but to future generations. Our use of the environment must be such as not to harm or unduly disadvantage human beings of the future as well as of the present.

Will such a concern for posterity suffice? Will it enable our society to provide adequate safeguards for the natural world? John Passmore, for one, argues that environmentalism can be accommodated within a traditional liberal framework [*Passmore, 1974*]. Governments in Western democratic states can legislate to prevent the kind of environmental degradation and exhaustion that directly harms present and future human beings, and parliamentary democracy provides opportunities for people with special environmental interests or concerns to have their case heard and their claims weighed by their political representatives. But within this framework the only ground for the protection of nature is human utility. And since the economic demands of developers are likely to outweigh the aesthetic and spiritual needs of 'nature lovers' in any utilitarian scheme of things, the 'nature' that will end up being conserved will be a managed, economically optimised one, rather than a wild nature. This will mean tree farms instead of native forests, gene banks instead of rainforests, domestic animals instead of wild ones. In other words there will be little incentive, within this framework, to protect the ecological diversity, stability and richness of life on earth. It may be that a new, biocentric or ecocentric ethic which respects the interests of other life forms and living systems for their own sake rather than for their human utility is necessary to provide such an incentive and, if the natural world is to receive adequate protection, such an ethic may need to become operative in public life. In other words, while it can be argued that morality has traditionally been superfluous in politics because the liberal democratic system satisfied our basic moral requirements without needing to appeal to the conscience of its members, this may no longer be the case in the context of the ecological crisis. While it may have been theoretically possible for the state to serve moral values – in the shape of the collective interest – while appealing only to the long-term self-interest of individuals, it may not be possible for the state to serve the moral values associated with the natural environment in the same way. A new moral dimension of life that cannot be encompassed within liberal ideology may have been brought into view by the ecological crisis.

The third question which was identified above asked whether the project of environmental reform is best served by the centralisation or the decentralisation of political power. Some authors argue that centralisation of power, with its attendant authoritarianism, is the inevitable response of governments to the ecological crisis [*Heilbroner, 1974; Ophuls, 1977*]. Others point to the emphasis on participative democracy within the contemporary environment movement itself.[4] But we may wonder whether either of these views really gets to grips with the issue. Those, like Ophuls and Heilbroner, who argue that only authoritarian regimes will have the political muscle to enforce the socio-economic restructuring the ecological crisis will require, fail to acknowledge that those who win power in authoritarian regimes are likely to be those least likely to exercise it responsibly in the interests of either the human or the non-human community. Those who are reassured by the democratic nature of the environment movement itself, on the other hand, fail to take due account of the fact that the environment movement has historically engaged only in rearguard measures and has concentrated its efforts on such conservation and preservation issues as pollution control and the protection of wilderness areas.

As it becomes increasingly clear that environmental problems are the outcome of ecologically unsound attitudes and practices in virtually all spheres of life, the relevance of the traditional environment movement fades. Rearguard measures will no longer suffice to solve problems which are a function of the fundamental organisation of society. Such problems can only be solved if ecological values are incorporated into the entire fabric of social life. But the transformation of the structure of society is a goal that is well beyond the scope and aspirations of the traditional environment movement, and is accordingly a goal which demands new strategies. The fact that the traditional environment movement has favoured democratic strategies therefore in itself fails to decide the issue of whether the new, transformative goal – which is in fact the goal of the recently emerged green movement – calls for democratic or non-democratic strategies.

I have already remarked on some of the limitations of liberal democratic systems *vis-à-vis* the ecological crisis. In light of these it seems doubtful that wholesale environmental reform can be achieved wholly within this traditional framework, even with the advent of green parties. The green movement itself, like its predecessor the environment movement, favours participative structures and strategies that are more reminiscent of anarchism than of liberalism. These strategies can be effective for specific campaigns, and the devolution of ecological responsibility to local communities can be highly effective for certain kinds of environmental issues, such as waste disposal and pesticide control in populated regions. But such strategies seem unlikely to succeed in transforming the socioeconomic structure of society as a whole, or in addressing either environmental issues in remote regions, such as soil degradation and desertification, or global environmental issues, such as the greenhouse effect or tropical deforestation. These goals appear to call for centralist strategies which defy the decentralist proclivities of the green movement.

These questions then – of political motivation, morality and the distribution of power – were those originally addressed by our research group. New questions of course surfaced as dialogue unfolded. But two common themes emerged in our 'conversation', and these were still identifiably, if tenuously, related to the original questions. These themes were, firstly, a concern with the relation between ecological morality (green values) and political structures or procedures: are certain political systems conducive to the development of a green moral outlook, or are the moral outlooks of citizens formed independently of political systems?[5] The second theme to emerge in several of the contributions was related to the centralisation/decentralisation issue, and involved an exploration of the idea of democracy without traditional boundaries. 'Unbounded democracy' was understood differently by different authors, but it was in each case seen as a key both to environmentalism, and to the re-vitalisation of democracy itself, in an ecological and transnational world. In the remainder of this introduction, I shall say a little about the approaches of each of the contributors to these and other questions.

In his contribution 'Political and Ecological Communication', John Dryzek argues that any political or economic system embodies imperatives or emergent properties that take effect whatever the intentions of agents within the system. This is true for both capitalism and liberal democracy, and neither of these systems is particularly conducive to ecologically desirable outcomes. What is needed is a new form of *communicative* rather than liberal democracy – that is, a form of democracy dedicated to the maximisation of communication rather than preference aggregation. This conception of democracy may be seen to lead to a dissolution of the traditional boundaries of democratic communities, and in particular, for ecological purposes, to a dissolution of the boundary between human society and nature: nature becomes a co-respondent in the new system, capable of sending signals which may be received and integrated into the deliberative processes whereby policy is formed. In this way, nature becomes a party to the democratic process. The forms that such unbounded democracy may take are prefigured by contemporary social movements, which are not limited by formal boundaries or jurisdictions, or 'obsolete notions of national sovereignty', but are variable in scope.

Janna Thompson offers a similar proposal. After considering the challenge to political systems implicit in the global ecological crisis, she concludes that this crisis, and the related crises of global poverty and war, call for a re-ordering of world society. The new order will be comprised of structures endowed with the flexibility required to respond to the complex and variable manifestations of the current global malaise; these structures will also be capable of motivating people to comply with far-reaching reform measures (that is, they will promote the flourishing of green values amongst their members). Thompson sees the germ of such structures in certain existing regionally unbounded forms of organisation, such as transnational activist networks and social movements, heritage preservation movements, and non-governmental organisations such as Greenpeace.

John Burnheim attributes the failure of our existing parliamentary systems to respond adequately to the environmental crisis not to their democratic nature, but to a characteristic which he sees as common to all political systems to date, namely their proclivity for encouraging power trading. Power trading involves each politician in trading her support in matters to which she is relatively indifferent for the support of others in matters in which she has an interest. This is a system which leads to sub-optimal outcomes across the board, as decisions are made neither on merit nor on relevant criteria, but in accord with the dictates of 'the numbers game'. Burnheim's remedy for this is an entirely new form of political organisation, which he calls 'demarchy', and which discards the traditional boundaries of democratic societies and distributes power on functional rather than on regional lines. Such a system would ensure that environmental policies were made and administered by informed decision-makers with a direct interest in the outcomes of their decisions. Demarchic organisations may be local or international, and to the extent that society is organised in this way it will consist of a variety of semi-autonomous but interlocking functional systems, each with its own set of tasks to perform, but each also depending on some of the other systems to maintain the conditions for its continued operation.

In my own contribution I start by looking for the kind of social conditions that might be expected to foster an ecocentric moral outlook in individual members of society, and I find these conditions in community rather than in liberal forms of democracy. Small face-to-face communities, I argue, unlike liberal societies, provide conditions for the growth of selves predisposed to empathy, and hence open to the possibility of an ecocentric outlook. (In this I am in agreement with Ian Barns.) I emphasise that such 'ecological selves' should be understood in relational rather than holistic terms, where this emphasis on relationality helps us to distinguish eco-communitarianism from abstract forms of collectivism, such as nationalism and globalism. However, in light of some of the shortcomings of eco-community in a local sense as a vehicle for ecopolitical resistance in a world of transnational corporate capitalism, I argue that communities can and should also take 'unbounded', transnational forms. Examples of such transnational communities include some of the activist networks alluded to by Dryzek and Thompson.

Ian Barns argues that communitarian forms of 'radical democracy', being participatory and dialogical, afford a favorable framework both for formulating, and for creating the kinds of selves capable of implementing, an ecocentric moral agenda. However he also argues that community itself depends upon an underlying moral and metaphysical (possibly spiritual) vision – or conception of the good – held in common by its members. If such a vision is to be adequate to the experience of the postmodern world, it must accommodate plurality and difference – without sacrificing itself to liberal relativism – and through this accommodation of otherness it is likely to open up new – potentially ecocentric – vistas in our relation to the natural world.

Val Plumwood mounts an extensive critique of liberalism based on its promotion, in its present capitalist forms, of extreme social inequalities, which are naturalised by a dualistic culture which identifies those in positions of privilege with reason and assimilates those in positions of disadvantage to nature. This failure of egalitarianism in liberalism then is intimately linked with a deep-seated philosophical contempt for nature, and this effectively entails a regime of environmental destruction or negligence. An ecological polity can thus only be achieved through forms of democracy which restore egalitarianism, yet egalitarianism in turn is realisable only through a reconceptualisation of nature: the project of realising a genuinely democratic polity is thus intertwined with that of achieving an ecological one.

In a departure from the critiques of liberalism advanced in most of the other contributions, Robyn Eckersley considers whether liberal democracy, taken to its logical conclusion, might not encompass ecocentrism, and in this respect turn out to be a logically appropriate vehicle for ecocentric politics. She proceeds by an examination of the notion of rights, and its applicability to non-human life. If liberalism is understood as the political expression of the moral assumption that every human individual has the right to be allowed to flourish in his or her own way without undue interference from arbitrary authorities, and if ecocentrism is understood as the view that non-human forms of life are morally entitled to flourish in their own way, without undue interference from human agencies, then it would appear that liberalism could be extended to accommodate ecocentrism: non-human forms of life would be granted the right to live and flourish just as human beings are, and appropriate constitutional or legal advocacy arrangements could be set in place to give political force and realisability to these rights. The difficulty with adapting the rights discourse to ecological ends in this way, however, according to Eckersley, is that rights can only meaningfully attach to individuals, and not all non-human life forms can be individuated. This discourse thus has a limited – though not for that reason discountable – utility as a vehicle for ecopolitics.

Where other contributors have evaluated various forms of democracy in terms of their capacity to foster ecological morality, Robert Young takes a particular 'moral' practice adopted by some radical ecologists, namely monkeywrenching, and considers whether or not it is democratic. Or, more accurately, he considers whether such a practice is morally justifiable, and in particular whether it is consistent with democracy. He dismisses the suggestion that monkeywrenching constitutes a form of terrorism, and characterises it instead as a form of civil disobedience. As such, it may be seen as both morally justifiable and as promoting the democratic process, by allowing those whose views have been under-represented in contemporary liberal forms of democracy to inform their fellow citizens, and possibly stir their ecological conscience. Young concludes that monkeywrenching represents a legitimate way in which individuals may seek to raise ecological awareness within the framework of existing societies.

Bronwyn Hayward (whose contribution was, incidentally, produced independently of the *Ecology and Democracy* research group) notes the disaffection of many radical ecologists with liberal forms of democracy, and their preference for participatory forms thereof, where this preference is based on the assumption that participatory forms of democracy are both more environmentally efficacious and more democratic than liberal forms. Hayward sets out to test this assumption. She draws on the democratic theories of John Dryzek and Iris Marion Young in an attempt to address practical problems that arose out of recent experiences with participatory forms of environmental decision-making in New Zealand. She finds that while the theories of Dryzek and Young do help to solve some of these problems, they conspicuously fail to solve others, including the most serious. It would seem to follow that the faith of radical ecologists in a pre-established 'fit' between ecology and participatory forms of democracy needs to be subjected to further scrutiny.

NOTES

1. Of course, leaving wetlands for the birds might entail certain aesthetic or psychological benefits for some humans, but in a hungry or greedy world, such benefits are not likely to weigh heavily in the scales against more material uses of the lands in question.
2. For further thoughts on this question, see my contribution in the present collection.
3. A great deal of feminist literature has focussed on the dualistic theory of human nature presupposed by liberal political philosophy. See, for instance, Jaggar [*1983*].
4. Eco-anarchists, such as Murray Bookchin, and bioregionalists, ecofeminists, deep ecologists and other radical ecologists all tend to insist on an intrinsic connection between the ecology movement and participative or face-to-face democracy. This position is investigated by a number of authors in the present collection.
5. This distinction – between ecological morality and political systems – echoes a distinction drawn by Goodin [*1992*] between 'green values' and 'green agency'. Goodin defines green values in terms of a set of ends related to the protection and preservation of nature, and green agency in terms of the political procedures and strategies by which these ends might be realised. He argues that green values are independent of green agency, and hence that environmentalism is not a matter of devising new political systems, but of bringing green values to bear on existing systems. Most of the authors in this collection in one way or another contest this view.

REFERENCES

Goodin, Robert (1992), *Green Political Theory*, Cambridge: Polity Press
Heilbroner, Robert (1974), *An Inquiry into the Human Prospect*, New York: Norton & Co.
Jaggar, Alison (1983), *Feminist Politics and Human Nature*, Totowa, NJ: Rowman & Allanheld.
Mathews, Freya (1991), 'Democracy and the Ecological Crisis', *Legal Services Bulletin*, Vol.16, No.4.
Naess, Arne (1989), *Ecology, Community and Lifestyle*, Cambridge: Cambridge University Press; translated by David Rothenberg.

Ophuls, William (1977), *Ecology and the Politics of Scarcity*, San Francisco, CA: W.H. Freeman
    & Co.
Passmore, John (1974), *Man's Responsibility for Nature*, London: Duckworth.

Political and Ecological Communication

JOHN S. DRYZEK

Democracy is a matter of effective communication, not just preference aggregation. Normally it is only communication among humans about human interests that is at issue. But democracy can also exist or be denied in human dealings with the natural world. Ecological democratisation is therefore a matter of better integration of political and ecological communication. Principles of ecological democracy can be used both to criticise existing institutional arrangements, and to inspire a search for alternative institutions that would better integrate politics and ecology.

We can, I believe, best explore the prospects for an effective green democracy by working with a political model whose essence is authentic communication rather than, say, preference aggregation, representation, or partisan competition. The ecological context means that the kind of communicative democracy that ensues ought to take a particular shape or shapes. This shape depends not on the set of values through reference to which democrats have always justified their projects, though such values have an important place in any contemplation of appropriate political structure. It is, more importantly, a question of some political forms being better able to enter into fruitful engagement with natural systems than others, and so more effectively cope with the ecological challenge.

Why we Need Green Structures, not just Green Values

Inasmuch as there is a conventional wisdom on the matter of ecology and democracy, it would draw a sharp distinction between procedure and substance. As Robert Goodin [*1992: 168*] puts it, 'To advocate democracy is to advocate procedures, to advocate environmentalism is to advocate substantive outcomes'. And there can never be any guarantee that

John Dryzek is Professor of Political Science in the Politics Department, University of Melbourne. For helpful comments, the author would like to thank the other participants in the Melbourne *Democracy and the Environment* Working Group, especially Robyn Eckersley, Freya Mathews and Val Plumwood; Robert Goodin; David Schlosberg; and audiences at Griffith University's School of Australian Environmental Studies, Australian National University's Research School of Social Sciences, and the Ecopolitics VII conference.

democratic procedure will produce ecologically benign substance. This distinction between procedure and substance forms the core of Goodin's [1992] treatment of green political theory. To Goodin, the green theory of value represents a coherent set of ends related to the protection and preservation of nature, whereas the green theory of agency addresses where and how these values might be promoted. Goodin argues that a green theory of agency cannot be derived from the green theory of value. Greens may still want to advocate, say, grassroots participatory democracy; but they should recognise that any such advocacy has to be on grounds separate from basic green values. This procedure/substance divide arises most graphically in the context of green advocacy of decentralisation and community self-control. Such decentralisation of political authority would have decidely anti-ecological substantive consequences in many places with natural-resource-based local economies. Many counties in the Western United States are currently trying to assert their authority against federal environmental legislation (so far with little success in the courts) in order that mining, grazing on federal lands, and forest clearcutting can proceed unchecked. Decentralisation will only work to the extent that local recipients of authority subscribe to ecological values or, alternatively, the degree to which they must stay put and depend for their livelihoods solely on what can be produced locally.

On this kind of account, political structure obviously matters far less than the adoption of green values on the part of denizens in that structure, or the occupancy of key positions (such as membership in parliament) in that structure by greens. Along these lines, Eckersley [1992] concludes that the key to green political transformation is the dissemination and adoption of ecocentric culture. In fairness, she also addresses the issue of political structure, though the kind of structure she advocates is quite close to what already exists in federal liberal democracies. Similarly, to Goodin the key to green politics is participation in electoral politics and coalition with other parties in an effort to ensure that governments in liberal democracies adopt, if only partially and incrementally, those parts of the green political agenda inspired by the green theory of value. As he puts it, 'we can, and probably should, accept green political prescriptions without necessarily adopting green ideas about how to reform political structures and processes' [Goodin, 1992: 5].

The trouble with Goodin's position here is that it regards political agency as essentially unproblematical. In other words, all that has to be done is to convince people in positions of political authority that X should be pursued, and X will be pursued. Goodin's 'X' is in fact a rather large one: he considers (and I agree) that the green programme merits adoption on an all-or-nothing basis. But there are good reasons why dominant political mechanisms cannot adopt and implement that programme, or even substantial chunks of it, irrespective of the degree to which green values are adopted by participants in these mechanisms. For any complex system, be it economic, political, ecological, or social, embodies imperatives or emergent properties that take effect regardless of the intentions of the denizens of the system. Such imperatives constitute values that the system will seek. Other values will be downplayed or ignored.

To begin with the currently dominant order of capitalist democracy, all liberal democracies currently operate in the context of a capitalist market system. Any state operating in the context of such a system is greatly constrained in terms of the kinds of policies it can pursue. Policies that damage business profitability – or are even perceived as likely to damage that profitability – are automatically punished by the recoil of the market. Disinvestment here means economic downturn. And such downturn is bad for governments because it both reduces the tax revenue for the schemes those governments want to pursue (such as environmental restoration), and reduces the popularity of the government in the eyes of the voters. This effect is not a matter of conspiracy or direct corporate influence on government; it happens automatically, irrespective of anyone's intentions.

The constraints upon governments here are intensified by the increasing mobility of capital across national boundaries. So, for example, anti-pollution regulation in the United States stimulates an exodus of polluting industry across the Rio Grande to Mexico's *maquiladora* sector. Thus irrespective of the ideology of government – and irrespective of the number of green lobbyists, coalition members, or parliamentarians – the first task of any liberal democratic state must always be to secure and maintain profitable conditions for business.

Environmental policy is possible in such states, but only if its damage to business profitability is marginal, or if it can be shown to be good for business. Along these lines, Albert Weale [*1992: 66–92*] discusses the ideology of 'ecological modernisation', which he believes has gained a toehold in German policy-making. More recently, United States Vice-President Albert Gore has pointed to the degree to which environmental protection can actually enhance business profitability. Yet it remains to be demonstrated that a systemic reconciliation of economic and ecological values is achievable here, as opposed to isolated successes on the part of green capitalists. If green demands are more radical, or 'all or nothing' in Goodin's terms, then 'nothing' remains the likely consequence in any clash with economic imperatives.

Even setting aside the economic context of policy determination under capitalist democracy, there remain reasons why the structure of liberal democracy itself is ultimately incapable of responding effectively to ecological problems. To cut a long story short, these problems often feature high degrees of complexity and uncertainty, and substantial collective action problems. Thus any adequate political mechanism for dealing with them must incorporate negative feedback (the ability to generate corrective movement when a natural system's equilibrium is disturbed), coordination across different problems (so that solving a problem in one place does not simply create greater problems elsewhere), coordination across actors (to supply public goods or prevent the tragedy of the commons), robustness (an ability to perform well across different conditions and contexts), flexibility (an ability to adjust internal structure in response to changing conditions), and resilience (an ability to correct for severe disequilibrium, or environmental crisis).[1]

One can debate the degree to which these criteria are met by different political-economic mechanisms, such as markets, administrative hierarchies, and international negotiations, as well as liberal democracies. My own judgment is that liberal democracy does not perform particularly well across these criteria. Negative feedback under liberal democracy is mostly achieved as a result of particular actors whose interests are aggrieved giving political vent to their annoyance, be it in voting for green candidates, lobbying, contributing money to environmentalist interest groups, or demonstrating. But such feedback devices are typically dominated by the representation of economic interests, businesses and (perhaps) labour. Coordination is often problematical because the currency of liberal democracy consists of tangible rewards to particular interests. Such particular interests do not add up to the general ecological interest. Further, complex problems are generally disaggregated on the basis of these same particular interests, and piecemeal responses crafted in each of the remaining subsets. The ensuing 'partisan mutual adjustment', to use Lindblom's [1965] term, may produce a politically rational resultant. But there is no reason to expect this resultant to be ecologically rational. In other words, interests may be placated in proportion to their material political influence, and compromises may be achieved across them, but wholesale ecological destruction can still result. Resilience in liberal democracy is inhibited by short time horizons (resulting from electoral cycles) and a general addiction to the 'political solvent' of economic growth (politics is much happier, and choices easier, when the size of the available financial 'pie' is growing).

Despite its inadequacies, I would argue that among the political mechanisms that have been tried by nations from time to time, liberal democracy is the most ecologically rational system [Dryzek, 1987: Ch.9]. But even setting aside the issue of the ecological adequacy of liberal democracy, and its relative merits compared to other systems, the fact remains that the way political systems are structured can make an enormous difference when it comes to the likelihood or otherwise of realising green values. And if this is true, then (to use Goodin's distinction) we should be able to derive a model of politics from the green theory of value, not just the green theory of agency. Let me now attempt such a derivation.

Biocentric and Anthropocentric Models, and their Inadequacies

What, then, might such a model look like? Would it be democratic? If so, in what sense of democracy? Presumably, what we are looking for is some kind of polity that could embed something more than short-term human material interests, and achieve more sustainable equilibria encompassing natural and human systems. Along these lines, Eckersley [1992] uses the term 'ecocentric' to describe her preferred kind of system. The term 'ecocentric' or 'biocentric' implies that intrinsic value is located in nature, and can connote an absence of regard for human interests, essentially shedding one 'centrism' in favour of another. But Eckersley herself is careful to say that she also wants the variety of human interests in nature to be sheltered under her ecocentric umbrella.

Does it make sense for us to speak in terms of ecocentric or biocentric democracy? In perhaps its most widely-used sense, 'ecocentric politics' refers only to a human political system that would give priority to ecological values. To advocate ecocentric politics in such terms is unremarkable, reducing as it does to advocacy of a biocentric ethic – one that accords intrinsic value to natural entities, irrespective of human interest in those entities. Beyond this ethical imperative politics is unchanged, and does not need to stand in any particular *structural* relation to nature. The problem with such a minimalist approach to ecocentric democracy is that it returns us directly to the position that was rejected in the previous section, where I tried to establish that we need green political structures as well as green values.

What more can ecocentric politics mean, beyond advocacy of biocentric values? A maximalist view here might emphasise the 'politics' created by and in nature, to which humans could adjust *their* politics. Now, Aristotle suggested long ago that what sets humans apart is that man is *zoon politikon*, the political animal. Primate ethology now suggests that there is something like politics that occurs in animal societies involving, for example, bargaining and trickery in the establishment of dominance hierarchies among males, though even here, one should be wary of anthropomorphising observed behaviour. Yet even if a quasi-politics can be found among primates or other animals, that kind of politics is one in which we humans cannot participate, just as animals cannot participate in our politics. Moreover, most of what goes on in the natural world (outside animal societies) would still be extremely hard to assimilate to any definition of politics.

The last century or so has seen the ascription of all kinds of political and social models to nature. Social Darwinists saw in nature a reflection of naked capitalism. Marx and Engels saw evolutionary justification for dialectical materialism. In 1915 the US political scientist Henry Jones Ford saw collectivist justification for an organic state. Nazis saw justification for genocide. Microeconomists see something like market transactions in the maximisation of inclusive fitness. Eco-anarchists from Kropotkin to Murray Bookchin see in nature models only of co-operation and mutualism. Roger Masters [1989] has recently suggested that liberal democracy is 'natural' in its flexibility in responding to changing environments. Ecofeminists see caring and nurturing, at least in female nature. And so forth. In short, just about every human political ideology and political-economic system has at one time or another been justified as consistent with nature, especially nature as revealed by Darwinism.

But this sheer variety should suggest that in nature we will find no single blueprint for human politics. And even if we did, that model would only prove *ecologically* benign to the extent that it could demonstrate that cross-species interactions were universally mutualistic and benign, rather than often hostile and competitive. Following Kropotkin, Murray Bookchin [1982] propounds exactly such a mutualistic, co-operative view of nature, to which he suggests human social, economic, and political life should be assimilated. But Bookchin's position here is, to say the least, selective in its interpretation of nature, and no more persuasive than all the other selective interpretations which have been used to justify all manner of human political arrangements. So a maximalist notion of ecocentric politics of the sort advocated by Bookchin should be rejected.

Yet nature is not devoid of political lessons. What we *will* find in nature, or at least in our interactions with it, is a variety of levels and kinds of communication to which we might try to adapt. The key here is to downplay 'centrism' of any kind, and focus instead on the kinds of interactions that might occur across the boundaries between humanity and nature. In this spirit, the search for green democracy can indeed involve looking for progressively less anthropocentric political forms. For democracy can exist not only among humans, but also in human dealings with the natural world – though not *in* that natural world, or in any simple *model* which nature provides for humanity. So the key here is seeking more egalitarian interchange at the human/natural boundary; an interchange that involves progressively less in the way of human autism. In short, ecological democratisation here is a matter of more effective integration of political and ecological communication.

On the face of it, this requirement might suggest that the whole history of democratic theory – and democratic practice – should be jettisoned, and that a truly green programme of institutional innovation should be sought under a different rubric than 'democracy'. For democracy, however contested a concept, and in however many varieties it has appeared in the last two and and a half thousand years, is, if nothing else, anthropocentric. One way to substantiate this point would be to go through all the major models of democracy (for example, as presented in Held [*1987*]), and test them for anthropocentrism. Obviously I have not the space to do that. But let me just note that inasmuch as democratic theory has been taken under the wing of liberalism in the last few hundred years (and most of it has been), then its anthropocentrism has been guaranteed. As Freya Mathews [*1991b: 158*] notes, 'liberalism as it stands is of course anthropocentric: it takes human interest as the measure of all value'. Liberalism does so because only reasoning entities are accorded political standing. The members of a liberal democracy might, of course, choose to enact positive measures for environmental protection, for example by granting legal rights to natural objects. Guardians for those objects might then make claims on political and legal systems. But any such representation might simply *down*grade nature to another set of interests, disaggregating and isolating these interests by assigning them to identifiable natural objects, thus ignoring their intrinsically ecological (interconnected) character.

If we take the major alternative to liberalism, we find that Marxism (and so its associated models of democracy) is equally materialistic and anthropocentric, seeking human liberation in part through more effective domination and control of nature [*Eckersley, 1992: 75–95*].[2]

The Communicative Rationality of Ecological Democracy

To attempt to move in a different direction here, let me return to the issue of the connection between democracy and reason, as highlighted in Mathews's mention of liberalism. Without wishing to get too involved in the various debates surrounding democracy and rationality [*Spragens, 1990; Dryzek, 1990a*], let me suggest that the best or most fruitful approach to the issue of how we might rescue rationality and perhaps democracy from anthropocentrism begins with Jürgen Habermas's analysis of the dialectics of rationalisation attendant upon modernity. To Habermas (notably, 1984, 1987), modernisation connotes two kinds of rationalisation. The first is instrumental: instrumental rationality may be defined in terms of the capacity to devise, select, and effect good means to clarified and consistent ends. The second is communicative: communicative action involves understanding across subjects, the coordination of their actions through discussion, and socialisation. Communicative rationality is the degree to which these processes are uncoerced, undistorted, and engaged by competent individuals. On Habermas's account, instrumental rationalisation has so far come out ahead, and with it the domination of money and power in political and social life, especially through bureaucracy and capitalism. One can imagine a democracy of instrumental or strategically rational individuals, and this kind of democracy is modelled in great detail by public choice analysis but, as public choice has itself shown, such a democracy is an incoherent mess, producing unstable and arbitrary outcomes [*Dryzek, 1992*]. Thus some degree of communicative rationality is crucial to *any* democracy. More important for present purposes, communicative rationality constitutes the model for a democracy that is deliberative rather than strategic in character; or at least one where strategic action is kept firmly in its place.

But could such a democracy be green? Eckersley [*1992: 109–17*] for one argues that it cannot. And in the terms in which she argues, she is entirely correct. She points out that for Habermas (just as for most liberals) the only entities that matter are ones capable of engaging as subjects in dialogue – in other words, human beings. In a belief carried over from his earlier work on the philosophy of science, Habermas considers that the only fruitful human attitude toward the natural world is one of instrumental manipulation and control. Indeed, the whole point of communicative rationalisation is to *prevent* human interactions with one another becoming like human interactions with the natural world [*Alford, 1985: 77*]. Human liberation is bought at the expense of the domination of nature, and so Habermas is as anthropocentric as orthodox Marxists here. And for this reason Eckersley dismisses Habermas as having any possible relevance to the search for an ecocentric politics.

Let me suggest that it would be more appropriate here to try to rescue communicative rationality from Habermas. The key would be to treat communication, and so communicative rationality, as extending to entities that can act as agents, even though they lack the self-awareness that connotes subjectivity. Agency is not the same as subjectivity, and only the former need be sought in nature. Habermas treats nature as though it were brute matter. But nature is not passive, inert, and plastic. Instead, this world is truly alive, and pervaded with meanings.[3]

Minimally, a recognition of agency in nature would underwrite respect for natural objects and ecological processes. Just as democrats should condemn humans who would silence other humans, so should they condemn humans who would silence nature by destroying it. But there are implications here for politcs, as well as morality. For this recognition of agency in nature means that we should treat signals emanating from the natural world with the same respect we accord signals emanating from human subjects, and as requiring equally careful interpretation. In other words, our relation to the natural world should not be one of instrumental intervention and observation of results oriented to control. Thus communicative interaction with the natural world can and should be an eminently rational affair [Dryzek, 1990b]. Of course, human verbal communication cannot extend into the natural world.[4] But greater continuity is evident in non-verbal communication – body language, facial displays, pheronomes, and so forth [Dryzek, 1990b: 207]. And a lot goes on in human conversation beyond the words, which is why a telephone discussion is not the same as a face-to-face meeting. More important than such continuities here are the ecological processes which transcend the boundaries of species, such as the creation, modification, or destruction of niches; or cycles involving oxygen, nitrogen, carbon, and water. Disruptions in such processes occasionally capture our attention, in the form, for example, of climate change, desertification, deforestation, and species extinction.

The idea that there may be agency in nature might seem to fly in the face of several hundred years of Western natural science, social science, and political theory. But perhaps the suggestion is not so far-fetched. Accounts of the actual practice of biological science often emphasise not manipulation and control, but rather understanding and communication. Examples here are especially prominent in work on animal thinking (notably by Donald Griffin), ethology (as in the work of Jane Goodall on chimpanzees), ecology [Worster, 1985], and even genetics (see Keller's [1983] discussion of the 'feeling for the organism' in the work of Barbara Mclintock).

Agency in nature on a grand scale is proposed in James Lovelock's Gaia hypothesis, which suggests that the biosphere as a whole acts so as to maintain the conditions for life. Lovelock does not suggest that Gaia has awareness, and so it cannot be described as a subject (still less a goddess). Rather, Gaia consists of a complex, self-regulating intelligence. But taking the hypothesis to heart 'implies that the stable state of our planet includes man as a part of, or partner in, a very democratic entity' [Lovelock, 1979: 145]. Let me suggest that Lovelock's words here may be taken more literally than perhaps he intends, and that his hypothesis can indeed help us conceptualise a non-anthropocentric democracy.[5]

All of these suggestions of agency in nature have their critics, especially among philosophers, probably less frequently among natural scientists. And it may often be hard to prove these positions scientifically. But that may not be the point. No democratic theory has ever been founded on scientific proof of anything, and there is no reason to seek an exception here. When it comes to the essence of *human* nature, political theorists can only disagree among themselves. To some, a utility-maximising *homo economicus* captures the essence of human nature; to others (mostly sociologists), it is a plastic, socialised conception of humanity in which there are no choices to be made, let alone utilities to be maximised; to others (such as critical theorists) a communicative and creative self; to others (such as civic republicans) a public-spirited and reflective self. In the present context, the idea of an ecological self [*Mathews, 1991a*] is perhaps more appropriate than these established paradigms of personhood. My general point here is that when it comes to an ecological democracy that opens itself toward non-human nature, we should not apply standards of proof which no other democratic theory could possibly meet.

I have tried to show that it is conceivable that processes of communicative reason can be extended to cover non-human entities. Communicative reason can underwrite a particular kind of democracy in purely human affairs – one that is discursive or deliberative in character, whose essence is talk and scrutiny of the interests common to a group of people, or of particular interests of some subset of that group. But of course non-human entities cannot talk, and nor should they be anthropomorphised by giving them rights against us or preferences to be incorporated in utilitarian calculation, still less votes. However, as I have suggested, there are senses in which nature can communicate. So what kind of politics or democracy can be at issue here?

Democracy Without Boundaries

To approach an answer, we first need to clear away some of the underbrush that has accumulated with the pervasiveness of liberal discourse in the last few centuries. In a liberal conception of democracy, the essence of democracy is preference aggregation [*Miller, 1992: 54–5*]. Liberals themselves might disagree as to what mechanisms for preference aggregation work best, or whose preferences should be aggregated, or to what extent aggregated preferences should be restrained by other considerations (such as basic human rights). But on one thing they all agree: preferences need to be aggregated, and if so, then a basic task is to define the population (society, or citizenry) whose preferences are to be taken into account. In practice, this can be done very precisely, with electoral registers and so forth. The liberal model of democracy requires a hard-and-fast boundary between the human and non-human world (not to mention a boundary between public and private realms, now challenged by feminists). For non-human entities cannot have preferences that we could easily recognise, or be at all confident in attributing to them. Thus ecological democracy cannot be sought in the image of preference aggregation in liberal democracy.

This liberal ideal of democracy as preference aggregation also presupposes the notion of a self-contained, self-governing community. But in today's world, that notion is becoming increasingly fictional, as political, social, and especially economic transactions transcend national boundaries. In which case, it might be productive to start thinking about models of democracy in which the boundaries of communities are indeterminate. Burnheim's proposals for demarchy can be interpreted as interesting moves in this direction. To Burnheim [1985], democracy and democratic legitimacy are not to be sought in geographically-bounded entities like nation states, but rather in functional authorities of varying geographical scope, run by individuals selected by lot from among those with a material interest in the issue in question. Now, Burnheim's functional authorities arguably establish different boundaries: between functional issue areas, rather than geographical territories. But the trouble here is that there are of course major interactions across issue areas. So interactions across issue areas, no less than interactions across state boundaries, force us to look for the essence of democracy not in the mechanical aggregation of the preferences of a well-defined and well-bounded group of people (such as a nation-state, or set of persons with a material interest in an issue), but rather in the content and style of interactions. Some styles may be judged anti-democratic (for example, the imposition of a decision without possibility for debate or criticism), some relatively democratic (for example, wide dissemination of information about an issue, the holding of hearings open to any interested parties, and so on).

A focus on the style and content of interactions fits well with the communicative rationality grounding for democracy to which I have already alluded. Now, some critics of deliberative democracy and its grounding in communicative rationality argue that it privileges rational argument, and effectively excludes other kinds of voices. But the solution to any such exclusion is obvious: the deliberative model should be extended so as to make provision for such alternative voices.[6] A similar extension may be in order to accommodate non-human communication.

Along with a recognition of the indefinite nature of boundaries of the political community, such extension means that we are now well-placed (or at least better-placed than liberal democrats) to think about dismantling what is perhaps the biggest political boundary of them all: that between the human and the non-human world. This is indeed a big step, and no doubt some people would still believe that it takes us out of the realm of politics and democracy altogether, at least as those terms are conventionally defined. Yet there is a sense in which human relationships with nature are *already* political. As Val Plumwood points out in her contribution to this collection, politicisation is a concomitant of the human colonization of nature. Such colonisation connotes an authoritarian politics; democratisation would imply a more egalitarian politics here.

Democracy is, if nothing else, both an open-ended project and an essentially contested concept; indeed, if debates about the meaning of democracy did not occur in a society, we would hesitate to describe that society as truly democratic. All I am trying to do here is introduce another – major – dimension of contestation.

At one level, it is possible to propose ecological democracy as a regulative ideal. This is, after all, how the basic principles of both liberal and deliberative democracy can be advanced [*Miller, 1992: 55–6*]. For liberals, the regulative ideal is fairness and efficiency in preference aggregation: the various institutional forms under which preference aggregation might proceed are then a matter for investigation, comparison, and debate. Similarly, for deliberative democrats, the regulative ideal is free discourse about issues and interests; again, various institutional forms might then be scrutinised in the light of this ideal. For ecological democrats, the regulative ideal is effectiveness in communication that transcends the boundary of the human world. As it enters human systems, then obviously ecological communication needs to be interpreted. However, unlike the situation in liberal democracy (or for that matter in Burnheim's demarchy), this communication does not have to be mediated by the material interests of particular actors.

The content of such communication might involve attention to feedback signals emanating from natural systems; in which case, the practical challenge when it comes to institutional design becomes one of dismantling barriers to such communication. With this principle in mind, it is a straightforward matter to criticise institutions that try to subordinate nature on a large scale. Think, for example, of the development projects sponsored by the World Bank, which until recently did not even pretend to take local environmental factors into account (now they at least pretend to). Yet it is also possible to criticise approaches to our dealings with the environment that do exactly the reverse, and seek only the removal of human agency. On one of his own interpretations, Lovelock's Gaia can do quite well without people. And a misanthrope such as David Ehrenfeld [*1978*] would prefer to rely on natural processes left well alone by humans.

With this regulative ideal of ecological democracy in mind we are, then, in a position both to criticise existing political-economic arrangements and to think about what might work better. I am not going to offer a blueprint for the institutions of such a democracy. The design of such a democracy should itself be discursive, democratic, and sensitive to ecological signals.

Moreover, idealist political prescription insensitive to real-world constraints and possibilities for innovation is often of limited value. And variation in the social and natural contexts within which political systems operate means that we should be open to institutional experimentation and variety across these contexts (though, as I noted earlier, an ability to operate in different contexts may itself be a highly desirable quality for any political-economic mechanism).

When it comes to criticism of existing political (and economic) mechanisms, it is reasonably easy to use the ecological communicative ideal to expose some gross failings. Perhaps most obviously, to the degree that any such mechanism allows internal communication to dominate and distort signals from the outside, it merits condemnation. So, for example, a bureaucracy with a well-developed internal culture may prove highly inattentive to its environment. And bureaucratic hierarchy pretty much ensures distortion and loss of information across the levels of hierarchy. Indeed, these are standard criticisms of bureaucracy as a problem-solving device, though such criticisms are usually couched in terms of a human environment, not a natural one. Markets can be just as autistic, if in different ways. Obviously, they respond only to *human, consumer* preferences that can be couched in *monetary* terms. Any market actor trying to take non-pecuniary factors into account is going to have its profitability, and so survival chances, damaged (this is not to gainsay the possibility of green consumerism). Conversely, the positive feedback of business growth (and the growth of the capitalist market in general) is guided by processes entirely internal to markets.

Above all, existing mechanisms merit condemnation to the extent that their size and scope do not match the size and scope of ecosystems and/or ecological problems. Under such circumstances, communications from or about particular ecological problems or disequilibria will be swamped by communications from other parts of the world. Here, markets that transcend ecological boundaries, which they increasingly do, merit special condemnation. The internationalisation and globalisation of markets make it that much easier to engage in local despoliation. It may be quite obvious that a local ecosystem is being degraded and destroyed, but 'international competitiveness' is a good stick with which to beat environmentalist critics of an operation. For example, they can be told that old growth forests must be clearcut, rather than logged selectively. Obviously, some ecological problems are global, as are some markets. This does not of course mean that effective response mechanisms to global ecological problems can be found in global markets. Market autism guarantees that they cannot.

Turning to the desirable scope and shape of institutions suggested by the ideal of ecological democracy, the watchword here is 'appropriate scale'. In other words, the size and scope of institutions should match the size and scope of problems. There may be good reasons for the predispositions toward small scale in ecoanarchism and 'small is beautiful' green political thought. Most notably, feedback processes in natural systems are diffuse and internal [*Patten and Odum, 1981*], and do not pass through any central control point. Highly centralised human collective choice mechanisms are not well-placed to attend to such diffuse feedback. Moreover, the autonomy and self-sufficiency advocated by green decentralisers can force improved perception of the natural world. To the degree that a community must rely on local ecological resources, it will have to take care of them. It does not follow that local self-reliance should be taken to an extreme of autarky. Rather, it is a matter of degree: the more the community is politically and economically self-reliant, then the more it must take care of its local ecosystems. Presumably the degree of self-reliance necessary to secure adequate care here depends a great deal on the level of environmental consciousness in the community in question. To the extent that environmental consciousness is lacking, then economic consciousness has to do all the work, so there are many places (such as resource-dependent local economies in the American West) where only autarky would do the trick.

But obviously not all ecological problems and feedback signals reside at the local level. Some of them are global, and hence demand global institutional response. There is no need in this scheme of things to privilege the nation-state, and every reason not to; few, if any, ecological problems coincide with state boundaries. There is only slightly greater reason to privilege bioregions. Bioregions are notoriously hard to define, and again many problems transcend their boundaries. For example, an airshed will not necessarily correspond with a watershed, and a single watershed may contain several radically different types of ecosystems. (I lived in the Columbia river basin, which contains both mid-continent deserts and coastal forests.)

Coordination through Spontaneous Order

An ecological democracy would, then, contain numerous and cross-cutting *loci* of political authority. The obvious question here is: how does one coordinate them, given that one cannot (for example) resolve air pollution problems while completely ignoring the issue of water pollution, or deal with local sulphur dioxide pollution while ignoring the long-distance diffusion of sulphur dioxide in acid rain? The way this coordination is currently accomplished is by privileging one level of political organisation. In unitary political systems, this will normally be the national state, though matters can be a bit more complicated in federal systems. The state (national or sub-national) will of course often contain an anti-pollution agency which (nominally, if rarely in practice) coordinates policy in regard to different kinds of pollutants. But, as I have already noted, this is an entirely artificial solution, and no more defensible than privileging the local community, or for that matter the global community.

The main conceivable alternative to privileging the state is to rely on the emergence of some spontaneous order that would somehow coordinate the actions of large numbers of bodies. One example of such an order is the market, especially as celebrated by von Hayek [*Goodin, 1992: 154*]. But markets, as noted, are not exactly an ecological success story. Nor are they much good at coordinating the activities of *political* authorities. Within decentralised political systems, coordination is achieved largely through the spontaneous order of partisan mutual adjustment, which to Lindblom [*1965*] is at the core of collective decision in liberal democracies. Such regimes may contain more formal and consciously-designed constitutions, but partisan mutual adjustment proceeds regardless of the content of such formalisms. This adjustment involves a complex mix of talk, strategy, commitment, and individual action devised in response to the context created by the actions of others. As I noted earlier, this kind of spontaneous order under liberal democracy leaves much to be desired when scrutinised in an ecological light.

Ecosystems, including the global ecosystem, are also examples of spontaneous order, so one might try to devise an imitation which included humans. Along these lines, Murray Bookchin [*1982*] attempts to develop a naturalistic justification for human political organisation. His eco-anarchist prescriptions might make some sense at the local level. But he can develop no *naturalistic* justification for the kinds of political order that would be needed to transcend localities, beyond relying on the spontaneous generation of structures whose specification is completely indeterminate (which is really no answer at all).

Let me suggest that there is a kind of spontaneous order which might perform the requisite coordinating functions quite well. Discussions in democratic theory are normally directed toward how the state, or state-analogues such as local governments and intergovernmental authorities, shall be constructed. What this focus misses is the possibility of democratisation *apart from* and *against* established authority [*Dryzek, 1996*]. This latter kind of democratisation is associated with the idea of a public sphere or civil society. Public spheres are political bodies that do not exist as part of formal political authority, but rather in confrontation with that authority. Normally, they find their identity in confrontation with the state (think, for example, of Solidarity in Poland in the early 1980s), though authority constituted at levels both higher and lower than the state can also be the object of their ire. Resistance here is often 'local' in the sense of being issue-specific. Such local resistance is celebrated by Michel Foucault, though he would not be interested in the constructive role for public spheres intimated here. The internal politics of public spheres is usually defined by relatively egalitarian debate, and consensual modes of decision making. Contemporary examples are afforded by new social movements, especially on behalf of feminism, ecology, and peace. Indeed, the green movement may be conceptualised in these terms – at least the parts of that movement that do not seek entry into the state through electoral politics.

Such public spheres fit well with communicative and deliberative models of democracy. But what do they have to do with coordination across geographical jurisdictions or functional issue area boundaries? The answer is that scope in these terms is unbounded and variable, possibly responding to the scope of the issue in question. To take a simple example, the environmental movement is now international, and organisations such as Greenpeace or Friends of the Earth International can bring home to particular governments the international dimension of issues, such as the consequences to Third World countries of toxic wastes exported by industrialised countries. Along these lines, Goodin [1992: 176–7] notes that green parties can assist in the 'coordination of international environmental policies', though as a green 'Realo' he appears to have only conventional party political participation in state politics in mind, rather than public spheres. To take another example, international public spheres constituted by indigenous peoples and their advocates can bring home to boycotters of furs in London or Paris the resulting economic devastation such boycotts imply for indigenous communities in the Arctic, which rely for cash income on trapping. A public sphere on a fairly grand scale was constituted by the unofficial Global Forum which proceeded in parallel with the United Nations Conference on Environment and Development in Rio in 1992. The point is that the reach of public spheres is entirely variable and not limited by formal boundaries on jurisdictions, or obsolete notions of national sovereignty. And they can come into existence, grow, and die along with the importance of particular issues. So, for example, it is entirely appropriate that the West European peace movement declined as cold war tensions eased in the 1980s.

Conclusion

In contemplating the kinds of communication that might ensure more harmonious coordination across political and ecological systems, there is an ever-present danger of lapsing into ungrounded idealism and wishful thinking. Yet green democracy is not an all-or-nothing affair, and it can constitute a process as well as a goal. As a goal, any such green democracy might appear very distant, given the seeming global hegemony of profoundly anti-environmental liberal democratic and capitalist ideas, celebrated by Francis Fukuyama [*1992*] as the end of history. But if the 'grow or die' system of capitalist democracy is ultimately unsustainable in the light of ecological limits, green democrats are well-placed to both hasten its demise and intimate political alternatives. This might not be a bad way to see history moving again.

NOTES

1. Greater detail on these requirements may be found in Dryzek [*1987*].
2. Curiously enough, fascism may do better than either liberalism or Marxism in the anti-anthropocentrism stakes; as Anna Bramwell [1989: 195–208] notes, the first green 'party' in Europe was actually a strand in Hitler's Nazi Party. But fascism obviously takes us quite a long way from democracy, and the arguments of eco-authoritarians such as Robert Heilbroner and Garrett Hardin have been too thoroughly discredited to warrant any attention here.
3. This point should not be confused with the green spirituality advocated by deep ecologists, goddess worshippers, and others who see divinity in nature. The choice here is not between an inert nature on the one hand and a nature populated by wood nymphs, sprites, and goddesses on the other. Nor does a recognition of agency in the natural world imply that its entities should be treated like human subjects.
4. Prince Charles may talk to his rhododendrons, but they do not talk back.
5. The Gaia hypothesis bears some resemblance to superorganismic and teleological treatments of ecosystem development, which have long been abandoned by most academic ecologists (except Eugene Odum), who are committed to more reductionist and stochastic models. But the superorganismic view lives on in the pages of *The Ecologist*.
6. Iris Marion Young points to the equal validity of greeting, rhetoric, and storytelling.

REFERENCES

Alford, C. Fred (1985), *Science and the Revenge of Nature: Marcuse and Habermas*, Gainesville, FL: University Press of Florida.
Bookchin, Murray (1982), *The Ecology of Freedom: The Emergence and Dissolution of Hierarchy*, Palo Alto, CA: Cheshire.
Bramwell, Anna (1989), *Ecology in the 20th Century: A History*, New Haven, CT: Yale University Press.
Burnheim, John (1985), *Is Democracy Possible?*, Cambridge: Cambridge University Press.
Dryzek, John S. (1987), *Rational Ecology: Environment and Political Economy*, Oxford: Basil Blackwell.
Dryzek, John S. (1990a), *Discursive Democracy: Politics, Policy, and Political Science*, Cambridge: Cambridge University Press.
Dryzek, John S. (1990b), Green Reason: Communicative Ethics for the Biosphere, *Environmental Ethics*, Vol.12, pp.195–210.
Dryzek, John S. (1992), How Far Is It From Virginia and Rochester to Frankfurt? Public Choice as Critical Theory, *British Journal of Political Science*, Vol.22, pp.397–417.
Dryzek, John S. (1996), *Democracy in Capitalist Times: Ideals, Limits, and Struggles*, Oxford: Oxford University Press.

Eckersley, Robyn (1992), *Environmentalism and Political Theory: Toward an Ecocentric Apporach*, Albany, NY: State University of New York Press.

Ehrenfeld, David (1978), *The Arrogance of Humanism*, New York: Oxford University Press.

Fukuyama, Francis (1992), *The End of History and the Last Man*, New York: Free Press.

Goodin, Robert E. (1992), *Green Political Theory*, Cambridge: Polity.

Habermas, Jürgen (1984), *The Theory of Communicative Action I: Reason and the Rationalization of Society*, Boston, MA: Beacon.

Habermas, Jurgen (1987), *The Theory of Communicative Action II: Lifeworld and System*, Boston, MA: Beacon.

Held, David (1987), *Models of Democracy*, Cambridge: Polity.

Keller, Evelyn Fox (1983), *A Feeling for the Organism: The Life and Work of Barbara McClintock*, San Francisco, CA: W.H. Freeman.

Lindblom, Charles E. (1965), *The Intelligence of Democracy: Decision Making Through Mutual Adjustment*, New York: Free Press.

Lovelock, James (1979), *Gaia: A New Look at Life on Earth*, Oxford: Oxford University Press.

Masters, Roger D. (1989), *The Nature of Politics*, New Haven, CT: Yale University Press.

Mathews, Freya (1991a), *The Ecological Self*, Savage, MD: Barnes & Noble.

Mathews, Freya (1991b), 'Democracy and the Ecological Crisis', *Legal Service Bulletin*, Vol.16, No.4, pp.157–9.

Miller, David (1992), 'Deliberative Democracy and Social Choice', *Political Studies*, Vol.40 (special issue), pp.54–67.

Patten, Bernard C. and Eugene P. Odum (1981), 'The Cybernetic Nature of Ecosystems', *American Naturalist*, Vol.118, pp.886–95.

Spragens, Thomas A., Jr. (1990), *Reason and Democracy*, Durham, NC: Duke University Press.

Weale, Albert (1992), *The New Politics of Pollution*, Manchester: Manchester University Press.

Worster, Donald (1985), *Nature's Economy: A History of Ecological Ideas*, Cambridge: Cambridge University Press.

Towards a Green World Order: Environment and World Politics

JANNA THOMPSON

Global environmental problems need a political solution. One of the most difficult problems for environmental political theory is to determine what this solution would be. There are two basic conditions that any proposed 'world order' must satisfy: it must ensure that individuals and communities comply with environmental prescriptions, and that decision-making is flexible enough to cope with environmental problems in all their complexity. Common conceptions of a world political order, centralist and anarchist, are not likely to satisfy these conditions. It must be considered also what developments in world society are most likely to bring about a world order capable of solving environmental and related problems.

Environmental problems are transnational problems. In some cases, the effects themselves reach beyond borders. But even problems that seem to be merely local, such as photochemical smog, or polluted lakes and rivers, are the result of a world-wide development of production and markets, the by-products of a struggle for economic prosperity or survival. The attempts of people within their neighbourhoods or national borders to solve environmental problems are likely to have limited success, for either the solution will be beyond their political means or their efforts will be thwarted by 'economic necessities'. The attempt of one country to live within environmental limitations, to impose strict environmental measures, to put a ceiling on production and consumption, will not have its desired effect unless other countries do the same. And if this seems unlikely then there will be little popular support for measures that are bound to be disadvantageous for those who adopt them.

Environmental problems are bound up with other global problems. It seems unlikely that environmental problems can be solved without also doing something about the problem of world poverty and under-development, for people who are caught up in the struggle for mere survival are not able to make sacrifices to save their environment. Nor are they likely

Janna Thompson teaches in the School of Philosophy, La Trobe University, Australia.

to give up the desire for a better life – their demand for 'development' – for the sake of remaining within planetary limits to growth, especially if the living standard in developed countries remains so much greater than their own.[1] It is unlikely that environmental problems will be solved without also solving the problem of war. For war is itself a serious cause of environmental devastation, and hostilities between people, even when they do not lead to war, make even minimal co-operation in dealing with environmental problems difficult to achieve.

These interrelated problems require a political solution. They are not likely to be solved as a matter of course by the free play of economic forces. Saving the environment requires intervention on a global scale to prevent environmentally disastrous 'external diseconomies' and to protect the interests of future generations (whose needs are generally discounted by economic calculation). Solving the problem of poverty and under-development may require massive aid programmes – a redistribution of wealth from west to east and from north to south. The resolution of hostilities is clearly a task that requires political will and political means.

Nor are these related problems likely to be solved simply by the promotion of good will. Even if all, or most, of the leaders of states were convinced of the urgent need to solve environmental and related problems, they would be hindered by a lack of appropriate means: the mechanisms required to control world economic affairs, to monitor and coordinate the use of resources, to redistribute goods in a way that ensures that the most needy people of the world benefit, the means to prevent hostilities and arbitrate disputes. Even if leaders were convinced of the need to act, they might not do so for fear that others would take advantage of their sacrifices.

What we really need, it seems, is a new world order: more effective world institutions or, perhaps, a total re-organisation of the political world. But what we need exactly, and how we can get it, are hard to envision. The possibility that the people of the world, or even the most powerful political actors, could come to an agreement about how global problems should be solved, or which should take precedence, seems remote. But what makes the political problems raised by environmental issues even more intractable is that there is no obviously right answer to the question of what an environmentally sound world society would be like. There is no agreement, even among environmentalists, about what political developments are a step in the right direction, about what counts as real progress as far as world affairs are concerned. For the same reason it seems especially difficult to answer in a global context the question posed by Freya Mathews: whether democracy is compatible with the measures which have to be taken to save the environment.

For some political thinkers, global centralisation of power is the obvious solution for problems that are global.[2] They look forward to the creation of a world state able to exercise control over what happens in the world in the same way that national states exercise sovereignty in their territory. A world state would presumably have the institutional means to manage the environmental affairs of the globe, to impose limits, re-distribute resources and enforce peace. No problem would be beyond its reach. Other proposals for world government reject, more or less radically, the centralisation of power which such a model embodies. A world government might instead be a confederal political society, similar to what the European Union is supposed to become – allowing considerable autonomy to member states or regions, but nevertheless having available central political institutions capable of making and enforcing decisions on matters which affect everyone – which will naturally include environmental and related issues. However, many environmentalists, inspired by anarchist ideas, are inclined to favour a much more decentralised political world: a world society consisting of communities, small enough so that face to face relations and participatory democracy are possible.[3] These communities would have ways of coordinating their affairs through representatives, but they would avoid institutions which centralise power at the expense of local autonomy.

Other proposals for global re-organisation do not fit either the centralised, confederal, or anarchist model. They include Burnheim's demarchy [1986], a system of interrelated functional organisations which, like anarchist communities, eschews a central state, but which is not based upon territory;[4] and ideas for a system based upon interlocking relationships between communities of various kinds rather than on coordination between autonomous territorial communities, whether local or national.[5]

The type of political society proposed, whether centralised state or a collection of small communities, should be distinguished from the mode of government. A centralised state can have a democratic government of one form or another; it can be a dictatorship or a system which removes some kinds of decisions from the pressures of popular sovereignty. A confederal structure can be more or less democratic at the various levels of government. Small communities can be democratic or authoritarian – though environmental anarchists have invariably advocated democracy, indeed democracy in its most radical and participatory form. Democracy in Burnheim's demarchy takes a very different form from democracy in a territorial society. The different ways in which democracy can be embedded in a political system, and the different meanings it can have, suggest that the question of whether a democracy can solve environmental and related problems can only be answered by considering and assessing these various proposals for world order and considering the role democracy could play in each.

However, my purpose here is not to advocate a particular model or put forward a detailed proposal for the re-organisation of the world. Given the speculative nature of all such exercises, this is probably not a very useful thing to do. Nevertheless, I want to be able to reach conclusions about what political processes and arrangements are conducive to solving global environmental and related problems, conclusions which are strong enough to be useful for assessing political models and able to give us an idea about what global developments we should favour. A proposed political solution must be appropriate to the nature of the problem. The best way of approaching the question of what changes in world society are required for solving environmental problems is to consider, first, what sort of problem for any political society, global or local, environmental issues pose – and then try to draw some conclusions about what kinds of political arrangements are likely to be best able to deal with them.

The two basic problems that environmental issues raise for any political order are what I shall call the problem of compliance and the problem of flexibility. Environmental issues are not alone in giving rise to these difficulties, but environmental matters do so in an obvious and extreme way. The problem of compliance is the well known problem of how to ensure that people obey the law, co-operate with each other and make the sacrifices necessary to achieve social ends. This problem is especially pressing in the case of environmental issues because the sacrifices that must be made by individuals and communities for the sake of environmental preservation (especially if this includes measures for alleviating world poverty) are likely to be considerable. At the global level the problem is compounded by mutual fear and suspicion between national societies.

The flexibility problem is the problem of dealing with causes and effects that are interrelated in a complex way and are likely to manifest themselves in unexpected ways at a number of different levels. Environmental problems are clearly problems of this sort. They have complex and non-linear causes,[6] they manifest themselves differently in different circumstances, they are often at one and the same time local and global; moreover, their causes and effects are inextricably bound up with other serious problems. A political system that cannot cope with such complexities will not solve environmental problems.

Those who worry about compliance have sometimes come to the conclusion that a Hobbesian solution is the only viable political means for imposing environmental restrictions on a reluctant world.[7] There must be political institutions capable of bringing about environmental sustainability by force or threat of force, and such institutions, it seems, are only likely to be possessed by a centralised state. Even a confederal system may not be appropriate if it allows too much autonomy or veto power to its constituent parts. A Hobbesian is also likely to doubt whether world (or national) politics can be democratic. For popular resistance to measures which require sacrifices is likely to be a barrier to making and implementing the decisions that have to be made. What we need in order to solve the compliance problem, it seems, is a world state with strong institutions, and perhaps one that is authoritarian in its decision-making about crucial matters.[8]

Whether an authoritarian central state really can solve the compliance problem is at least doubtful. It is hard to imagine a world government so powerful that it is able to prevent rebellion and civil war among people who would rather die than give up their own ways of doing things, or which is able to implement measures that require powerful economic interests to alter or even give up profitable activities. But even if this could be done, the compliance problem will not necessarily be solved. For force to be an effective means, there must be not only ways of exerting it, but also ways of detecting and preventing attempts to circumvent it. Authoritarian measures may be easier to enforce in some cases than others. It is possible to suppose that a world government could effectively enforce birth control measures: pregnancies and their results are difficult to hide. (Nevertheless, local corruption and the need to make compromises with ethnic minorities have prevented the Chinese government from achieving its population planning goals.)

Controls over production and disposal of wastes, use of resources, limitations on production or consumption are likely to be much more difficult to police. Violations are harder to detect, and corruption among administrators is likely to be more widespread. (In socialist countries, the 'black' illegal economy was often more significant than the official one.)[9] The world government would have to be a kind of '*Khmer Vert*' with officials at all levels fanatically dedicated to policing central directives. But the more tightly controlled such a system becomes the less it seems likely to solve the flexibility problem. For a rigid bureaucratic system ruled from the centre is not likely to be able to respond adequately to local developments or to cope with the unexpected ways that environmental problems manifest themselves. Even a democratic world state, in which most people are convinced of the need to solve environmental problems, is likely to be too top heavy in its use of political power, too bureaucratic in its implementation of decisions, to respond in the flexible way that environmental problems require.[10]

Force is not generally the best way of solving the compliance problem. If things can be arranged so that most individuals have an incentive to do the right thing, as far as the environment is concerned, then the problems associated with policing will not be so overwhelming. Incentives can, and have been, effectively used to tackle some environmental problems, and it would be a great accomplishment if we could develop, or at least imagine, a world-wide system of institutions and measures which would encourage desirable behaviour without having to assume that everyone is converted to environmentalism.

As I understand it, Burnheim's demarchy is a creative attempt to devise such a scheme; it assumes that there is a way of coordinating the attempts that people make to pursue their interests which will promote, or at least be compatible with, environmental protection and other desirable social ends (whether people generally act for the sake of these ends or not). The system is decentralised, democratic and yet is set up in a way that is supposed to make it possible to fulfil tasks which require global coordination. It is designed to be flexible. Whether it would indeed be able to solve global problems is difficult to say (Burnheim's examples all have to do with the much simpler and overseeable affairs of smaller communities). But it seems to me doubtful that any arrangement of incentives can solve problems that require individuals to give up some of their important objectives (rather than finding a different way of fulfilling them or making them compatible with the objectives of others). A political system that relies principally on incentives will probably not solve the compliance problem, and perhaps not the flexibility problem either. For what we need is not merely a system of coordination that is able to carry out global tasks, but one that is able to change its conception of a task and its ways of performing it; one able to discontinue certain kinds of activities. We need to know much more about how a system like Burnheim's would respond to conditions which can change in complex, and unforeseen, ways.

So far I have been assuming that the compliance and flexibility problems have to be solved in a world society of people who often have priorities and interests incompatible with environmental sustainability. In such a world it is not surprising that the compliance problem seems insuperable. But if compliance cannot be assured by force or by incentives, then we have to rely on the willingness of most people to obey the law, co-operate and do the right thing – whether out of habit or moral conviction. If most people are law-abiding, then coercive institutions will have the more manageable task of detecting and controlling those relatively few who have criminal intentions. Many environmentalists therefore regard it as their basic task to persuade people to adopt environmental values. The problem of compliance, as they see it, is primarily a moral and not a political problem.

This understanding of the matter is promoted by Robert Goodin [*1992: 15ff.*] who insists on separating the green theory of value, and the basis on which it rests, from the green theory of agency, and argues that it is a mistake for greens to treat their values as if they were inseparable from the promotion of particular social relations. A focus on green values does not make political concerns irrelevant. Dryzek makes the point that the lack of appropriate political institutions can make environmental problems difficult or impossible to solve, whatever desires and values people have. There is also, I believe, something wrong, or at least misleading, about the idea that politics is a mere means for achieving the moral objectives that we have somehow acquired.

One reason for thinking that it is wrong is that very few people are persuaded by argument alone. The best arguments for environmental values often fail to make an impression, or when they are accepted, do not get a proper grip on people's motivations. When it comes to the point many people prefer to fulfil goals other than environmental goals. These failings cannot, I think, be attributed simply to irrationality, selfishness or weakness of will. If sympathies direct our moral convictions (as Hume believed), then the failure to accept or act on a good moral argument may have to do with a lack of feeling for what we are supposed to value, or the impression that the acts that we are supposed to perform are too unconventional or pointless, or simply alien to our idea of who we are. Our sympathies and our identity are, in turn, influenced by our social relations and the conventions of our society. An environmentalist who wants people to accept and live by environmental values has to turn her attention to the social factors which affect their predisposition or ability to do this.[11]

There can be a number of ways in which social practices and relationships affect moral attitudes and inclinations. First, making political agreements, living within a political order, can encourage individuals to treat each other with respect. Kant [1795] plausibly argued that the moral progress of a population, and therefore the acceptability of universal moral objectives such as perpetual peace, depend upon the habits people acquire in a constitutional state where individual rights are recognised and the rule of law prevails. Rawls [1987] similarly suggests that a political *modus vivendi* can, as the result of custom and practice, become a source of moral conviction and obligation. Secondly, political participation can encourage the acceptance of moral responsibility for achieving social objectives. Mill argued [1861] that democracy is more likely to encourage in individuals a sense of social responsibility than authoritarian forms of rule. The fact that environmental problems are much more serious in former socialist countries than they are in liberal democratic countries provides some evidence that he is right. Thirdly, co-operative social and political relations can encourage people to sympathise with others and regard themselves as having a responsibility for each other's well-being – a predisposition that every distributive theory of justice depends upon.[12]

Let us assume that these attempts to connect moral conviction to social relations are basically correct. They do not imply that moral argument plays no role in moral persuasion. But if political relations can make people more receptive to certain ideas about what their moral duties are, and more prepared to tolerate sacrifices, environmentalists cannot afford to treat political relationships as merely means – neutral techniques for achieving the goals that agents have somehow acquired. To solve the compliance problem they must turn their attention to the question of what kind of political relations and practices provide a good environment for encouraging the adoption of environmental values, and what sort of political society makes it likely that people will retain these values and act on them. This means that proposals for re-ordering world society should be judged according to how well they are likely to promote and perpetuate the attitudes and relations in which environmental values can develop and flourish.

The political philosophers of the environment who have been most centrally concerned with this question are the environmental anarchists. Their ideas of community are based upon the idea that in small, independent and democratic associations people are most likely to develop and maintain a respectful and caring attitude toward nature and co-operative relations with each other. They make a number of important points about the connection between social relations and moral and political goals which are worth appreciating and trying to incorporate into our ideas about the developments which ought to be encouraged.[13]

The first is that relations of co-operation, living and working together, sharing common ends or a common heritage, encourage the acceptance of mutual obligations. Those who belong to such networks are likely to acknowledge, without the need for supreme acts of moral will, or the application of political force, a duty to make sacrifices for the sake of others in their community, including those who cannot care for themselves: the young, the old, the ill. A small face-to-face community is not necessarily the only (or the best) place for generating such a sense of duty. The obvious question is whether and how such relationships can embrace everyone in the world, underwrite and make practical the idea that concern for other's needs is a duty of justice.

The second important point that these utopian stories make is that attachment to a place, having roots, can encourage a desire to protect one's own environment and a willingness to take responsibility for it. Those who are transient, whose relation to a place is merely a business relation, those who can simply move on when they have exhausted its resources, are not so likely to know or care what happens to the environments that they affect or to think that they have a duty to do so. Political boundaries that discourage migration or put limits on business activity can thus have a good environmental effect, and some environmentalists have suggested that there should be more boundary restrictions rather than fewer.[14] But the imposition of boundaries is not likely to solve either environmental problems or the problem of poverty unless measures for distributing resources are also politically possible (indeed, the increasing number of illegal migrants in North America and Europe shows that policing boundaries is another example of the difficulty of using force in an effective way when a lot of people have strong motivations for circumventing it). Moreover, boundary restrictions on movements and interventions should not be allowed to discourage what is in fact a healthy development: the concern that people can develop for environments not their own (for the Antarctic, the Pacific Ocean or the Amazon Basin, for example). That people develop such concerns and be able to act on them seems to me a necessary condition for the preservation of the global environment.

The third important aspect of the environmental anarchist view is the stress it places on the role of democratic political relations in solving both the compliance and the flexibility problems. Democracy is supposed to encourage people to co-operate, appreciate each other's needs, take responsibility for community tasks – the virtues that Mill also associates with a democratic society. But in addition it is supposed to enable people to respond effectively to local environmental problems. Democracy, as the anarchists understand it, is a feedback arrangement which enables local knowledge and ideas to affect decisions at higher levels, for policy made at higher levels to be properly interpreted and applied to local conditions. They reject a conception of democracy that regards it as a way of forcing a central government to respond to popular pressure. They see it as a way of bringing together the knowledge, points of view and expertise of individuals on whatever problem lies at hand. Democracy so employed constitutes a plausible attempt to solve the flexibility problem.[15]

Nevertheless, anarchist models must find a way of coping with flexibility problems at a global level. Environmental anarchists never really explain how independent communities can manage to coordinate their activities so that they can solve common environment problems or deal with the effects that the activities of one community are likely to have on another. They are, to be sure, willing to countenance the existence of higher level bodies to coordinate the affairs of communities, but they say little about how these bodies are supposed to perform this task, and what this means for the autonomy of a community. If too much stress is placed on preserving community autonomy then it seems difficult to imagine how inter-community problems can be solved. On the other hand, if higher level political relations are developed to the degree that seems to be required to overcome such problems, then community autonomy will be seriously compromised and the anarchist model may not differ significantly from proposals which accept or advocate centralisation of political power [*Goodin, 1992*]. This does not mean that the problem cannot be solved within the anarchist framework; all plausible proposals for a new environmental world order are going to require some compromise between local autonomy and global institutions. But more attention has to be paid by anarchist thinkers to the question of how we are going to act, as well as think, globally.

It can also be doubted whether anarchist communities can secure the compliance necessary to carry out inter-community measures for preserving the environment. For if our principal social relations are with others in our local community, then we are not so likely to develop sympathies for outsiders or an inclination to take responsibility for their well being. The less responsibility we feel, the less inclined we will probably be to put limitations on our activities for the sake of outsiders or to help them in need. So environmental or other projects which require co-operation among communities may not get done – either through lack of means or lack of will; nor will related problems of poverty and hostility be solved.

Anarchist models of political society are not the only ones that suffer from these difficulties. Confederal governments might find it just as difficult to win acceptance for measures that compromise national or regional autonomy or require individuals and communities to make considerable sacrifices for the sake of others outside their national community. Burnheim's demarchy, by ensuring that the democratically managed parts are integrated into a whole, may be more successful in coordinating the activities of individuals. On the other hand, an individual who is primarily concerned with the way in which groups perform tasks which further his or her interests may not be inclined to accept measures which require her to sacrifice the fulfilment of her interests, either for the sake of the environment or for that of distant strangers.

These assessments have to be regarded as tentative, especially when we have a limited idea of how a political model would work and of its potential to overcome difficulties. But the exercise at least gives us some idea of what relations and institutions an environmentally sound society should contain or promote. To solve the compliance problem what we seem to need, as far as world political organisation is concerned, is a social order that imposes boundaries on activities of certain kinds and encourages the development of bounded communities of people who are prepared to take responsibility for their own environment and well-being. But at the same time we need to encourage co-operative relations of people across borders, the development of a universal sense of justice and global environmental concerns – objectives that are strong enough to motivate people to accept sacrifices for the sake of the environment, future generations and the less well off people of the world. To solve the flexibility problem we seem to need a system that encourages the development of local knowledge and local problem solving, but which is also able to make good and effective regional and global decisions – a system where problems are tackled and solved at the appropriate level, and feedback at every level of decision-making is effective. One of the problems that environmental political theory must face is whether these demanding, and apparently contrary, requirements can be realised by any imaginable political system. The influence of political relations on moral attitudes raises a difficulty about motivation. If people are not likely to have the right attitudes until they live in the right kind of society, then what makes desirable moral and political change possible?

The best way of tackling these problems is, I think, to begin by considering developments or possibilities that actually exist in world society or seem to be coming into existence: new forms of organisation, developments in relationships and attitudes, new possibilities for environmental action. We can then try to determine which of these developments are likely to fulfil the compliance and flexibility requirements, or at least seem to be moving in the right direction – whether people recognise and desire this or not. The result of the exercise may not be a clear vision of a good and environmentally sound world society, but it could at least provide environmentalists and others with an idea of what they should be struggling for – of what counts as progress as far as world social affairs are concerned. It may also reveal a way of solving the problem of motivation. Developments can occur which are favourable to moral progress without people actually willing this result.

There are two developments in the world as a whole which seem to be of significance and which, I think, environmentalists should, and sometimes do, take as central in an assessment of future possibilities. The first is the increasing concern of people all over the world to maintain and preserve their cultural uniqueness and their community integrity in the face of world market forces, neo-colonialism, or centralised political decision-making which ignores local interests. The desire of people to preserve community integrity can encourage an attachment to their land, an appreciation of its uniqueness and its environmental treasures, and a desire to protect and preserve this environmental heritage. The demand of indigenous people for 'land rights', the desire of ethnic and cultural groups for greater autonomy, demands for the de-centralisation of political decision-making, are all examples of regional movements for cultural preservation which often have environmental implications.

The second development seems to move us in a contrary direction – toward centralised federal and world institutions in an increasingly interdependent world. It seems likely that trans-national organisations will be required by governments and political pressure groups to take more and more responsibility for dealing with environmental issues which national states and smaller communities do not have the political means to solve (this has already happened to some extent within the European Union), to impose environmental limitations on development projects (as the World Bank now does for projects that it sponsors), to rule on environmental disputes (as the World Court is sometimes expected to do). It is likely that the federal and world bodies which are supposed to deal with environmental matters are going to become more numerous, and probably more powerful and independent of the authority of any particular national government.

These two contrary world developments are of obvious interest to environmentalists, but neither by itself (or even in conjunction with the other) is likely to lead to an environmentally sound (or just) world society. Demands for community power can simply be a means for protecting the privileges of wealthy communities, or they can be an expression of chauvinistic attitudes which are not likely to encourage co-operation or sacrifice for the sake of solving world environmental problems. The development of regional or world political bodies may turn out to be a means of protecting a *status quo* in which the wealthy continue to exploit world resources at the expense of people in the less well-off parts of the world. What seems to offer a possibility for real progress, as far as environmental politics is concerned, are not these developments themselves, but other possibilities that they open up.

One of these is the encouragement of trans-national environmental organisations and pressure groups. In order to save their own environment from the political or economic forces that seem likely to destroy it, local people have to enlist the support of others, including, in some cases, people beyond their national borders. To save the whale or the rain forests, to put pressure on national and international bodies, environmentalists find it useful to form international links, whether these are formal organisations or merely informal exchanges of ideas. Given the nature of the problems that have to be solved, the most important of these are organisations or networks designed to bring together people from both developed and under-developed countries, and organisations which are concerned with social as well as purely environmental interests. A good example of a network that does both of these things is the rain forest action groups which bring together environmentalists, mostly from developed countries such as Australia and the US, with native people who live in or near rain forests and want to preserve their own life and livelihood. These organisations aim to put pressure on both the governments that encourage exploitation of rain forests and those that allow the import of rain forest timber and other products, and to bring the attention of the world to the environmental and human problems that destruction of the rain forests cause. They are truly international movements.

However, it is not just transnational environmental movements that environmentalists should look on with favour and try to promote. Other movements or networks which unite people across borders, particularly those which bring together people from east and west, north and south should be welcomed: peace groups, organisations of indigenous people, trade union links, church and ethnic organisations, as well as the functional organisations favoured by Burnheim.[16] For they not only encourage exchange of information and co-operation among people. Their existence also promotes a world society in which people have connections and sympathies with those outside their borders, networks of mutual aid which can result in a more demanding idea of what justice requires, and relations which enable people to help each other in a direct and practical way. Any movement or organisation that can accomplish this, even in a small way, should be welcomed by environmentalists as a means of promoting relationships that are likely to be favourable to the solution of world environmental problems.

Another kind of development that environmentalists should also, generally, welcome are movements that aim to bring to the attention of a population the uniqueness and preciousness of their heritage. People who learn to value their heritage are also likely to be receptive to the idea that this heritage includes their land, their wilderness areas, the plant and animals species which are unique to their area. Even nationalist movements can provide a fertile ground for encouraging environmental values, providing these movements are not merely excuses for chauvinistic behaviour, and providing that there is a way of concentrating the attention on soil rather than blood. Attempts to protect an environmental heritage are especially important if they link the struggles of one group of people with those of another, or if they emphasise the world significance of attempts to protect local environments. The successful struggle of the Tasmanian Wilderness Society to save the Franklin River not only encouraged people everywhere in Australia to regard a previously unknown wilderness area as an important part of their heritage. It brought this area, and its unique features, to the attention of the world and caused it to be recognised as a World Heritage Area.

Another welcome development is the existence of groups or networks, such as Greenpeace, which attempt to make use of existing international and regional structures in order to campaign for environmental and other objectives – those that focus their activities on influencing international organisations like the World Bank or the United Nations, take their case to the World Court, focus public attention on the virtues and shortcomings of international agreements, put pressure on governments to keep existing agreements and to make better ones in the future. These efforts not only make use of the structures for influencing international affairs that already exist; they also encourage people to be aware of the importance and possibilities of trans-national spheres of political activity.

These favourable developments do not amount to a new environmental world order, and they may never do so. But it is not absurd to suppose that they could be the beginning of a process which will bring about political and social structures much more favourable to the solution of environmental and related problems – structures that provide an effective political means for dealing with global and local problems and which also encourage people to recognise and fulfil global obligations to others and to the environment. How this could happen, and what the result might be, can only be a subject of speculation. The Marxist idea that present necessities determine future outcomes is not a helpful one, especially in a case where the outcome of existing developments is so uncertain, and Marx's comforting idea that history only poses for itself problems that it can solve may well be wrong. Nevertheless, it is not impossible to imagine that things could go right – partly as the result of human intentions and partly because of developments that have results different from what people intend. In imagining how world society could become more conducive to environmental protection, my approach will be more in the spirit of Kant [*1795*], who attempted to show how favourable developments in politics and moral consciousness could enable humankind to progress from a state of affairs in which war and tyranny prevail, to universal peace in a world of constitutional republics. Kant's account of the future was based upon hope – not on a view about historical necessity – but on what he nevertheless thought was a realistic assessment of existing possibilities. So let us in the same spirit consider what might be the outcome of present developments in world society if things go as well as they could go.

Let us suppose that transnational organisations and popular movements of various kinds become more prevalent and prominent, that regional and international organisations will in the future take over some of the functions that national governments now exercise (as has happened already in the European Union), and that the people of national societies become more aware of transnational affairs and more concerned about the fact that important political decisions are being made by bodies over which they have little control. This will encourage the formation of transnational pressure groups and attempts to make trans-national bodies more accountable and more democratic. Let us assume that this effort can succeed, and let us also assume that some, at least, of these transnational bodies are international, and not merely regional.

At the same time we can suppose that movements for local autonomy and the protection of heritage also become more prevalent. Local people will want to ensure that decision-making about some matters remains in their hands, though they will also have to acknowledge the necessity of higher levels of decision-making about some matters. There will be continual struggles and experiments, some which favour more local autonomy than others; but the general assumption will be that communities should have a wide scope for decision-making on matters that affect their survival and heritage.

However, communities based upon territory and cultural heritage will not be the only groups or even, necessarily, the main communities that international developments encourage or bring into being. People who live in a particular territory will be associated with others through a multitude of national, regional and international organisations – through environmental movements, religious groups, businesses, trade unions, political parties, cultural unions. Some of these will be international organisations which bring together people in wealthy and poor areas of the world. At first these groups will operate primarily as pressure groups or informal organisations, but as their activities become more important to people, they will develop a more representative, and perhaps democratic, structure. We can imagine that some of them will take on the function of distributing wealth, providing social security and networks of support, carrying out environmental tasks or monitoring environmental projects. In any case, they will encourage people to appreciate the needs and concerns of others, including their environmental concerns, and to accept moral obligations of care for people and environments in other parts of the world.

The individuals who belong to this complex system of interrelations are likely to be the kind of individuals who can address both local and global problems. They will have an attachment to their own local community and its heritage, but on the other hand they will have other loyalties and associations which force them to take into account the needs of people outside their borders, whether local or national. They will be concerned with global political issues and with the activities of regional and international bodies which are supposed to represent their interests. This does not mean that people in general will be much more concerned with political issues than they are now, but their political consciousness will include a much greater awareness of what is happening in the world as a whole, and if they do become concerned about a particular issue, there will be organisations and groups at various levels which can be made responsive to their needs and can do something effective about them.

In this multi-layered interlocking world society there will be conflicts of loyalties and clashes of interests. Communities will sometimes be confronted by groups who have opposing ideas about how their own resources should be used. Environmental interests will not be the only matters of concern and sometimes environmentalists will lose their battles. No social order is bound to save the world. My claim is only that a world order that is pluralist, as far as organisations and interests are concerned, and democratic in its processes is most likely to provide the appropriate political means for solving both the compliance and flexibility problems.

On the other hand, a pluralist world society might make demands upon resources which will lead to environmental destruction. Or it may act too late, or ignore the needs of future generations. Or most people in it may choose temporary affluence over the long term preservation of environmental heritage. There may be, as some pessimists suggest, no way of solving environmental problems short of radical political and social changes, short of a revolutionary break from the forms of political life which have developed in the last 300 years. The Kantian exercise I have engaged in assumes that the situation is not so desperate that it cannot be solved through evolutionary political changes. It also recognises that a favourable change of moral consciousness is not something that can be guaranteed by any political order. Political theory at most can provide an account of what kind of political and social environment is most favourable to the creation of a good will and to its effective exercise.

NOTES

1. Robin Attfield [1992] argues that those who support environmentalism ought also to support demands for international justice (and *vice versa*). Michael Jacobs [1991: 187] argues that there are also strong pragmatic reasons why we ought to give aid to the poor of the world: 'It is certainly unlikely that Third World countries will agree to any international convention on global warming unless very substantial aid is provided to enable them to comply'.
2. Proposals for world government, of one form or another, were particularly common after the Second World War. See, for example, Clark and Sohn [1958]. Most of those who favoured world government were primarily concerned with solving the problem of war. Environmentalists, for one reason or another, have not found the idea so attractive.
3. This is such a common idea among environmentalists that Goodin [1992] regards it as the green political orthodoxy. Advocates include Edward Goldsmith [1972], Val and Richard Routley [1980], Rudolf Bahro [1986], Theodore Rozak [1986], Kirkpatrick Sale [1980].
4. See also Burnheim's contribution to the present collection.
5. They include the world order I advocate [1992] which is based upon both territorial and non-territorial communities.
6. Keekok Lee [1989: 52ff.] regards the non-linear nature of environmental causation as a particularly significant factor to take into account in any attempt to avoid environmental problems. A non-linear cause involves a feedback loop: A causes changes in B which alter A, and so on.
7. Those who have developed this line of thought include Garrett Hardin [1968], Robert L. Heilbroner [1974], William Ophuls [1977].
8. This is not the same as advocating world dictatorship. Authoritarianism may be compatible

with some form of 'guided democracy' or with measures designed to remove some matters from the reach of democratic decision-making.

9. Hugh Stretton [1976] presents a more detailed argument for thinking that a green dictatorship, even if it could be imposed, would probably fail to achieve its environmental objectives due to corruption of officials, or the incentives that would have to be offered to them in order to prevent corruption.

10. It is Murray Bookchin's thesis [1982, 1990] that authoritarian or centralised political formations cannot solve environmental problems because of the very nature of ecological systems. This seems basically right. Complex systems are capable of creating complex problems.

11. A person who accepts and lives by certain moral values regards them as essential to her idea of herself. The problem of compliance thus raises the question discussed by Ian Barns: how is the development of the self and its idea of the good affected by social relations?

12. Sandel [1982] makes the point that Rawls's theory of justice, which requires that goods be distributed to the advantage of the least well off, presupposes that people of a community have relations with each other that predispose them to accept sacrifices for the sake of others in their society. The more tenuous these relationships, the less acceptable to them will be a theory of distributive justice.

13. Both Goodin [1992] and Eckersley [1992] find anarchist views unrealistic as far as their political prescriptions are concerned. In particular, Eckersley accuses eco-anarchists of confusing the potential nature of individuals with their essential nature [1992: 171]. Anarchists do tend to have questionable views about human nature, but her criticism does not do justice to the idea that new ways of living and relating might give rise to attitudes and values that are favourable to environmental protection.

14. This is suggested by Brian Barry [1992] (though not primarily for environmental reasons): 'A counterfactual America combining state-level controls over immigration and strong federal policies to bring economic development to the South while ensuring legal and political rights to the Blacks would surely be a better one than that which actually exists. And that is, in broad terms, the formula that I advocate for the world as a whole.'

15. Environmental anarchist democracy is essentially what Dryzek [1990] calls discursive democracy – it depends upon communication among people of ideas, points of view and knowledge, and agreements reached collectively by taking the contributions of everyone into account. Ian Barns in his contribution to the present collection also stresses that democracy ought to take into account different points of view and encourage discussion about substantial social issues and ideas of the good.

16. It is true that the views of some of these institutions are not all that favourable to environmentalism. But what seems important to me are not what opinions these groups now advocate (which can change), but the kind of links that they establish among people.

REFERENCES

Attfield, Robin (1992), 'Development and environmentalism', in R. Attfield and B. Wilkins (eds.), *International Justice and the Third World,* London, New York: Routledge.

Bahro, Rudolf (1982), *Socialism and Survival,* London: Heretic Books.

Bahro, Rudolf (1986), *Building the Green Movement,* London: Heretic.

Barry, Brian (1992), 'Quest for Simplicity: a Sceptical View', in Brian Barry and Robert E. Goodin (eds.), *Free Movement: Ethical Issues in the Transmigration of People and Money,* University Park, PA: Pennsylvania State University Press.

Burnheim, John (1986), 'Democracy, Nation States and the World System', in D. Held and C. Pollitt, *New Forms of Democracy,* London: Sage, pp.218–39.

Burnheim, John (1989), *Is Democracy Possible? The Alternative to Electoral Politics,* Berkeley, CA: University of California Press.

Bookchin, Murray (1982), *Ecology of Freedom: The Emergence and Dissolution of Hierarchy,* Palo Alto, CA: Cheshire.

Bookchin, Murray (1974), *Post-scarcity Anarchism,* London: Wildwood House.

Bookchin, Murray (1990), *Remaking Society: Pathways to a Green Future,* Boston, MA: South End Press.

Clark, Grenville and Louis B.Sohn, (1958), *World Peace through World Law,* Cambridge, MA: Harward University Press.

Dryzek, John S. (1990) *Discursive Democracy* Cambridge: Cambridge University Press.

Eckersley, Robin (1992), *Environmentalism and Political Theory: Toward an Ecocentric Approach,* Albany, NY: State University of New York.

Frankel, Boris (1987), *Post-industrial Utopians,* Cambridge: Polity.

Goldsmith, Edward *et al.* (1972), 'Blueprint for Survival', *The Ecologist,* Vol.2, No.1 pp 1–44.

Goodin, Robert E. (1992), *Green Political Theory,* Cambridge: Polity.

Hardin, Garrett (1968), 'Tragedy of the Commons', *Science,* 162, pp.1243–8).

Heilbroner, Robert L. (1974), *An Inquiry into the Human Prospect,* New York: Norton.

Jacobs, Michael (1991), *The Green Economy,* London and Concord, MA: Pluto Press.

Kant, Immanuel (1963 [1795]), 'Perpetual Peace', in Lewis White Beck (ed.), *Kant on History,* New York: Bobbs-Merrill.

Lee, Keekok (1989), *Social Philosophy and Ecological Scarcity,* London and New York: Routledge.

Mannison, D. *et al.* (eds.) (1980), *Environmental Philosophy,* Canberra: Research School of Social Sciences.

Mill, John Stuart (1861), *Considerations on Representative Government.*

Ophuls, William (1977), *Ecology and the Politics of Scarcity: Prologue to a Political Theory of the Steady State,* San Francisco, CA: W.H. Freeman.

Rawls, John (1987), 'The Idea of an Overlapping Consensus', *Oxford Journal of Legal Studies,* 7, pp.1–25.

Rozak, Theodore (1986), *Person/Planet,* Garden City, NY: Doubleday.

Routley, Val and Richard Routley, 'Social Theories, Self Management and Environmental Problems', in Mannison *et al.* (eds.) [*1980*].

Sale, Kirkpatrick (1980), *Human Scale,* New York: Coward, Cann & Geoghegan.

Sale, Kirkpatrick (1985), *Dwellers in the Land: The Bio-regional Vision,* San Francisco, CA: Sierra Books.

Sandel, Michael (1982), *Liberalism and the Limits of Justice,* Cambridge: Cambridge University Press.

Stretton, Hugh (1976), *Capitalism, Socialism and the Environment,* Cambridge: Cambridge University Press.

Thompson, Janna (1992), *Justice and World Order,* London and New York: Routledge.

Power-Trading and the Environment

JOHN BURNHEIM

It is not democracy, but politics that is the problem in arriving at sound common decisions in ecological matters, as in many others. Politics, democratic or not, is a matter of generalised power-trading. Every political player has some say over many outcomes, only a few of which have a direct effect on his or her welfare. The political game consists largely in power-trading, selling one's power in matters to which one is relatively indifferent in order to secure the exercise of power in one's favour in more 'important' contexts. In this game, ecological considerations inevitably fare badly in most cases. Even where there is agreement about the need to act, there is no agreement about who is to bear the costs. In ordinary discourse we usually call a decision 'political' to the extent that it is the result of power-trading. The basic principle of sound democracy is that decisions on any matter should be made only by agents who are genuinely representative of those who are directly and materially affected by those decisions. This involves a *functional* decentralisation of power to specialised authorities, not necessarily local communities, but a network of communities of interest. One crucial question then is, how to represent the interests of those who cannot speak for themselves? Suggestions are offered about appropriate selection procedures. Another is, how to finance an ecologically and democratically sound system? The answer lies in charging heavily for the use of land and natural resources. Finally, the practical questions are always very specific ones. In order to act well we do not need to share the same ecological vision, much less to enforce it by massive political action, but only to empower those who bear the consequences of particular actions and failures to act.

Environment politics, like other areas of political action, is a matter of forming the appropriate public opinion and seeing that it issues in appropriate action. So far, the environmental movement has concentrated on the first stage, tending to assume that there is no special difficulty about the second. Of course it is naive to assume that our political processes naturally

John Burnheim formerly taught in the Department of Traditional and Modern Philosophy, University of Sydney.

deliver what the public wants in any area of government, but there are features of typical environmental and ecological problems that make our usual political problems especially acute. Obvious difficulties are that environmental problems are especially likely to involve the interests of those who can have no direct representation in our present electoral systems, mute nature and future human beings. Moreover, many ecological decisions are completely irreversible, extinguishing species and initiating processes that cannot be stopped.

Electoral politics necessarily concentrates on immediate issues while politicians pay ritual deference to the long-term ones. Almost any group with a substantial immediate interest in opposing a sound environmental practice can exercise more political power than the more diffuse environmental lobby, which is saddled with a seemingly endless list of demands. Politicians can buy off the loggers, but the environmentalists are 'insatiable'. This leads to a tendency among environmentalists to moralise about the dirtiness and deceptiveness of political activity at the expense of analysis in depth and constructive thinking. Environmentalists must stop wringing their hands at the selfishness, myopia and idiocy of political decisions and look carefully at the problem of putting in place institutions and procedures that might be expected to generate and implement appropriate decisions in the matters that concern them. Even if all our political agents shared those same concerns, it is not likely that that would result in sound environmental action through our present political processes.

It is almost universally recognised now that the market is incapable of providing a range of public goods, including protection of the environment, that a tolerable market society needs. This is not so much a matter of self-interest as of the sort of coordination the mechanism of the market can achieve. The 'tragedy of the commons' will occur even if all the participants are altruists as long as they have no means of rationing access to the commons. Each will feel justified in exploiting the commons for the best of motives, with results quite as disastrous as if they were utterly selfish.

Environmental questions involve great uncertainties and gambles. We live in an evolving universe every aspect of which is in unstable balance. What needs to be done is obvious only to the ignorant and dogmatic. Almost everything we can do has its costs as well as benefits. Confrontational politics stresses conflicts of interest, opinions and values. There is almost always conflict over who is to bear the burdens of measures that almost everybody supports, and often no way of resolving it. Each group attempts to shift the responsibility on to some other group, and the measures are not put into effect. Different systems of government have different weaknesses in this area. What I want to suggest is that there is a fundamental problem in all political systems up to the present that we need to understand if we are to meet the challenge of providing public goods, especially the protection of the environment, which is the greatest of all public goods in the long term. Political theory must become as central to environmentalism as biology is today.

It is not democracy as such that is unlikely to result in sound decisions about environmental matters, but current forms of democracy, because of a feature they have in common with all forms of government that have existed up to the present.[1] This crucial feature is that people are given power to determine what is done in matters in which they have no legitimate material interest. So they use that power to advance other interests they have by trading power.

In all politics past and present, decision-making depends crucially on generalised power-trading. All the active day-to-day players in the political game have a certain amount of power through control of resources such as knowledge, loyalties, money, official positions, prestige and votes. Even the so-called absolute monarch has ministers who play power-games amongst themselves and with him. Players buy support they need on one issue from others who have some power in that area, usually by promising to return some equivalent favour in the future. Vote-trading is the most obvious example, but there are ways of trading most exercises of power. The point of the game is to maximise one's power by subjecting the powers of others to one's control as cheaply as possible. Power has its own satisfactions and can bring rich rewards. But no matter how noble one's aims, achieving those ends in politics means playing the power-game. Occasionally one may succeed by persuasion, but the serious politician will always try to exact a price for support.

In existing democratic states, voters hand over to elected representatives their votes on everything that comes up for public decision. The representatives trade favours among themselves in the light of their judgements about what is best from their own point of view and what the electorate will wear. The outcome is determined by the skill of politicians in power-trading.

The Trouble with Power-Trading

We are so accustomed to politics as generalised power-trading, much though we may complain about it, that it is difficult to see through the rationalisations that legitimise it, or at least make it seem inevitable. People complain about politics in which issues are decided, not on their merits, but in virtue of the power strategies of the politicians. Most theoretical discussion, however, takes it for granted that realistic political structures must work through generalised power-trading, and that the problems are those of securing better control over abuses of power and more accountability. One of the simplest forms of power is threatening violence, especially if it can be done plausibly and legitimately, or with impunity. There are strong resemblances between this particular form of power and most other forms that will help us sort out some of what is wrong with power-trading.

We normally regard threats of violence as justified only as deterrents from wrong-doing, and even then only on the basis that the threatener has some particular entitlement to deter the potential malefactor. Threatening violence against others merely to get our own way with them is robbery or rape or some other invasion of rights. We are not entitled to threaten what we are not entitled to do. Violence is inherently destructive. It can on occasion remove certain evils, but it rarely produces good. A regime in which some agents secure what they want by intimidation rather than by producing it or exchanging some equivalent for it is unproductive and unjust. Indeed, any system that allows some people to appropriate either private or public goods without fair exchange or compensation is unjust and unproductive.

In so far as agents in the power game can appropriate for themselves and others goods they have neither produced nor bought, these proceedings resemble the use of violence to get what one wants. They require justification. If I am uninterested in the outcome of a certain issue that concerns you and use my voting in your interest on that issue to get from you some substantial favour for myself, I am taking something from you under duress at no cost to myself. Even if there were substantial equality and reciprocity in the game, it would be unsatisfactory. Gains and losses might average out, but there would be many unnecessary losses arising out of decisions made on inappropriate grounds, unrelated to the merits of the case. It might be fair, though everybody would be worse off than they would be where decisions were taken only on relevant grounds.

But power games are not all like a free market, or even a free-for-all. In a free market it always costs one to act destructively or punitively towards another. For example, one may threaten to move one's custom from one firm to another, but in a market where everybody charges the market price, it is unlikely one can extract a return that warrants the effort. The firm that is threatened can attract other customers, and no one customer is crucial to its survival. Even where monopolies exist, they are open to challenge and probably will be challenged. In the political power game, by contrast, the number of players is limited by the number of positions in the power structure, seats in parliament, places in the party hierarchy, or the administrative structure. Entry is difficult and often involves payments to those already in positions of power. There is no open market, no competitively set prices, power grows out of power even more certainly than money grows out of money. The cost of the *quid pro quo* that the power broker gives for his power is borne not by himself, but by the public or that portion of it that loses the vote. Of course, his vote has its opportunity cost. If it is used to extract some favour from one group, another is correspondingly alienated. But in a well-constructed strategy one may in fact gain from depriving one's enemies of what would otherwise have gone to them, while a single vote may win the gratitude of several groups.

Power can be both profitable and costless. Even when it does not reduce the amount of good available by making less than optimal choices and rewarding itself inappropriately, it almost inevitably maldistributes it, because who has the numbers on a particular issue is largely unrelated to the merits of the case, however they are assessed. There are in practice many bad effects of the system. Minorities that focus almost exclusively on a particular issue can get their way at the cost of using their power on other issues simply to buy support, irresponsibly. So, notoriously, a small, intense interest group concentrated in a few electorates can exercise enormous power, while a much larger number spread throughout all electorates is virtually powerless. Again, in all power-games the time scale tends to be short. If you want to be effective it is wise to concentrate on short-term objectives. Long-term debts get written off. Even the honest politician does not stay bound for long.

In most situations it is the more general, remote or diffuse interests that suffer, ecological ones especially, and those of animals and future generations. Even where there is much good will towards the more general or remote interests, particular interest groups will try to pass the cost of meeting the general interest onto others or use support for the general interest as a bargaining chip in their own interest. Different plans to protect the environment will impose different and unequal costs on different groups, and each will try to suit itself and blame the other if nothing is done to attain the goal that both profess to share.

Instead of Power-Trading

Power-trading decisions will normally be very different from decisions in which only those strongly affected by the decisions have a say, because in such a case only relevant considerations are likely to be given any weight. No free-floating power has a foothold. In so far as there is a direct conflict of interest the parties must look for a package that maximises the utilities of all concerned. Where the decision is taken by a representative committee, as a committee they will have to be able to represent that decision as fair to all concerned. They cannot shift the blame on to others or on to irrelevant issues.

At the same time, especially if, as I argue in *Is Democracy Possible?* [*Burnheim, 1985*], they are statistically rather then electorally chosen, their negotiations are freed from other irrelevancies that commonly handicap elected governments. They are not tied to any particular general prejudice or ideology. Unlike bureaucrats, they need not be concerned about setting precedents in other areas of public administration. Their concern is simply to make the most of the resources available to them for the purposes they are charged to look after.

A rough example may help, for the sake of simplicity taken at the level of local government. You and I are members of the town council. I want to direct the public library to spend more on hobby books, and similar practical publications, in the hope of interesting the young in such things. You want more spent on literary classics in the hope of raising cultural standards in the community. Since the council has to take a policy decision, each of us goes to various of our colleagues to enlist their support. Typically the responses we get are: 'I'm undecided. There is a lot to be said on both sides, but I suppose I owe you one for your support at the last meeting. You can count on my vote.' When I try another, the subject will be switched to the proposal for upgrading the swimming centre until it becomes clear that a trade would be in both our interests. Whether you win or I win is a matter of who can strike the more deals tying up more votes.

Suppose, by contrast, that the decision is to be made by a library committee representative of those directly affected by the decision, the library staff and the users. If we are members of that committee, our approach will need to be different. We shall have to look for common ground on which to construct a majority entirely in terms of considerations relevant to the library. We will take a much closer look at ways in which we might both get as much of what we want as possible. In the process of negotiation each strives to find ways of offering advantages from his or her point of view. Imaginative and creative proposals tend to come out of such contexts, given a will to arrive at an optimal solution. If a solution cannot be found by negotiation, we have to fall back on adjudication, which is usually less desirable because it is less creative. Either is preferable to power-trading.

Conflicts of Interest and Representation

In generalised power-trading sub-optimal outcomes tend to occur whether the interests in play are selfish or noble, narrow or broad. What skews the outcome is the introduction of costs and pay-offs that are not related to the question at issue. Moreover, public discussion is undermined. Politicians rarely admit that their decision on a particular matter has been determined mainly by political strategies. They attempt to justify it on the merits of the case, even when it is obvious that these are being sacrificed to political expediency. The result is widespread cynicism, not only about politicians, but about politics, which is damaging to the public good in a host of ways. The politicians are trapped. No matter how good their intentions, they do have to trade against each other interests that have almost nothing in common. They have no answer that those adversely affected can accept to the question: Why should our interests suffer in order to advance that other interest we do not share?

In most contemporary democracies representatives are elected by geographically defined constituencies. They have to satisfy a majority or plurality of voters that they and their parties are more likely to advance the interests of those voters than are their rivals. Not only do different groups in the electorate have conflicting interests, but all individuals have many interests that conflict. As a motorist I want a new freeway; as a householder I do not want it adjacent to my property. What I want to suggest is that what I need is not someone to represent *me*, but a variety of people to represent my different interests. For the most part, the best available solutions to problems of conflict of interests are likely to be achieved by concretely focused negotiations between those who are concerned with those interests. They alone have the capacity and the motivation to develop creative solutions.

Even the most impartial arbitrator is limited to considerations of fairness, adjudicating recognised claims rather than developing new ideas. In the same way, even the best planners in a planned economy are almost certain to be mistaken about what to produce, no matter how attentive they are to what consumers say they want. What consumers buy is the product that best fits their preferences as they emerge from a situation that is the result of changes in what is produced. Only decentralised and risk-trading initiative can provide this sort of change, and it is one of the great virtues of the market that it does so, at least where private goods are concerned, by a process of trial and error. Similarly in science and the arts the best developments come not from planning, but from decentralised risk-taking initiative concentrated on a particular problem. I would argue that the disenchantment of many with public provision of goods and services is due in great measure to the political process as we know it. Voting is a very conservative context, dominated by the present preferences of voters and the past performances of the politicians. We need a system of providing public goods that can be much more experimental. As advocates of the market constantly remind us, the public sector is a mass of unnecessary rigidities. The solution is not to minimise its scope, as they would do, but to change the structure of decision-making.

Two Principles of Democracy

The basic principle of democracy, I suggest, is that each of a person's legitimate interests should be represented in a given context of decision to the degree that they are materially and directly affected by decisions in that domain. By materially here I mean not simply in virtue of a person's beliefs and feelings, however justified these may be. The point is not that only objective or material considerations should have any role in determining what is to be done. Those empowered to decide may do so on the basis of sentiment or ideology if they think that is what is appropriate. The point is that they must bear the effects of their doing so and justify themselves to their colleagues and to public opinion. I return below to the question of interests other than those of existing persons, notably those of the environment and of future generations.

When it comes to deciding what are legitimate interests or deliberately changing existing patterns of legitimate interest, representation of existing interests cannot be an appropriate basis of proceeding. The wisdom of the community, and especially its moral resources, has to be brought to bear on the problems to be solved (a distinction that resembles Hayek's distinction between law and legislation). I am not suggesting that there are theoretically determinable right answers to such questions, much less that the wise will generally agree about them. People will differ about the likely consequences and about the relations between consequentialist and deontological considerations. What one would hope is that in coming to some compromise the determination of those charged with making the decision would reflect informed and responsible opinion in the community. This presupposes a context of public discussion and tradition. It is entirely inappropriate that such matters be decided by power-trading or by violence, though they very often are. I can only refer the reader to my book *Is Democracy Possible?* [*Burnheim, 1985*] for suggestions about the appropriate institutional procedures to embody such principles.

Very briefly, I argue that decision-makers should be chosen by lot from a pool of people who have commended themselves to their peers on the administrative committees that oversee the provision of everyday public goods as having the attributes appropriate to making decisions about the legitimacy of interests and the relative weighing of interests, including those of future generations and of non-human beings.

The point is that there is a multiple indeterminacy as well as a host of moral problems here. Like it or not, our collective behaviour constitutes a population policy, determining the composition of future generations as well as what resources we shall hand on to them. (I do not for a minute suggest that we should have some unitary population policy, but only that people who make decisions need to be aware of what they are doing in its broadest context.) Wisdom, knowledge and intelligence are as necessary as integrity and good intentions. There is a certain elitism in such a proposal, but the elite would be generated from below, and it would not be self-reproducing. Nor would it assign its own rewards. On the other hand, whatever one thinks of mass voting as a means of representing present interests of the electorate, there is no reason to think that it can, much less will, represent adequately interests that cannot have a vote.

Money and Majority Rule

It may be objected that power-trading is appropriate where goods and services that cost money are concerned. At least all taxpayers should have a say in how their taxes are spent. Even if public money is not derived from taxation but, say, from rents, it is our common property to spend as we collectively determine. A little less crudely, there is a large cost that each of us has to bear in regard to any public expenditure, namely the opportunity cost of that money being unavailable for other public purposes we may value more. In fact most political decisions about public goods are usually represented as budgetary decisions, and power-trading is very naturally expressed in monetary terms.

The almost vacuous answer to the question why we cannot have any particular thing is that there is no money, which inevitably elicits the retort that money is being wasted on certain other things. Money can give us a rough measure of costs and of certain kinds of benefits, and it is important that these factors are made fully explicit. We have to know what things cost. But if a certain educational programme and a certain health programme have similar monetary costs and benefits, and we cannot afford both, we have to decide which is to be preferred, putting certain specific needs and benefits before others. So-called priorities, which we are exhorted to get right, or abstract values are no help either. I may believe the community spends too much on health services, and too little on education, but still favour this health expenditure over that educational proposal. The generalities in terms of which these questions are presented to the electorate are almost meaningless.

Even if there were a clear majority will on the specific issue, not everything is properly to be decided on that basis. Minorities have rights; in practice, of course, public matters are rarely decided by legislatures and administrations simply on the basis of winner takes all. They attempt to give at least some substance to the claim that they are concerned with the welfare of the whole community, not just those who support them. To deny any recognised legitimate interest is normally seen as an abuse of power and a threat to the legitimacy of the government. Of course there may be important interests whose legitimacy is not generally recognised and some interests that are accepted as legitimate on morally unacceptable grounds. Nevertheless, nobody allocating public money dares to admit to any other basis of decision than attempting to balance all legitimate claims on the basis of need and public benefit in accordance with recognised moral values and principles. Public opinion exercises considerable restraint on what people can get away with in any matter where there is genuine informed debate and a sense of community. Nevertheless power-trading in these decisions does result in great weight being given to more immediate cost-benefit considerations involving the politically powerful.

We need a mechanism for allocating public monies that is much more appropriate to the rationale of fairness than majority rule.

Public Goods

I do not propose to dispute the view, dubious though it is, that ultimately the value of public goods can be measured completely in terms of their effects on the welfare of individuals. What needs emphasising is that most fully public goods not only can be shared by everybody, but are normally enhanced by being shared. The knowledge, mutual understanding, cultural sensibility and traditions that make a fully fledged community are validated, developed and enhanced by being shared. Taken together they are the core components of a civil social life which is both the matrix and often the object of the individual's spiritual life. Such goods cannot be bought and sold. They have no monetary value, though their value may be reflected in real-estate prices or in what people are prepared to forego to share more fully in them. Not so long ago it was fashionable to deplore a tendency to submit such goods to purely economic assessments. Today the pendulum has swung to the other extreme and we are told that our economic well-being is at risk when people value cognitive and aesthetic achievement and satisfactions more highly than economic goods. I shall not try to refute this pernicious view here.

Critics of public support for cultural goods are on stronger ground when they insist that the most important of these goods are essentially by-products or favourable externalities. They are not the result of deliberate attempts to produce them, but arise out of the ways in which people pursue a host of more specific and limited goals. Nevertheless, they do not require material economic support in many instances and, since there can be no useful predictability in these matters, there can be no valid measure of cost-effectiveness. In strictly economic terms no rational decision is possible. The question is whether we value these things enough to risk wasting money on them. To the extent that power-trading prevails we are unlikely to do so.

What I would hope is that in the sort of policy that I am advocating more diffuse and general concerns would be provided for, because the first step in either adjudication or negotiation is to secure those things on which the parties are agreed, and also because it is usually not very costly to support such public goods.

The Ecosystem

In important ways the health of the ecosystem is a public good like those just discussed. We cannot produce it by direct action, but only harm it. Precisely because its benefits are so accessible they have no market value, even though they have enormous value, which is turned into economic value as soon as access to them is blocked. Unfortunately, there is very often a direct and substantial economic incentive to do things that damage the health of ecosystems. Counteracting these incentives is difficult even where the need to do so is clear in terms of existing interests. In some simple cases prohibitions against doing certain things may be appropriate and adequate, but most of the more general problems involve limiting population pressure and cutting down on the uses we make of endangered and non-renewable resources. In a market economy the only effective way of doing this is by making them more expensive. Obviously, as long as the only costs of using natural resources are the costs of extracting them and a rent to their owners reflecting the relative ease of exploitation here rather than there, these resources will be exploited to the hilt. Regulations governing their consumption have only minimal effects, especially where each particular use seems perfectly legitimate.

Indeed, in any democratic society, and for that matter in any authoritarian one, it is going to be exceedingly difficult to control the innumerable uses to which natural resources are put, unless we can feed into the market prices of those goods at the source an economically arbitrary, but ecologically rational, price differential over the open market value large enough to reduce drastically the level of consumption by making ecologically sound alternatives competitive. We have to make those costs percolate right through the system. This is part of the point of insisting on feeding them in at the source. It may well be the case, for example, that a technology that uses a great deal of fossil fuel at the consumer end is still ecologically efficient because the alternatives use so much in their construction or in their side effects. The market can adapt much more appropriately to such base-price inputs than to a host of taxes and prohibitions.

Even so, getting our societies to accept such a regime is going to be extremely difficult. What I suggest is that the growing threat to the ecosystem is going to produce a strong consciousness of it, as the common heritage and responsibility of all present and future human beings. What could be more natural than that we should provide for the various public goods we need by charging rents on the use of our natural resources to fund them? Income and consumption taxes are always more or less arbitrary in their incidence, and very often regressive. If we could at the same time make more equitable provision for our public revenue and control the biggest single cause of ecological deterioration, that must have a powerful appeal.

International Bodies

The greatest of the many difficulties in such a proposal is that it could work only on an international scale.[2] In regard to each kind of extractive resource it would be necessary to get the agreement of all the producer states to hand over to the relevant international body the pricing of that resource. This might not be so difficult if there were no question of quotas, and if each were assured of a revenue better than they might expect from market pricing. In order to ensure international acceptance of the system, they might well agree to most of the surplus over market price being disbursed on international public goods. In that case it might not be difficult to orchestrate a system of trade sanctions to enforce compliance.

The key, I believe, to such developments is to remove them as far as possible from international power-trading by ensuring both that the committees[3] that control these authorities are not representative of states but of the kinds of people affected by their decisions, and that the scope of each body is strictly limited, so there is no danger of its forming the nucleus of a new super-state. So, for example, it seems undesirable that raising funds in this way and disbursing them be in the same hands. As I have argued elsewhere, it is not too difficult to imagine such a system working well once established. The problem is getting there.

Beyond the Will of the People

There is, however, one difficulty that encumbers any democratic theory in ecological matters. Classical democratic theory of all sorts is concerned to make government as accountable as possible to the will of the people, subject, perhaps, to certain restrictions respecting the rights of minorities. The will of the people, however determined, is quite likely not to have sufficient regard to the rights of future generations and the well-being of non-human things. In regard to those who are not represented in the political process, we who are represented are at best in the position of benevolent despots, having responsibility for them among a host of other more immediate concerns. Yet, in the abstract at least, their welfare and rights ought to weigh equally with ours. It seems to me important that in each context where a specific interest of future generations or of the ecosystem is involved there should be representatives whose specific job it is to defend and promote those interests. Such representatives should be as far as possible otherwise disinterested, capable and knowledgeable. As I have said, I would have them chosen by lot from a pool of people nominated by their peers on committees they had already served on as having the qualities that would suit the task. In the context of public discussion and scrutiny they would be rewarded by the respect of those whose opinions they value. It is part of this scheme that people are not normally eligible for reappointment to the same committee, that committee members are replaced one at a time to ensure continuity and that the material rewards of office are essentially compensation for income forgone while in office. One would expect there to be other advantages to those who performed well. Their abilities might attract the attention of potential employers, for example.

A judicious, decentralised, functional, unelected set of public bodies would take the grand drama out of politics. It would lose the adversarial conflict, the razzamatazz and the portentousness of politics as we know it, and we are reluctant to lose our illusions, particularly the illusion of power. However, since illusions of power are almost wholly both morally and practically dangerous, we can discard our illusions, not wearily or cynically, but critically, looking for the causes of our failures and for the locus of our responsibilities in things we can do something about. Unfortunately, this prescription is revolutionary without having the glamour that revolutions feed on. Still, my contention is that we shall not solve our problems until we face up to the inherent dynamics of the institutional arrangements and procedures that make solution difficult. Right ideas can become effective in political life only if they are freed from the distortions of power-trading and expressed in relevant institutional procedures of negotiation and arbitration.[4]

If the new system were merely a matter of advocating a form of polity fairer and more efficient than our present arrangements, it would not be of much practical interest. The only clearly identifiable interests it favours are of those who do not yet exist. There are no existing models to exhibit its benefits. It would work only where nationalism and other forms of totalising chauvinism were largely discredited, and so on. There is a familiar circularity here. If it did operate, this system might be expected to generate the conditions it needs to work in. But if the existing decision processes are as badly flawed as I suggest, how are those conditions ever to come about?

One cannot attach very much weight to the likelihood of a reaction against power-trading being of much assistance. It is so pervasive, not only in political institutions, but in business and bureaucracies of all sorts ('it's not what you know but who you know'), that even those who condemn it think of it as ineradicable, certainly beyond the reach of any structural or procedural reforms. We are all aware of the problems of changing conventions. Ultimately there could be great benefits from rationalising English spelling, but the costs falling on the generation that did so would greatly outweigh any benefits they might receive from it. As the cynic put it, 'What has posterity done for me?'

One important mitigating factor is that the change to what I call 'demarchic' structures does not need to be sudden or total. The crucial thing is to get some working models in place in particular areas, and to get their appropriateness recognised in the key areas where considerations that transcend the interests and the competence of politicians and voters as at present constituted should be decisive. One place we might start is in the administration of resources that are largely ungoverned, such as those of the sea and polar regions [*Burnheim, 1986*].

Ecological issues are the most obvious examples, and the most urgent and difficult. Unfortunately, the ecologically aware are subject to two temptations to reject the suggestions I have been making. The ecological predicament is often seen as a whole that must be dealt with as a system, rather than by a multitude of independent authorities. Secondly, the emphasis on interests and on not imposing one's values and beliefs on other people smells of an individualistic liberalism.

A Model of Polity

One of the great obstacles to sound thinking in these matters is the polarisation of thinking between atomism and holism both in biological and political contexts – on the one hand reductionism to the individual, the cell or the selfish gene, as the case may be, on the other the absolute spirit, Gaia or the mystic whole. I shall not attempt to dismiss all such conceptions in the name of some religious, metaphysical or otherwise privileged competitor. What I would suggest is that both in ecological and in political contexts, at the level of abstraction and of practicality of the present discussion, models derived from modern medical science may prove helpful.

The human body, for example, contains a variety of systems, all with great importance for some of the others, and with some relation to and dependence on nearly all of them. They are all made up of cells, each of which has a similar core but which develop in very different ways in different circumstances. The various operating systems have a good deal of flexibility and autonomy as long as the others provide the conditions necessary for their functioning, such as blood supply, appropriate electrical and chemical signals and so on. Each has its specific pathologies and forms of vulnerability, as well as defences and means of recuperation. The most important thing that each needs from the others is their own healthy functioning. Granted that, it can usually look after itself. Similarly an ecosystem consists of a host of chains of food and fertilisation, each dependent on but relatively autonomous from the others in different ways and to different degrees. Even the central nervous system in the more complex animals is not very highly centralised in its functioning. It exercises no direct control over the development of the whole. Insofar as anything performs that role it is the genes that do so in interaction with the internal and external environment of the organism. There is an increasing number of things we can do to interfere with various functions and even with the genes themselves, but the only sober and achievable aim is to defend, rectify and enhance the performance of what is already there in relatively limited ways.

The analogies I would like to make between biological systems so conceived and polities as I would like them to be are obvious, and I shall not labour them. Instead, I must address the obvious omission from my picture. Granted it is a roughly satisfactory picture of the biological level of functioning, it omits the higher functions that are built on the biological but operate in quite a different way. In particular it omits human thought and action. We live, not just to preserve and reproduce ourselves as biological organisms, but to produce all those human achievements that we call culture. At the level of individual human lives these achievements are not just by-products of biological functioning. They involve deliberate thought and action in which we use our biological resources for ends that transcend biological survival. From the earliest states until very recently it has been assumed in theory and in practice that the organisation of society should be directed not just to its healthy functioning as a social organism but to great and glorious deeds, magnificent self-affirmation, the service of the divine in deliberately organised action to which all lower levels of activity are subjected. From this perspective the conception I have outlined appears myopic, debased and petty.

The obvious retort is to point to the megalomania, barbarity and destructiveness of most of what has been counted as glorious in most cultures. The better answer is to deny that there is any privileged analogue of the individual human being at the level of thought and action. We can and do group ourselves into a great variety of collective agents and as such do many things no individual could do, some of them humdrum, others glorious, none of which eclipses or guides all the others.

Some of these associations will be concerned with matters of great importance, but still operate in a voluntary mode. There are in fact very many bodies that exercise substantial authority without having any power to enforce their decisions other than from their prestige and acceptance. Examples range from the Red Cross to professional and sporting bodies, churches and scientific organisations. Many authorities, such as environmental ones, will certainly need the backing of other powers. But this backing need not necessarily come from state power if the authority in question can call on sufficiently powerful support and sanctions from other independent authorities. A group of recognised international authorities backing each other up could be powerful enough to exercise decisive sanctions even over most states in most circumstances. They need not constitute a super-state, and it is undesirable that they should. All that is needed is mechanisms of coordination, adjudication and joint action for specific purposes that derive their power entirely from mutual agreement, not from any overriding sovereignty. Indeed, the broader point of demarchy is to chip away and ultimately destroy sovereignty at all levels of social life. The myth of sovereignty is something that democracies have taken over from authoritarian regimes and incorporated in the ideology of the will of the people conceived as the nation-state. A fully defensible democracy must be conceived as a set of institutions and procedures that secures for all human and non-human beings the best natural and social environment that can be achieved with the means available to us. That involves producing a rich variety of public goods. Its being democratic must consist in its permitting and encouraging the active participation of people in decision-making, sometimes as representatives of specific interests they themselves have, but often too as trustees of interests that cannot speak for themselves.

To summarise: liberal democracy, being a form of power-trading, is inadequate to deal with environmental problems. Only a system designed to give due weight and representation to interests that go beyond the normal horizons of electoral politics can do that. The morality we need would develop in the process of discussion once we recognised that a defensible democracy cannot be just a matter of the interests of the present generation of human beings. Like any morality, it will depend for its practical force on its appeal to people's self respect.

NOTES

1. In addition liberal democracy has specific disabilities as Dryzek, Plumwood, Mathews and other contributors to the collection argue.
2. My focus here is very limited. For a wider perspective see Thompson's contribution in this collection.

3. These remarks may suggest indifference to the ways in which market relations generate and amplify inequalities, as Plumwood (this collection) reminds us. A market economy must be tempered by the generous provision of public goods and some redistributive mechanisms
4. I am assuming the continuance of conceptions of self, nature, rationality and morality that are typically liberal. If, for example, eco-feminists manage to change these assumptions of current political discourse, that could trigger radical change. However, I believe that institutional change is normally indispensible if a change in consciousness is to become stabilised and effective.

REFERENCES

Burnheim, J. (1985), *Is Democracy Possible?*, Cambridge: Polity Press; Berkeley, CA: University of California Press.
Burnheim, J. (1986), 'Democracy, Nation States and the World System', in Held and Pollitt [*1986*].
Held, D. and C. Pollitt, (eds.) (1986), *New Forms of Democracy*, London: Sage.
Pollitt, C. (1986), 'Democracy and Bureaucracy', in Held and Pollitt [*1986*].

Community and the Ecological Self

FREYA MATHEWS

Small face-to-face communities provide conditions for the growth of relational selves, which, unlike the individualistic selves of liberalism, are predisposed to empathy, and hence arguably to an ecocentric perspective. The relationality of community in this sense, however, needs to be distinguished from abstract forms of holism, such as nationalism and globalism. Community can nevertheless to some extent meet the challenges of transnationality by itself assuming certain transnational features, without thereby losing its roots in particularity and concreteness and assuming the abstract character of globalism.

In this contribution I shall explore some of the tensions between liberal democracy and the requirements of thoroughgoing ecological reform, where by this I mean a degree of reform commensurate with the current world-wide ecological crisis. I propose to adopt an ecocentric rather than an anthropocentric yardstick of reform since, as is explained in the introduction to this collection, ecocentrism affords an exacting standard for ascertaining the true environmental potential of political systems. I shall argue that liberal democracy fails to provide the kind of social conditions conducive to the large-scale emergence of an ecocentric consciousness, and hence that ecocentric environmentalism is bound to remain a minority concern in liberal regimes. I shall then outline the kind of social conditions which I consider generally to be a necessary (though not sufficient) condition for the emergence of an ecocentric outlook.[1] Up to this point my paper recapitulates, though in an ecological vein, some of the lines of argument developed by communitarian, socialist and feminist critics of liberalism. Thereafter, however, I subject the notion of eco-communitarian selfhood, developed in the first half of the study, to closer scrutiny, distinguishing it from abstract forms of collectivism or globalism, yet also expanding it into a transnational frame. It is also worth noting that the overall argument is largely programmatic, as space does not allow the full development and

Freya Mathews teaches in the Philosophy Department, La Trobe University, Australia. The author is very grateful to Tony Coady, Robyn Eckersley, Janna Thompson and Robert Young for helpful comments on an earlier draft of this contribution.

defence of all the claims and inferences involved along the way.

Liberal Democracy and Morality

What are the underlying principles of democracy? There is of course no agreed-upon answer to this question. But I would suggest that the basic aim of democracy, as it was understood both in classical Greece and in Europe in the seventeenth and eighteenth centuries, was for the individual members of society to achieve some degree of control over social decisions that affected their lives. That is, the aim was to take the power to make those decisions out of the hands of absolute authorities, and to place it, to varying degrees, into the hands of the people whom those decisions affected. In other words, people were to be given the power to conduct their lives as freely as possible from the control of 'higher' authorities. Indeed no 'higher' authority was recognised: individuals themselves in principle had the final authority over their own lives. In this sense, all individuals were equal: no individual or class of individuals was of a higher order than any other. A certain notion of equality is thus implicit in this conception of democracy. But even more deeply embedded in this conception, I think, is the value of autonomy. Advocates of democracy insist on individual freedom from higher authorities not so much because they think that this is the best way to get what they want, in the sense of satisfying their immediate needs and desires, but rather because they value self-rule for its own sake. Hence even were they offered a political system in which everything they wanted would be granted to them by a benevolent, paternalistic authority, they would not be satisfied, for the point of their preference for democracy is not so much that it delivers what they want, in a material sense, but that it provides some degree of self-rule.[2]

Following a number of feminist, socialist and communitarian critics [*Sandel, 1982; Poole, 1993; Jaggar, 1983; Pateman, 1988; Nye, 1988*], I would argue that democracy in this sense valorises individualism, where this is understood as a particular sense of identity on the part of the members of the society in question. Or rather, it presupposes such individualism in theory, and helps to create or reinforce it in practice. Members of societies which are democratic in this sense see themselves as ultimate social units, of which society as a whole is merely the aggregate. The interests of these units are logically given independently of, and prior to, the interests of society; indeed the function of society, from this point of view, is merely to facilitate the unfettered self-realisation of such individuals – to enable these individuals to pursue their conception of their own good in their own way.

I propose to call democracy understood as a system of governance dedicated to individual freedom and self-rule 'liberal democracy', though I understand such a form of democracy to be capable of taking direct and indirect forms – from the participatory democracies of the ancient world to the representative or parliamentary democracies of the modern West. However, I am using the term 'liberal democracy' here, and in what follows, to denote an ideal type, rather than any actual flesh-and-blood historical society, for I am stripping the notion of its institutional and procedural and even economic[3] particularities, and focusing only on its ideological base – that is, its over-riding commitment to individual freedom and autonomy (where this, as I argue below, also implies a contractarian view of the foundations of society). In this sense, my use of the term 'liberal' is narrower than that of some liberal theorists, and the critique of 'liberalism' that I offer may not apply to some more encompassing theorisations of liberalism.[4]

It is liberal democracy understood in the sense of this ideal type that is, in my view, in tension with the requirements of an ecocentric outlook. This is for at least two related reasons, the first pertaining to morality, the second to identity. I shall examine the problem of morality in the present section, and that of identity in the next.

The view of human nature that I am here characterising as 'liberal' implies that people come together in democratic societies for the purpose of securing the conditions for self-rule, rather than on account of fellow feeling, or a desire to create social bonds or relationships as ends in themselves or for altruistic purposes. In other words, such democratic forms of society might be seen as having a contractarian rather than a moral basis. Adapting Rawls's veil-of-ignorance strategy to this purely contractarian end, it might be argued that if our ultimate interest is individual self-rule, then democratic organisation is simply prudentialism of the highest order – it involves our setting up society so that whatever happens to me (or my children) – however my fortunes (or those of my children) change – I shall still be free, to some degree, to pursue my own good in my own way. (However rich I am, I may become poor; however powerful, I may become weak; however able, I may become incapacitated; whatever social roles accrue to my gender now, they may give way to others; whatever my sexual orientation now, it may change; whatever my own race, that of my children or my grandchildren might be different. Given the inevitable uncertainty of the future, I can best secure my own long-term autonomy, or freedom to legislate for myself, by granting such freedom to all.)

Democracy in this contractual sense, then, has the satisfying characteristic of *appearing* to be 'moral' – it appears to rest on a principle of disinterested respect for the autonomy of all – without in fact requiring any moral or altruistic commitment from its members. It can be justified purely in terms of the interest of each individual in ruling themselves, and of their fitness to do so. Indeed such democracies *cannot* consistently require any common moral or altruistic commitment from their members – they *cannot* be founded on a public morality – since if they were, this would in itself violate the autonomy of their members, such autonomy entailing as it does the freedom of individuals to choose their own conception of the good.

It is this implicit lack of moral basis in liberal forms of political organisation that presents an obstacle to ecopolitics. For if the justification for individual self-rule or autonomy for all is that each individual is thereby assured of their own autonomy in any circumstances, then since neither I nor my children can ever become non-human, my interest in securing my own autonomy under all circumstances will not lead me to grant autonomy (in the sense of freedom from undue interference) to non-human beings: there is no reason for me to insist on their protection from the rest of society, since I can never be in their place.

In other words, in the absence of any common moral or altruistic underpinning to society, which might be generalised to non-human beings, there are no grounds intrinsic to liberal democracy for protecting the non-human world for its own sake.

Of course this is not to say that individuals in a liberal society are free to interfere with the environment in whatever ways they please. Some human actions have consequences for the environment that encroach on the autonomy of other human beings. Thus liberal democracies may attempt to deal with the problem of environmental protection by treating nature anthropocentrically as a set of resources which must be distributed and conserved in accordance with liberal principles of justice. Contemporary liberal philosophers seek to limit the destructive use that individuals and corporations make of the environment basically by appeal to the 'harm principle'. The freedom of a timber company to make commercial use of a forest 'resource' has to be offset on the one hand against the freedom of other groups to make, say, recreational use of the forest and on the other hand against the harm that, say, pollution from the timber mill may entail for residents downstream. The main innovation that liberal philosophers introduce into their arguments in addressing the problem of environmental degradation or resource exhaustion is the idea that the harm principle applies not only to present individuals but to future generations as well. Our use of the environment must be such as not to harm or unduly limit the choices of human beings of the future as well as of the present. But this concern for future generations need not be interpreted in a strongly moral sense if we take my interest in self-rule to include the interest of my children therein.

However, although liberal societies are not founded on a public morality, but on a particular form of individual self interest, namely the interest in self-rule, this is not to say that individuals, in exercising their freedom, might not commit themselves to moralities of their own choosing. That is, the 'good' that individuals are free to pursue in their own way may of course be a moral good as much as an egoistic good – so long as the realisation of such a 'moral' good does not contravene the harm principle or compromise the individual's own freedom to rule himself.[5]

From this point of view then, it is open to an individual with an ecocentric conception of the good to pursue this conception of the good in a democratic society, but on the understanding that this good is part of *her* interest, and counts for no more than that in computations of the collective good. In other words, her concern for the well-being of other life-forms is not taken at face value in this scenario, but is in effect converted into a kind of psychological interest of the individual in question. Her concern for other life forms is taken into consideration, if at all, out of respect for her freedom to pursue her own interests as she sees fit, and hence it is taken into consideration for *her* sake rather than for that of the other life forms themselves. Liberalism thus collapses the interests of multitudes of non-human beings and systems into a portion of the interests of perhaps no more than a handful of human advocates, and to the extent that those interests are taken seriously, it is out of a calculated deference to human autonomy.

In reply to this, however, a defender of liberalism might point out that liberal forms of democracy are not incompatible with communicative mechanisms within society. To the principle that each individual should be free to pursue her own conception of the good in her own way may be added the principle that as a society we should have mechanisms for communicating about significant conceptions of the good (Dryzek, this collection). In other words, the liberal might take the view that it is simply up to those who hold an ecocentric perspective to persuade the other members of society to share this perspective. If they are successful in inducing everyone to share it, the liberal might argue, then liberal democratic societies would have no difficulty in implementing an ecocentric polity, since human interest would in this case be enlarged to encompass the interests of the non-human world.

However, while it is true that if a majority of individuals in a liberal democracy adopted an ecocentric worldview, then an ecocentric polity might be forthcoming, it is unlikely – for reasons that will become apparent below – that most individuals in a purely liberal democracy *would* adopt an ecocentric worldview. And as long as there is significant conflict over ecocentric and anthropocentric perspectives, ecocentric outcomes are bound to be less likely than anthropocentric ones. This is because the ecocentric interests of individuals will always appear relatively lightweight compared with the direct material interests of their opponents: the 'psychological' or 'aesthetic' desires of wilderness *aficionados*, for instance, are always likely to seem trivial compared with the direct bread-and-butter interests of workers in the timber and mining industries. The freedom of the wilderness *aficionado* would seem to be less compromised by the logging of a forest than the freedom of a timber worker would be by the preserving of it. Thus when ecocentric values are subsumed under the interests of the human individuals who subscribe to them, the prospects for the protection of non-human life for its own sake are likely to remain bleak.

Liberal Democracy and Identity

I have argued in the previous section that there is a tension between liberalism and an ecocentric environmentalism, in so far as the foundation of liberal societies is not altruism – which might in principle be extended to the non-human world – but rather individual self-interest, specifically an interest in self-rule. This lack of an intrinsic or definitive concern for others on the part of liberal individuals is, I think, precisely a function of their individualism, the individualism implicit in the liberal premise – that is, that individual self-rule is the ultimate desideratum in politics. The priority of the principle of individual self-rule in liberalism means that in a liberal society people are neither expected to be altruistic, nor determined to be so through the structure of their social institutions. They are rather expected to conform to a view of human nature which is, *au fond*, individualistic and basically egoistic rather than altruistic, at least in the social and political domain (Plumwood, this collection), and liberal institutions shape them in such a way as to fulfil these expectations. How do these institutions achieve this?

Liberal institutions foster individualism by allowing social status to be won (or lost) through competition, rather than inherited through bloodlines or custom. In this way liberal societies historically broke up the fixed patterns of premodern societies, and set each individual in motion. Competing with their fellows to climb the ladders and avoid falling down the snakes of an hierarchical social structure, individuals could no longer define themselves in terms of permanent relationships with particular communities or places. In a world in which everything was potentially in flux, and no social destiny was guaranteed, individuals were forced to fall back on their own personal attributes and private relationships for their sense of identity.

However, the fact that liberal individuals are disposed to be self-interested and hence competitive does not, as observed in the previous section, entirely obviate the possibility of their contingently forgoing competition in favour of co-operation or even service-to-others, if these courses are sanctioned by reason or instilled by socialisation. But in this event, reason and/or socialisation will have to overpower the egoistic disposition of the individuals in question. In short, in liberal societies individuals are neither expected to be, nor constituted so as to become, disposed to fellow-feeling, empathy, spontaneous identification with others and their interests.[6] Without such an innate disposition, it is unlikely that more than a minority of such individuals will ever arrive at that perhaps most altruistic of all commitments – that is, the commitment to protect the non-human world for its own sake, as well as for the sake of its human beneficiaries.

Let us look a little more closely at the idea of the liberal individual. Liberal individualism may in fact be seen as exemplifying a principle of individuation that is quite general in its application, in the sense that it may be used to define what it is to be an individual across a range of domains, including physics, society and psychology [*Mathews, 1991*]. This principle, which is at bottom metaphysical, may be characterised as one of separation or division: it gives rise to *atomistic* realities, realities made up of ultimate units, where these units are, or are analogous to, substances in the traditional metaphysical sense – they are logically capable of standing alone. In such a substance scenario, it is the individuals that are given – it is they which have ontological priority. Assemblages of such individuals are mere aggregates, whose identity is derived from their constituent units. Moreover, since each individual is logically independent of all others, its properties belong to it, and it alone. Hence it is quite possible for a particular class of individuals, defined in terms of a common property, to be considered as categorically distinct from another class, whose members lack the property in question. If the property in question is a highly valued one, the class of individuals that possesses it might then be ranked above the class that lacks it. In this way, separation or division as a principle of individuation permits dichotomisation and value hierarchism (and hence reason/nature dualism, as we shall see below) to inform ontology.

It is easy to see how such a substance criterion of individuation is translated into social terms in liberal philosophy. From a liberal point of view, society is made up of discrete, independent individuals (social atoms), which can logically exist asocially, but who choose to place themselves in social settings with a view to furthering their own individual interests. Social structure is ultimately explained in terms of the actions and intentions of such individuals – that is, individuals are given; the identity of societies is derived from that of their constituents – that is, the individuals or the individuals or social atoms.

Liberal individualism is an abstract form of individualism in the sense that, in the shift from metaphysics to politics, liberals simply presuppose that human individuals, like metaphysical atoms, are logically capable of 'standing alone'. That is, they simply presuppose that people are logically capable of existing as rational (and therefore human) beings, independently of society, even though, from an empirical point of view, rational beings of course never are simply 'given', independently of social relations.[7] In this sense, liberal notions of human identity are based on an abstract idea of 'the individual', and liberal identity is accordingly an abstract form of identity, rather than one that is grounded in our actual experience of the process of identity formation. On the other hand, however, liberals so arrange society as to vindicate to some extent their presuppositions with regard to human nature. Through institutions that promote competition and social mobility, and which to a significant extent instrumentalise and contractualise relations (at least between adult people), liberal society goes some way towards countering the relational aspects of early (and later) identity formation and making actual the abstract individuals prefigured in its theory.

Understanding the way a substance criterion of individuation is used in liberalism also helps to throw light on another aspect of its worldview for, as noted above, the division of the world into discrete, self-contained units makes it possible to treat mind and matter as separate metaphysical categories – attributes which some individuals possess and others lack, absolutely. Since mind is valorised by liberal, and other Western, philosophers, the class of beings that possess mind may be set apart from, and above, the classes of beings that lack it. In this way, the substance principle of individuation permits a dualistic ranking of mind over body, and humanity over nature, where this has been seen as a hallmark of liberalism by feminist critics [*Jaggar, 1983; Plumwood, 1993*]. Such a dualistic ranking of mind over body, and humanity over nature, also clearly vitiates liberalism as a vehicle for ecocentric politics.

Let me explain the latter point a little more fully. From a liberal point of view, human beings earn their political status, and are entitled to the political prerogative of individual self-rule, on the strength of their capacity for reason. It is reason that qualifies us to legislate for ourselves in matters that affect us directly. But in liberal thought reason is understood dualistically, as that which sets human beings apart from, and above, nature. It seems to follow, then, that the whole edifice of *modern* liberalism, at any rate, is raised, from the very start, on the ideological ruins of nature: human beings are invested with 'natural rights' to freedom and equality on the grounds that they, *qua* human beings, transcend nature.[8] The substance principle of individuation thus generates a tendency towards dualism and hierarchism in liberal thought, which vitiates liberalism as a vehicle for a polity based on respect for nature.

However, liberal individualism, based as it is on a substance principle of individuation, does not exhaust the possibilities of human identity. Alternative modes of identity may offer more promising ontological foundations for human empathy with, and compassion for, both the human and non-human worlds. And there may be forms of society which mould human identity along lines more conducive to such an altruistic, and hence potentially ecocentric, outlook than liberal democracies do.

Ecological Identity as a Function of Community

I wish to suggest that a form of human identity defined not in terms of its independence from others but rather in terms of its relationships with them would provide a more appropriate ontological foundation for an ecocentric polity than liberal individualism does. It is the 'relational self', rather than the 'separate self' of liberalism, that regards the interests of others as inextricable from its own, and is accordingly imbued with fellow-feeling.

How to understand this contrast between the 'relational self' and the 'separate self' of liberalism? One way is to consider the metaphysical principle of individuation which underlies the 'relational self', in the same way that we have just considered the principle which underlay the 'separate self'. The principle of individuation which produces 'separate selves' is, as we saw, a principle of separation or division, which, like a pastry-cutter, carves reality up into substances or substance-like entities. That which results in 'relational selves', in contrast, may be characterised as a systemic or relational principle [*Mathews, 1991*]. From a relational perspective, reality is not divisible into units. It is rather a system or web of relationships. Individuals are, in this scheme of things, constituted by their relations with other individuals – it is these relations that determine their identity. Such individuals cannot stand alone – their identities are logically intermeshed with those of others.

In this scenario, then, it is the system of relations as a whole that is given, or has ontological priority. Though the identities of individuals are 'real', in the sense that they are objectively determined rather than nominal or illusory, they have a derivative status: without the system as a whole, the individuals would not exist.[9]

Since the attributes of any element of such a system are in fact a function of the attributes of other elements, or of the system of relations as a whole, the credit (or blame) for attributes that happen to be more prized (or reviled) than others cannot be assigned exclusively to the individuals who manifest those attributes, but must be distributed more diffusely throughout the system. Hence attributes cannot properly be dichotomised, nor the classes which ostensibly possess them ranked one above another.

Now the relational principle of individuation is, of course, invoked in contemporary ecological metaphysics, which is relational to the core [*Naess, 1973, 1979; Mathews, 1991*]. But how is it to be translated into social terms? Before answering this question, it might be worth pointing out that it is not my intention here to attempt to legitimate a particular social order (in this case, as it happens, community) by arguing that it reflects a particular (in this case, ecological) order of nature. Dryzek criticises this well-worn ideological strategy ('social structure P is right because it is natural') in his contribution to the present collection. While I do not entirely agree with Dryzek on this, since I think there is a sense in which our notions of personhood and society do need to be aligned with the metaphysical, physical, biological and ecological facts of our world if our arrangements for living are to be viable in the longer term, I do not need to settle this issue here. For my present aim is only to discover the sociopolitical conditions that will produce the kind of selves capable of experiencing themselves and their relation to nature in a way that is likely to induce in them an attitude of sympathetic concern for the natural world, and hence an ecocentric outlook.

How then, returning to our earlier question, is a relational principle of individuation to be translated into social terms? If, as we have seen, a separate self lacks a sense of involvement in the identity of others, and is hence capable of arriving at concern for the interests of others at most through reason, a relational individual is likely to enjoy a sense of self which encompasses others, and hence includes concern for their interests, independently of the dictates of reason. One way of characterising this contrast in the grounds of the respective moral outlooks of the two types of self is through the distinction between rationalistic (justice) and empathetic (care) perspectives in epistemology and ethics.[10]

According to a number of feminist psychologists,[11] the rationalistic perspective emanates from a psychology that foregrounds the self and backgrounds others and the self's relations to them (this corresponds to what I am here describing as a separate self). The empathetic perspective emanates from a psychology of relatedness, which backgrounds the self and foregrounds the self's relations to others (where this corresponds to what I am here describing as a relational self.) Of course, the main danger associated with a psychology of separateness is that it will not emanate in a moral outlook at all. But if it does, it will tend to be an outlook formed by reason – a 'justice perspective', which seeks primarily to lay down the rights and duties of individuals, abstractly and impartially, in such a way that it is not even in principle necessary for us to know others in order to discover what is right or wrong for them.

From the empathetic perspective, morality is not the rather cold-blooded business of working out that to which others are rationally entitled, whether one likes it or not, and whether one knows them or not, but is rather a matter of *responding* appropriately to those we do know – those with whom we are in communication, in relationship. In other words, morality from this perspective does not rely on tablets of commandments, or rules of conduct, but trusts our own responsiveness to those we know and about whom we accordingly care. Its primary goal is the preservation of the web of relationships which define or sustain both the self and others.

To draw a distinction between these two perspectives is not to say that they are mutually exclusive, or that one is right and the other simply wrong-headed. I would indeed argue that moral sentiment – nourished through sustained relationships with particular others – is a necessary condition for any kind of moral outlook: we have first to learn through experience to care for others before moral argument can have any force. However, once I have learned to care about a particular being of a certain kind, I am more likely to arrive, through reflection, at a generalised concern for beings of that kind than I would if I had never been acquainted with any of the beings in question (this point is particularly important in an ecological connection, as we shall see below.)

If the separate self, with either its unapologetic egoism or its merely intellectual appreciation of justice, is constituted through liberal regimes of individual self-rule, with their concomitants of competition and conflict, what are the sociopolitical conditions for the emergence of a relational self, with its disposition to empathise with others?

I would suggest, along with some communitarians, anarchists and feminists [*Sandel,1982; Ritter, 1980; Elshtain, 1981, 1986; Held, 1987*], that a society in which individual identity was constituted through relations with others would be one in which self-realisation would be achieved through reciprocity and interdependence rather than through autonomy. Co-operation and communion rather than competition and conflict would be the fundamental principle of such a society. This principle suggests the idea of *community*, for it is in small, face-to-face communities that people can achieve genuine interconnectedness through sustained experiences of mutuality and reciprocity.

That community is a logical expression of an empathetic perspective, the moral perspective of a relational self, might be explained as follows: empathy is, from the feminist perspectives of Benjamin, Belenky *et al.*, Gilligan, Fox Keller and others, a function of relationship. Clearly, however, 'relationship' must be intended in a special sense in this connection: the term cannot refer merely to instrumental relationships, or relationships of convenience or expediency, let alone of domination or exploitation. It refers rather to relationships based on mutual recognition, on a mutual understanding of the true needs and desires of the other. For this reason, relationship, in the present sense, requires communication: we can know others, and in this sense 'relate to' them, only by communicating with them. However, when we know others in this sense – when we understand the forces that drive them and the sources of their various forms of self-expression – it is impossible not to feel compassion for them, as spiritual traditions invariably attest. (It is not necessary that we delve into the specific secrets of others' psyches to know them in the present sense; it is sufficient that we establish a certain *rapport*, and a corresponding sense of the reality of their subjectivity, to know that they are feeling, striving, hurting beings, just as we are, where it is this insight that generates empathy on our part, and elicits our sympathy.)

In light of the importance of communication in this scenario, a major moral imperative, from this point of view, is to *keep the channels of communication open*. As long as we are genuinely communicating with others, we shall feel appropriately towards them – that is, communication will help to ensure empathy. An obvious way to ensure that the channels of communication remain open, at a social level, is to organise ourselves into small communities – communities on a human scale, in which it is possible for each individual to communicate effectively with all others.

So it would seem that community is a clear socio-political expression of and condition for relational selfhood, and that relational selfhood provides an ontological foundation for an empathetic outlook and the moral sensibility which accompanies it.

However I would like to dwell a little longer on the ideal of community and the notion of relationality that underpins it. For community may be dismissed as an ontological basis for a moral outlook on the grounds that many traditional communities have been hierarchical in structure. Individuals in such communities may indeed have been interdependent, and constituted by their relations of interdependence, but these relations were often those of the master-to-slave type. In other words, it seems pertinent to ask whether domination and subordination are not forms of relationship which can inform the identities of those who are party to them, and if so, whether relationality is not compatible with hierarchy, and hence inadequate as an ontological foundation for an altruistic outlook?[12]

In describing a relational self as one constituted by its relationships with others, I have already remarked that the relationships referred to in this context must be of a special type. But it is now imperative to specify this type more precisely. The relations connoted by 'relationships' in the present context are, I would suggest, not contingent relations but in some sense necessary ones: they are essential to the identity of those who are party to them. But this implies that the relationships in question are such that they contribute to the *self-realisation* of those who are their relata: the individuals in question could not come into being, and flourish, as the kinds of individuals they are, in the absence of these relationships. A certain reciprocity or mutuality is, as I indicated earlier, thereby implied: A depends on B to realise itself, but B also depends on A. Such reciprocity need not be directly one-to-one: A may depend on B without B's directly depending on A, yet A may be necessary to other elements of the system which are in turn necessary for the self-realisation of B. An example drawn from ecology might serve to illustrate the type of relationship in question here: in some parts of Australia, the bettong (a small kangaroo-like marsupial) appears to depend on truffles for its 'self-realisation', though the truffles themselves do not seem to need to be eaten by bettongs. However the *forest* depends on the digging-out activities of bettongs for the health of its root system. When the bettongs die out, as a result of predation by feral species, for instance, the forest dies-back. In this way, it transpires that truffles are indirectly dependent on bettongs for the maintenance of their habitat. Bettongs and truffles may thus be seen as mutually constitutive within a wider framework of relationships.

When this analysis of relationality is applied to the human case, it becomes clear that a relational self is one that depends on certain kinds of relationships with others for its self-realisation, for its coming into being and flourishing as a self. What is it to flourish as a human self? Without digressing for a hundred pages or so, it seems reasonable to say that a minimal condition for human self-realisation is the full realisation of subjectivity: a self can scarcely be regarded as self-realised if it lacks a sense of itself as subject, but instead experiences itself as an object-for-others. In light of this we might redefine the relational self as one whose subjectivity – the essence of its selfhood – is constituted intersubjectively: the self becomes aware of herself as subject by recognising the subjectivity of others and by having her own subjectivity simultaneously recognised and affirmed by them [*Benjamin, 1990; Poole, 1993*].

It now becomes clear that selves in this sense cannot be constituted by relations of domination and subordination. Hence although master and slave may be logically co-defining, under the descriptions of 'master' and 'slave', they are not mutually constituting *qua* selves – that is, their relationship is not conducive to their mutual flourishing as selves. For, following Hegel, Sartre, de Beauvoir, Benjamin and others, we might expect the master to objectify the slave, and the slave to have little sense of her own subjectivity – she may identify her master as subject, and, in her fantasies of subjectivity, imagine herself doing as he does (that is, dominating others). No intersubjectivity occurs in such a situation of denial and illusion, and there is certainly no self-realisation for the slave. Even the subjectivity of the master rings hollow, resting as it does on denial, on an inability to confront the reality of the other, where this implies the master's lack of belief in the reality or adequacy of his vaunted 'subjectivity'.

In any case it seems clear that relations of domination and subordination are not the kinds of relationships through which selves, *qua* selves, are mutually realised. So communities which permit relations of domination and subordination will not give rise to relational selves – that is, to the kinds of selves that are given to empathising with one another, and taking each other's interests as seriously as their own. In other words, communities must be *egalitarian* if they are to produce relational selves. Community as a foundation for an empathetic outlook then must be understood in an egalitarian sense.[13]

But how is this empathy and moral sensibility to be extended from the human to the natural world? Clearly community needs to be understood here not merely in human terms, but also as community with nature. That is to say, the eco-community will be such as to facilitate relationships not only amongst its human members, but also between its human members and their biotic neighbourhood. Human individuals will in this way come to experience themselves as constituted through their relationships with the natural world as well as with the human world. But what will such relationships consist in? Clearly I have in mind here something more than purely biological relationships, such as those defined by the food chain: such relations are already, perforce, in place, yet they conspicuously fail, in and of themselves, to generate empathy on our part for those beings who comprise our food.

What I have in mind is rather face-to-face relationships with a variety of particular non-human beings on a day-to-day basis, relationships which enable us to come to know those beings in all their variousness and individual uniqueness. How could we come to know them in this way? Presumably we could do so through communication, where communication is to be understood in a relatively straightforward manner in relation to the so-called 'higher' animals, and in a more figurative manner in relation to the so-called 'lower' animals, and plants, and plant communities such as forests. In making sense of the notion of communication in the latter case, we might appeal to epistemologies of 'attentiveness', invoked by some theological and feminist thinkers [*Weil, 1962; Buber, 1970; Fox Keller, 1985; Ruddick, 1984; Holler, 1990; Warren, 1990; Mathews, 1994a*]. These point to forms of human-to-non-human encounter, in which each party discovers the subjectivity of the other, through a process of overture and response. Clearly it is the relational self, with its readiness to recognise the subjectivity of others and receive their affirmation in return, that is likely to be open to the possibility of the subjectivity of non-human others. And since it is only through readiness to recognise the subjectivity of the other (through addressing it as a 'thou' rather than an 'it') that one is likely to receive the response that will indeed confirm its subjectivity, it is the relational self that is best placed to discover the putative subjectivity of non-human others, and to feel appropriately towards them in consequence.

Communication in the above sense is possible only with *particular* others. Hence to communicate with the natural world, and thereby come to empathise with it, is to be engaged in ongoing encounters with particular others – where this means, in practice, nature as it is embodied in a particular place. The eco-community will thus be a situated community, tied to place, as deep ecologists, social ecologists and bioregionalists attest.[14]

When we have engaged in sustained, face-to-face relationships with a range of non-human others, and recognised them as complex and responsive centres of subjectivity, with their own unique and mysterious purposes and imperatives, we shall be much more likely also to take seriously the interests of non-human others who lie beyond our ambit. Thus while eco-community may draw us into emotional and moral involvement with the lives of those in our immediate biotic neighbourhood, it will also tend to awaken in us a more generalised concern for nature.

It is worth pointing out that eco-communities need not necessarily be located only in rural areas. Community-with-nature may of course be more readily realisable in the countryside, but it is also eminently realisable in cities. There are numerous ways in which we can cultivate a sense of community with the natural world in urban neighbourhoods [*Plant, 1989; 1990*]. One of the more imaginative ways is to devise new forms of totemism, by, for example, declaring each child, at birth, a 'guardian' of some local species, perhaps including the name of that species amongst the child's given names. Other more hands-on ways include acquainting ourselves with the natural and indigenous history of our own area; greening streets and vacant land; restoring rivers or creeks; establishing neighbourhood gardens and permaculture projects; initiating alternative technology projects, compost and sewerage systems. Particularly important, I think, is the establishment of 'mixed communities' [*Naess, 1979; Devall, 1988*] of humans and animals, via urban and backyard 'farms' and sanctuaries, where these would provide opportunities for us to share our life world with non-human beings, and thereby discover for ourselves their complexity and individuality, their intelligence and capacity for responsiveness. (Modern western cities are increasingly becoming animal-free zones, where even such 'honorary persons' as dogs are barely tolerated any longer, so strong is the public sense that all living space should be for the exclusive use of humankind.) Through efforts such as these, urban eco-communities can eventually come to emanate a 'magic', and command a passionate loyalty, that even their rural counterparts cannot match, precisely because of their significance as beacons of hope and 're-enchantment' in a spoiled and uncaring world.[15]

My overall suggestion in this section, then, is that community, rather than liberal democracy, is the primary political prerequisite for the development of the kind of identity conducive to an ecocentric outlook (in this I am in agreement with Barns, present collection.) I do not wish to suggest however that eco-community is a *sufficient* condition for such an outlook. People may live in small rural communities, in daily face-to-face interaction with the natural world, yet, if they have been taught to regard non-human beings as mere objects, and means-to-ends, rather than as subjects, and ends-in-themselves, they may never experience the kind of intersubjective relationship with the natural world which I have described. Relationality facilitates open-ness to the possibility of inter-subjective engagement with the natural world, but does not guarantee it. On the other hand, a merely reasoned or taught belief in the moral considerability of non-human beings would not have much force in the moral field of action, unless it were underpinned by a deeply felt, concrete sense of the living receptivity and responsiveness of such beings. My conclusion, then, is that an ecocentric outlook is rendered possible, maybe even probable, but certainly not inevitable, by eco-communitarianism. It will generally be the case that, in Western societies at any rate, anthropocentric prejudices will have to be challenged before people will become open to the possibility of the kinds of *encounter* with the natural world that I have described. So although I have argued here that some experience of relating to nature is a necessary condition for an ecocentric outlook, such experience cannot, of course, be taken as conceptually unmediated: different understandings of nature will vitiate or enhance the possibility of human-to-nature relationships.

Having now conveyed something of the meaning I wish to assign to the notion of community in the present context, I would like to clarify further the relation between community and liberal democracy. Earlier I characterised liberalism in terms of individual self-rule, but I suggested that self-rule could be achieved to varying degrees in different types of liberal democracy, ranging from the direct and participatory to the indirect and representative. However, many authors equate participatory forms of democracy with community. How then can liberal democracies which take such participatory forms be distinguished, in practice, from communities in the present sense?

The short answer is that they cannot be so distinguished, at least not in any black-and-white way. This is because in fostering individual participation, small-scale direct democracies also incidentally tend to foster social relationships, while small-scale communities, in fostering social relationships, tend incidentally to induce individual involvement in public affairs: the two forms of political organisation thus in practice tend to converge. It is none the less important to bear in mind that they are dedicated to different ends: the end of liberal forms of democracy is to free individuals from political domination and to enhance their sense of autonomy, while that of community is to bring individuals out of self-absorption, into sympathy with others. Both envisage a form of self-realisation for individuals, but they conceive of the conditions for such self-realisation in different ways. The distinction may be illustrated by the significance attributed to consensus decision making from the two perspectives respectively. Some advocates of small-scale societies, such as Bookchin [*1981*], insist on the importance of consensus in community contexts, but see that importance as residing in the status of consensus as an extension of self-management and self-determination: in the absence of consensus, individual wills are over-ridden and individual autonomy accordingly diminished.

Feminists and ecofeminists [*Plant, 1989; Trinh T. Minh-ha, 1989*] who insist on consensus, however, tend to do so with a view to the opportunity for extensive communication that the process of consensuality affords: in the lengthy discussions which the process entails, mutual understanding amongst the participants is increased, and relationships tested and strengthened.[16] Since I am arguing that it is community that is conducive to an ecocentric outlook, it will make a difference in the long run whether a small society is conceived as first and foremost a direct democracy or as a community. The eco-anarchism of a theorist such as Bookchin, whose small direct democracies seem to be conceived primarily as vehicles for self-management and self-determination, exhibits strong liberal tendencies, which may militate against the possibility of its also serving as a vehicle for an ecocentric environmentalism.

In this connection I think it is important to notice that community, in the present sense, is not at all compatible with the modern ideal of individual freedom. The aim of community is to cultivate and preserve social bonds. But social bonds do bind – they create responsibilities and obligations from which one is not supposed to walk away. An individual woven into a web of such relations will indeed have a place in the scheme of things – she will 'belong', she will never be alone, she will be assured of human succour in all circumstances. But she will not have much room to move. She will be supported by the web, but also caught by it.

Community, then, does have its price. To take the communitarian path in the present sense is very much to forfeit autonomy, at least in the sense of individual freedom. One forfeits this autonomy not to 'higher' authorities, but to the needs and expectations of one's own people, the people with whom one's own destiny is interwoven.[17]

Although I have argued that eco-communitarianism is the primary political prerequisite for the development of ecological identities, such eco-communitarianism must be qualified in various ways if it is to be effective as an instrument of ecocentric environmental reform. I shall explore two of these ways.

First, the relational form of identity constituted through community must be distinguished not only from liberal individualism, but also from identities based on abstract identification with greater wholes or unities – that is, wholes or unities which have a basically abstract significance for the individual in question (for example, the nation).

Second, given that many ecological problems are now global in scope and result from forces which are themselves transnational in character (such as the forces of corporate capitalism), small local communities will be of limited efficacy as instruments of either innovation or resistance in the face of these problems [Eckersley, 1992]. Can new forms of community evolve to meet these challenges posed by globalism? Is transnational community possible, and, if so, would it be a match, politically speaking, for the transnational forces of environmental destruction currently arrayed against it?

I shall discuss each of these questions in turn, under separate headings.

Relational vs. Holistic Identity

When individual identity is described as being a function of community, this is sometimes understood to imply a holistic form of collectivism. That is, when I say that the community is logically prior to its members, I might be understood as saying that the identity of individuals is subsumed under that of the collective – that the individuals in question are no more than individual bearers of the collective identity, and in this sense have no independent identity of their own. Similarly, when ecophilosophers speak of the 'ecological self', they are sometimes understood holistically, as declaring that individuals are constituted by such identification with the biotic community as a whole, and accordingly lack any independent ontological status.[18] But this is not how I intend the notion of the relational self to be understood in the present context. Relational identity does provide an alternative to the individualism of liberalism, but this alternative should not be read in over-simplified holistic terms. The relational self is constituted by a system of relations – it is a nexus within the wider web. The wider web does indeed constitute a whole, in the sense that it is indivisible – it cannot be broken down into self-subsistent parts, since when we attempt to excise parts from it, the entire system begins to unravel. Hence while the web of relations is holistic in the sense of indivisible, its holism is systemic in nature, rather than substantival (block-like).

Individuals are identified through the system inasmuch as they come into existence through interaction with other elements of the system – they do not 'stand alone', in the manner of substances. Their identity is thus a function of that of the system. But this is quite different from saying that they are simply one-with, undifferentiated within, a block-like whole. Relational selves enjoy unique individual identities – they are what they are as a result of their unique positioning in a dynamic web of relations. Holistic selves, in contrast, are uniform in nature, in that in so far as they achieve identity at all, it is only as bearers of that of a greater homogeneous whole.

How to illustrate this distinction between relational and holistic selves? Consider an indigenous person whose identity, let us suppose, has been constituted through her relations with her people. Her people are part of her, they are her life-blood. But this is because she has been in continuous interaction with them since infancy. Her identity is based, not on an abstract identification, but on a lived interaction with concrete particulars. It would not make any difference to this identity, *qua* relational identity, if the woman in question were unaware that the people amongst whom she had lived were in fact members of a particular tribe, with a particular name and cultural identity. They are 'her people' primarily because they inform her very being, rather than because she has conceived of them as an abstract unity, and identified with her concept of them. Moreover, since the identity of this woman is a function of her own unique history of relations with particular individual members of the tribe, her identity will be different from those of other tribe members, even though the identities of all members are a function of their positioning within a single greater whole – that is, a particular field of relations.

Nationalism would qualify as an example of the contrasting case, that of holistic identity. In this connection, individuals identify with an entity which has only abstract significance for them, since no individual can experientially encompass a nation in all its concrete particularity. Indeed it is doubtful whether the idea of a nation can be exhausted by concrete particulars in any case. It seems to include an abstract dimension – an abstract unity, and perhaps value, which are not grounded in any of its concrete features. In any case, when seized by the sense of nationalism, entire populations do indeed become 'as one': as Australians, or Americans, or Japanese, they are uniform in nature, mere bearers of a common abstract – national – identity.[19]

The dangers of such holistic identification are manifest. When the identity of individuals becomes subsumed under that of wholes in this way, the interests – and rights – of individuals may become subordinated to the perceived interests – and rights – of the abstract whole, where this immediately summons up fascistic and totalitarian associations.

But this familiar danger of holistic identity is not the only one. When an individual identifies, not with particular others but with an abstract entity, she comes to see others not as particular living presences inextricably intertwined with her own living being. Rather she tends to view them under abstract categories – as instances of this or that abstract identity, congruent or dissonant with her own. Perceiving others in this way does not generate fellow-feeling for them – it does not induce a sharing of one's immediate sense of aliveness – and vulnerability – with them. This is not to say that it may not elicit *sentimental* attitudes towards the others in question – as bearers of *this* cherished abstract identity, or *that* despised one – but these attitudes are sentimental rather than authentic precisely because they are based on hollow preconceptions rather than on direct encounter with the reality of the others in question. Identification with abstract wholes or unities can thus have a dehumanising effect, allowing the true needs and nature of others to be ignored in favour of abstract stereotypes.[20] Another – more fashionable – way of putting this point is to say that when individuals identify with abstract wholes – whether these be as large as the cosmos itself, or 'Gaia", or the cosmopolis, or the nation, or as small as one's own city or neighbourhood – *difference* will be suppressed, the manifold real differences amongst individuals will be dissolved in homogenising or exclusionary abstract categories.[21]

This is not the last of the dangers of holistic identification in this abstract sense. When an individual subsumes his identity under that of a greater abstract entity or unity, one might expect him to suffer a sense of diminution, but in fact the opposite seems typically to take place: the individual becomes subject to inflation, or ego-aggrandisement – he feels as big and important and perhaps as powerful as the greater entity or unity purportedly is. Such a sense of omnipotence works, again, against the possibility of empathy – although again it might express itself in grandiose acts of charity or aid, as well as in a deadly hubris or arrogance.

In light of these remarks about the nature of holistic identity, I think it is clear that the abstract individualism of liberalism on the one hand, and a form of abstract holism, such as nationalism, for instance, on the other, can ultimately appear as flip sides of the same coin. As I have already explained, the identity of abstract individuals is abstract in the sense that it rests on the abstract idea of a pre-social individual, an individual who can logically exist as a fully rational, and therefore fully human, being independently of social relations with others. This idea is abstract inasmuch as such an individual is not – originally, at any rate – encountered in experience, since from an empirical point of view human individuals are invariably formed through social relations of interdependence.[22] (However, as I have already remarked, later exposure to liberal institutions can to some extent counter the relational aspects of the early processes of identity formation.) The liberal individual thus arrives at a sense of self not so much through attending to the data of his own experience, which reveal the irreducibly relational bedrock of his identity, as through identifying with an idea.[23]

The identity of holistic individuals is, I have suggested, abstract in a similar fashion: ideas of greater wholes – such as 'the nation' (or indeed 'Gaia', or the 'world society') – with which holistic individuals identify are also abstract in the sense that these wholes are not encountered in experience. An entity such as 'the nation' is not encountered in experience in two senses: it cannot be *encompassed* in the experience of a single individual; and as a unity it cannot be experienced because it does not *exist*; all that exists is a field or manifold of heterogeneous elements. (The latter objection may not apply to all contenders for the title of 'greater whole'. Gaia, for instance, may have a unity which is objective rather than nominal. However the former objection will still apply: from the viewpoint of the individual it is abstract because it cannot be encompassed in experience.)

A deeper contrast than that between the relational and the holistic self is here emerging. This is the contrast between concrete and abstract selves; while the concrete self is relational, the abstract self may take individualistic or holistic forms. The idea of self with which the relational individual identifies is based on processes which it has encountered in its own experience. These processes include relations of interdependence with others. Being dependent on others, and being identified with this dependence, the relational individual has to try to understand the reality of others, in all their concrete particularity: in other words, in order to understand himself, he must seek to understand others. The abstract individual, on the other hand, is 'out of touch' with his experience. Whether he sees himself as a liberal individual or as a bearer of a national identity, he has no need, logically speaking, to understand the real nature of particular others, since their nature – whatever it is – will make no difference to his own identity: he does not need to understand them in order to understand himself.

Finally, returning to the issue of holism again, I think that the significance of this distinction between identities that are concretely relational and those that are abstractly holistic is particularly important to appreciate in the present era of 'globalisation'. People from various different ideological camps are today anxious to identify themselves as 'global citizens'. Clearly such a global identity involves identification with an abstract concept of a global whole, since individuals cannot interact concretely, in face-to-face fashion, with all the (human and non-human) particulars included in the global domain. It matters little, in this connection, whether the abstract global unity with which one identifies is the system of corporate capitalism or the biosphere or planet itself. Global identity in either form would presumably be subject to the dangers I have just enumerated. However, the undeniably global nature of certain ecological processes and problems and threats to the environment, do seem to call for some kind of expansion of locally-based identities towards wider horizons. Whether or not this can be achieved without entraining holistic identity in the above sense will be considered below.

Transnational Communities

The idea of eco-communitarianism has a *prima facie* connotation of political decentralisation and regionalism. These are positions in favour with many of the more radical ecological thinkers, such as deep ecologists and bioregionalists: when people 'dwell in place', and live in true community with their own biotic neighbourhood, they are expected to become responsive to, and responsible for, that neighbourhood [*Sale, 1985; Naess, 1989; Plant, 1990*]. However, the suitability of small local communities for all ecopolitical purposes may be challenged on a number of grounds [*Eckersley, 1992*], including the following:

(i)   Since ecological processes are not confined by national boundaries, many ecological problems are now international in scope, and therefore not manageable by local agencies.

(ii) External authorities are occasionally needed to over-ride regional authorities that wittingly or unwittingly fail to meet their ecological responsibilities, either to their own bioregion, or to those downwind or downstream.

(iii) The political power of small local communities is no match for the forces of transnational capitalism currently arrayed against the environment world-wide.

These objections to small, local communities as the privileged vehicle for ecopolitics may lead to calls for more centralised or more global forms of political organisation, or both. I propose to concentrate here on the third problem, which is a problem of power, and the seeming inadequacy of small local communities to function as effective instruments of resistance to the forces of transnational capitalism, where these now arguably constitute the major threat to the world's environment.[24] My question is whether political formations are conceivable which retain a relational – that is, communitarian – structure yet which also demonstrate a capacity to resist the forces of transnational capitalism. If such formations are indeed conceivable, they might prove to be adaptable to management and coordination roles as well (Dryzek, Thompson, this collection).

The question I have posed is, I think, particularly important at the present time because of the accelerating pace of the processes of globalisation. These processes are driven by the increasingly stark imperatives of capitalism, where the ultimate such imperative is simply that of profit maximisation. The bedrock requirements of social life are, as we know, at the present time increasingly being subordinated to the bottomless requirements of capitalism. Societies in the grip of global competition, for instance, can no longer 'afford' such fundamental social goods as welfare and publicly-owned utilities and amenities. In this climate, the function of the state itself is seen to be that of ensuring conditions favourable to commercial enterprise. Since profit-making tends to be optimised as the scale, level of mechanisation and computerisation, and monopolising potential of companies increase, states find themselves dedicated to facilitating the rise of corporate colossi, which rival the states themselves in economic, and hence ultimately in political, power. Principles of economic natural selection ensure that such corporations in due course become transnational in scope and structure. Since such transnational organisations easily gain control of the economies of smaller states, their operations cannot be effectively controlled by those states. This process of corporate giantism accordingly seems self-reinforcing and therefore set to continue. In the middle future we might envision a situation in which states have faded into the political background, except as auxiliaries to corporations, and the corporations themselves have become not only the major economic players, but the primary political formations as well. States would no longer then be in a position to protect either their citizens or their environments from corporate agencies – they could no longer insist on either human or ecological rights, or even on the rights of states themselves to the means of their own self-perpetuation, such as taxes.[25]

In this scenario, then, the state as an independent regulatory power would wither away, although individual states might linger on as puppet-like enforcers of the will of corporations. As the state *qua* independent political agent withered away, so would the nation, until individual countries retained their identities only as geographical entities. This dissipation of national identity, together with the thoroughly transnational character of the corporations themselves, would ensure that individual members, or employees, of corporations would no longer identify themselves either in terms of nationality, nor even in terms of regionality, since they would have to stand in readiness to move from post to post around the world at the behest of their companies. Such individuals would accordingly be likely to identify directly with the companies themselves, in the abstract way I described in the previous section: the true 'corporation man' and woman would finally be born!

The scenario I have outlined here might be characterised as a kind of *corporate feudalism*. To the extent that corporations would still have to compete with one another for personnel, they could be expected to look after their employees – providing them with training (but not necessarily a general education), accommodation, health care, pensions, and so on. To this extent the corporation might effectively take over the social functions of the by-this-time defunct state. But those individuals whose services were not needed by the corporations would simply drop through the net of social provision, where this would mean that whoever was not supported by kin would fall into social oblivion.

Those whose services were not needed by the corporations would include any who were, for whatever reason, unemployable and, even more significantly, any who simply constituted surplus labour. The class of those who would satisfy the latter description is likely to be extremely large – to include entire populations, in fact. For as production of all kinds (primary as well as secondary) becomes – in the interests of economic efficiency – increasingly mechanised and computerised, and accordingly centralised, the requirements for labour (at manual, technical and managerial levels) progressively diminish.[26] The combination of exploding populations in Third World countries with the dwindling need for labour on the part of the corporate capitalist interests which have appropriated the resources of the countries in question poses a truly terrifying prospect. As noted, entire populations could be discarded in this scenario, and those individuals who were not so discarded would be effectively owned, body and soul, by their corporate providers, since these individuals, like the vassals of the medieval period, would depend on their corporate masters for their very survival.

The picture I have painted here – of corporate feudalism – is undoubtedly an apocalyptic one, but my intention has been merely to highlight a particular trend in current events, where the world is, thankfully, sufficiently complex to contain all kinds of other, countervailing and tangential trends as well. However, in light of the particular trend in question it would seem to be important, from environmental and other, social, perspectives, to develop transnational structures of resistance now – structures which by-pass the state in order to apply direct pressure to corporations themselves. My question here is again, can such structures be developed in such a way as to preserve and reinforce the relational identities of their members – identities which have been formed in genuine eco-community – or will they inevitably reinforce, at the existential level, the very processes that led to the kind of thinking they are attempting to resist? In other words, will transnational structures of resistance inevitably foster

that abstractness of identity which allows us to become 'out of touch' with
the real, felt needs of others, human and non-human alike?

I think the key to this question lies in discovering a type of political
formation which is not bounded in the conventional way – that is not
defined in terms of regional, national or even global boundaries, but rather
retains its connective or relational structure. To this end I would like to
propose here two models of political structure.

(1) The substance or nuclear model: This model depends upon the notion of
a boundary: political formations are bounded, either in space or by formal
means, such as legal incorporation. It is relative to such a boundary that a
centre can be defined. Hence it is only within the terms of this substance
model of political structure that the dichotomy between centralisation and
decentralisation arises: investing political power in the centre of course
gives rise to centralised political structures; when power is returned to
elements at, or closer to, the periphery (the boundary), however, the
structure becomes decentralised. Such patterns of the distribution of power
may be illustrated as follows:

FIGURE 1

SUBSTANCE OR NUCLEAR MODEL

centralised

decentralised

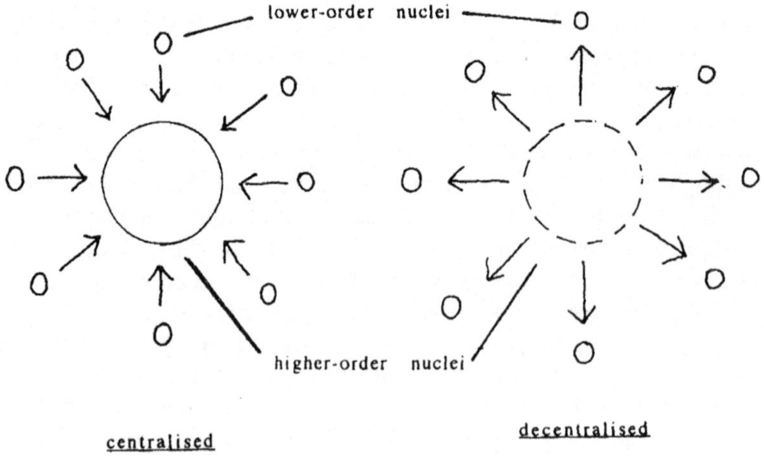

It is apparent from this, I think, that centralisation and decentralisation, as conventionally conceived, are merely different modalities of the same basic model of political structure – decentralisation is not the radical alternative to centralisation it is generally taken to be. In either case, political power is invested in larger or smaller political units – substance-like entities which, logically speaking, stand on their own. Autonomy is still the operative notion here. Decentralisation involves devolution of power away from larger nuclei to smaller ones. However, whether larger or smaller, these nuclei are still centres of power in their own right, centres of self-rule, not subject to interference from without. Even when such an organisation is decentralised to the point of returning power to mere individuals, the individuals are conceived as units of sovereignty, mini-centres of power, capable of making for themselves the kinds of decision relevant to the aims of the organisation. In political structures of this type then, power is located in autonomous or semi-autonomous centres, or nuclei.

When political structure is understood in this way, there will be a tendency for the individual to see herself both as a liberal individual (ultimate unit of political power and hence smallest potential unit of decentralisation) and as the bearer of the abstract identities of the higher order units under which the individual is subsumed – whether these be regional entities (such as municipalities, cities or nations) or functional organisations, such as corporations. In light of this, we might expect liberal individuals to exhibit tendencies to abstract forms of holism, such as nationalism.[27]

(2) The lattice or relational model of political structure: In a lattice structure, power is invested not in the elements of the structure themselves, but in the relations between them. Such structures accordingly cannot be described in terms of either boundaries or centres, but rather in terms of the lines of communication between the elements. Nor can they be characterised as either local or global, because they traverse geographical space, rather than encompassing it. The distribution of power in such structures may be illustrated as shown in Figure 2.

The centralised/decentralised dichotomy does not apply to structures of this lattice or relational type. Autonomy is no longer the operative notion in this context. Decisions are made neither by large nuclei at the centre of the organisation nor by small nuclei at the periphery, but rather in the lattice itself, as a result of everyway communication and information transmission.

Structures of the lattice or relational type are, of course, more familiarly designated as 'networks'. Network structures are already favoured by activists on many political fronts. However, the term 'network' is used loosely, and may not always refer to the kind of structure I have outlined

here. I have used the term 'lattice' to provide a more precise designation for
the structure in question.

FIGURE 2

LATTICE MODEL

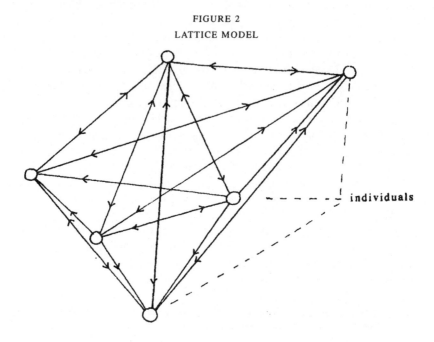

To the extent that lattice structures are effective in shaping or modifying
identity, they will clearly promote relational rather than substantival
(whether individualistic or holistic) forms thereof. Our question here then
is, can such lattice or relational structures take transnational form? Can we
in effect establish transnational *communities* of individuals, dedicated to
specific environmental ends?

For lattice structures to qualify as communities in the present sense they
would have to be such as to permit face-to-face interaction between
members. Clearly this is not possible in a transnational context. However to
the extent that individuals have access to computer and telecommunication
facilities, sustained person-to-person interaction is feasible for members of
networks. Such concrete, though technologically mediated, interaction
between individual members of a transnational network may be expected to
reinforce existing relational aspects of identity, forged in local communities,
while adding important new, transnational dimensions to them. These will
not be the abstract dimensions implied in the ideas of 'global citizenship' or
'global cosmopolitanism' currently in vogue in political theory [*Archibugi*

and Held, 1995]. They will rather be aspects of identity grounded in actual relations with particular others, relations that will add, in a small but real way, particular transnational threads to the existing fabric of our identity. In this case I shall no longer be merely an Australian of European descent, for instance, for I might blend a few strands of Bardi, Penan, Sioux, New Yorker, Icelander, and so on into my sense of self.[28] This is important, I think, for two reasons.

First, ecosystems themselves are relatively unbounded. Hence if our goal is an ecocentric polity, our loyalties cannot be too fixated on our own local bioregion – we must be aware of and responsive to wider ecological horizons. Yet simply to identify with wider and wider (and hence less and less concretely known) circles of nature, as some deep ecologists [*Fox, 1984; 1990*] advise, is surely to court the dangers of abstract holism, explored above. Perhaps transnational lattice structures afford an opportunity to expand our sense of ecological selfhood, without risking abstraction and inflation. To the extent that we are communicating in an ongoing, sustained way with individuals actively involved with ecological issues in their own regions or countries, we might achieve more meaningful forms of identification not only with the individuals in question, but with particular parts of the natural world beyond our own biotic neighbourhood.

Second, the forces presently threatening the environment worldwide are largely, if not predominantly, transnational in character. As I remarked earlier, small local eco-communities appear to be politically insignificant in the face of such forces. Transnational networks or communities of resistance, however, are potentially highly effective, even though small in terms of membership. Part of the secret of the strength of transnational corporations is, of course, that when political pressure is applied to them in one country, they simply transfer their operations to another. The availability of this option protects them even from strong state pressure within any given country. However, although a transnational activist network can generally bring to bear only pinpricks of pressure within any given country, it can apply its pressure directly to markets (for example, through picketing), and – unlike nation states themselves – it can reproduce this pressure in many countries. Even a relatively small pressure, reproduced in this way, is likely to provide sufficient irritation to induce a corporation to comply with the political demands in question. In other words, transnationality confers on organisations of resistance precisely the same kind of strength it confers on corporations themselves – a strength that cannot be computed in terms of the size (or scale of membership) of the organisation in question.[29]

So the present age of transnational corporations, which have largely escaped the rule of law – this being still essentially a function of the nation state – calls forth organisations of resistance which are themselves transnational in structure, and which seek to exercise some control over the corporations not through law, but by applying painful stimuli directly to those most sensitive of corporate nerve-endings, the retail outlets. With their lattice structures, these organisations can hopefully begin to address the global aspects of the environmental challenge without reproducing in their own structures the very forms of identity which result in the abstractness, the 'out-of-touchness' with the urgent living reality of other beings, that arguably underlies our present epic blindness to their needs.

Is There a Role for the Liberal State?

In this study I have questioned the appropriateness of liberal democracies as vehicles of an ecocentric environmentalism. I have argued that they provide neither the moral nor the ontological basis for ecocentric consciousness, and that small egalitarian communities are more suited to this end. Such communities, which may be local or transnational in their scope, help to cultivate relational – and hence ecological – identities. In their transnational guise, they also constitute a political instrument well adapted to resisting the environmentally destructive forces of transnational capitalism, and perhaps to assuming environmental administrative and co-ordinative roles as well.

There are many problems with such a communitarian scenario in addition to those which I have addressed here. These include problems concerning institutional and procedural arrangements both within and across communities. I do not have space here to offer a total picture of a communitarian world. Nor is my intention in any case so utopian. I am interested rather in the steps that we can take towards achieving a general ecocentric will, and devising political tools for such a will, within the framework of existing liberal democracies. I have argued that the creation of communities of various types would take us some distance in this direction. The shape that politics would take thereafter probably cannot be anticipated from the present point in time.

I do not wish to claim here, then, that there is no role for liberal democracies in a green future. On the contrary, although the emphasis on individual freedom and autonomy that is characteristic of liberal regimes works against the emergence of ecological identity and consciousness, the safeguarding of individual freedom remains important for ecopolitical purposes. For it is this commitment to individual freedom – and 'human rights' generally – that makes it possible for us to form ourselves into the ecological communities and to create the transnational structures of resistance that I have been advocating in the previous sections. As the corporate titans gain a stronger grip on states, they will – if my forecast of corporate feudalism is at all on track – tend either to replace existing liberal states with repressive 'puppet' states, or establish a directly corporate world order amongst themselves. In either case, individual participation in communities of ecological initiative or resistance is likely to be curtailed, whether through legal means or economic reprisals. It would seem to be necessary, then, to try to protect our liberal freedoms, even while seeking to create less individualistic, more relational identities for ourselves in communities of our own making. There is a tension in this position, but it is not a paralysing one.

Ironically, it is not only the environment but the liberal state itself which is at risk from that state's present one-sidedly economistic course. For, as I argued earlier, that course is likely to strengthen corporate formations, which may in time come to rival states themselves as the primary locus of power. One of the first steps towards protecting the liberal state then, with the opportunities for experimenting with communitarian initiatives that it affords, is surely to try to ameliorate its present excessive economism – to try to awaken it to the fact that if it continues down its present path, it will eventually no longer be in a position to ensure the autonomy of its citizens, nor hence to discharge its definitive duty as a liberal state: it will no longer be a liberal state, and possibly not even a state at all.

Moreover, as long as the liberal state is in place, there is every reason to green it to the best of our ability, through green parties, social movements, lobby groups, and so on, as long as we do not invest all our hope for an ecocentric sea change in these mechanisms, but rather continue to work on the ontological foundations for an ecocentric consciousness. Even centralised international agencies, such as Greenpeace, Worldwide Fund for Nature, and so on, are not ideologically ruled out by my argument. Although centralised and hierarchical in structure, and hence not in themselves conducive to the development or reinforcement of ecological identities, they may be effective tools of resistance or initiative in international forums for those who have already arrived at ecological consciousness by other means.

My argument then is that, while liberal forms of democracy do not in themselves provide conditions likely to foster widespread ecocentric consciousness, they do provide a starting point and a safe space, politically speaking, in which we can begin to create such conditions for ourselves. To that extent, liberal democracy remains important to ecocentric environment-alism, even though we shall have to attempt to counteract its individualistic effects in the limited space of political freedom that it makes available to us.

NOTES

1. Throughout this study I take the position adopted by Dryzek in his contribution to this collection, namely that, in environmental matters, at any rate, particular forms of political organisation tend to induce (or pre-empt) particular types of policy outcome, or that 'green values' cannot be fully separated from 'green agency' [*Goodin, 1992*] .

2. In this sense I think that a purely utilitarian conception of democracy – which seeks to maximise individual utilities – misses an important part of the original point of democracy, since 'the greatest happiness (or satisfaction) for the greatest number' could in principle be realised under a benign dictatorship.

3. Such a conception of liberalism of course entails its eminent compatibility with capitalism, but my intention here is to investigate the environmental implications of liberalism as such, rather than of liberal capitalism.

4. Those theorists, such as Kymlicka [*1993*], who regard liberalism as a theory about the state and its limitations rather than about society, are a case in point. From such a point of view, society might take communitarian forms and give rise to non-individualistic modes of identity in its members, while still falling within the framework of a liberal polity. This is not altogether unlike the sort of provisional compromise with liberalism that I reach at the end of my paper.

5. Recall Mill's well-known refusal to countenance any exercise of freedom intended to extinguish freedom itself eg the selling of oneself into slavery.

6. In Kant's terminology, they might, through reason, arrive at *moral* judgements, but they will not be capable of *beautiful* acts (see Naess [*1993*]).

7. In fact, as feminists such as Pateman [*1988*] have shown, the individuals who were deemed party to the social contract in the original social contract theories, such as those of Hobbes and Locke, were male heads of families. It was tacitly recognised, then, that individuals are formed through relationships with others, but the sphere of such 'domestic' relationships was relegated to the 'state of nature'. In so far as individuals are members of society, they were considered by liberals as logically independent of others. The actual original (and ongoing) social interdependence of individuals was thus glossed over in favour of an abstract ideal of autonomy. The whole question of how women, with their greater enmeshment in domestic relationships, could match this ideal was of course not even raised by the early contract theorists: autonomy was understood to be an ideal for men.

8. Plumwood (this collection) makes the point that though this dualistic elevation of reason above nature serves as a rationale for equality in the rhetoric of liberalism, it at the same time serves to inferiorise a whole range of social groups which are, in liberal societies, associated with nature. In this way, such reason/nature dualism naturalises and justifies social and political *inequality*.

9. There is, in my view, more to the metaphysical story than this: a purely relational ontology does not account for the the substantiality – in the sense of concreteness – of things. A field of relations is only actual, and hence constitutive of a world of concrete particulars, if it is in some way embedded in a substance continuum, such as space. For further metaphysical elaboration, see Mathews [*1991*].

10. The contrast between purely rational and more emotionally informed ways of knowing, and ways of thinking morally, has been explored by a number of feminist thinkers, for example, Gilligan [*1982*]; Belenky *et al.* [*1986*]; Fox Keller [*1985*]; Benjamin [*1990*]; Benhabib [*1992*]; Catherine Keller [*1986*]; Noddings [*1984*]; Ruddick [*1984*]; Hartsock [*1985*]. However the contrast may also be found in Hume, who argued that the basis of morality is moral sentiment rather than moral reason.

11. Feminist object relations theorists, such as Nancy Chodorow [*1978*] and Jane Flax [*1990*], originally provided models of the separate and relational selves. These models have been refined by Benjamin [*1990*], and applied by psychologists such as Gilligan [*1982*] and Belenky *et al.* [*1986*].

12. This is an important question because many commentators have shied away from communitarianism on the assumption that it is a basically conservative ideal. Certainly many of the values implicated in communitarianism have been embraced by conservative thinkers.

The contrast between interconnected or relational social organisations and aggregate or individualistic ones has a long history and was elaborated most notably perhaps by Ferdinand Tönnies, in the nineteenth century. In his book, *Gemeinschaft and Gesellschaft*, he distinguished between 'community' and 'society' in the following terms: community (Gemeinschaft) is to be understood as real, interacting, face-to-face community, where people are known to each other in many different roles, and are accordingly perceived by one another as whole persons, ends-in-themselves, rather than as mere functionaries. Community in this sense is held together by custom, ties to locality and bonds of kinship and inherited status. In society (Gesellschaft), in contrast, relationships between persons are formed as means-to-ends, and based on contract rather than custom, habit or affection. People encounter one another in limited, functional and often transient roles, and accordingly form no conception of one another as whole persons. Society in this sense is built on an instrumental and contractarian foundation.

Tönnies's own preference is obviously for community, which, sustained by bonds of kinship, status, locality, affection and affinity, creates a way of living conducive to a sense of wholeness, or fulfilment, and instils in people a sense of belonging, of their own inalienable place in the scheme of things. Tönnies's vision has striking affinities with that of contemporary communitarians, yet the communities to which Tönnies nostalgically looks back for inspiration are the feudal and patriarchal communities of the pre-modern era. It is clear in the light of this that we need to scrutinise more closely the notion of community that I have advocated here as a foundation for an altruistic and hence potentially ecocentric polity.

13. This conclusion – that relational selves require egalitarian forms of community as a precondition for their very existence – dovetails with my earlier observation, that relationality, when it is an established fact, compels an admission of equality. For when it is understood that the identities of others permeate my own, and *vice versa*, then it is also understood that no attribute of mine is referable to myself alone: my attributes, like those of all other elements of the system, are a function of the relations which constitute them, and hence of the system as a whole. No element of the system can count itself 'higher' than any other, nor on that account in a position to dominate another. Hence any community which in fact achieves a relational structure will *ipso facto* also achieve egalitarianism, at least at an ontological level – though the logic of this will not necessarily be reflected in peoples' perceptions, or their politics. However, since relationality can only be achieved in an egalitarian context, according to the above arguments, the egalitarianism of peoples' perceptions in such a community is already assured on other grounds in any case.

14. Deep ecologists [*Naess, 1989; Devall, 1988*] and bioregionalists [*Sale, 1985; Plant, 1990*] enjoin us to 'dwell in place'.

15. Ursula Leguin's novel, *Always Coming Home* [*1988*], is a treasure trove of ideas as to how human beings can live in community with the natural world. Admittedly the novel is set in the distant future, and in a rustic ambience, but it is a wonderful study in mixed communities. The novel is also noteworthy in this connection in that, although it depicts an eco-communitarian utopia, it does not suggest that the problem of evil has been solved therein, but rather shows how such a society manages and contains, but does not eliminate, human tragedy.

16. This also seems to apply in some indigenous communities. See Rose [*1992*].

17. Some of the more traditional Aboriginal communities illustrate this point. Individuals are indeed woven into an extensive and complex web of blood and customary relationships [*Rose, 1992*], but nor can they escape these relationships and the obligations they entail [*Graham, 1992*]. Lacking individual freedom and being beholden to others in this way effectively militates against not only a liberal ethos of individual freedom, but the capitalist ethos as well: one cannot simply follow the trail of opportunity wherever it might lead, and one's relatives will help themselves to whatever wealth one happens to attract in any case. Community in this sense then seems to imply a trade-off between freedom and belonging, between material wealth and social wealth.

18. This has been pointed out by Cheney [*1987*]; Plumwood [*1993*]; Kheel [*1990*].

19. Mary Daly [*1979*] makes an interesting (though typically rhetorically loaded) distinction between male comradeship, which involves loss of individual identity, and female sisterhood

or friendship, which results in mutual individual self-realisation.
20. Identification with abstract classes may occur as well. Racism, sexism and classism may rest on such a form of identification.
21. Some authors have raised this objection to communitarianism itself – that is, they have argued that communities homogenise their members, in the sense of making individual difference unacceptable [*Young, 1990*]. I hope to have shown here that this objection can only apply if community is understood in a holistic rather than a relational sense.
22. In saying that human individuals are invariably formed through social relations, I am not ignoring wolf and gazelle children, and such like. To the extent that these children do acquire a coherent sense of self, it is presumably more likely to be as honorary wolves or gazelles, though they will not of course perform entirely satisfactorily as such.
23. I am not intending to set up a sharp division between (abstract) ideas and experience here. All ideas are abstract, and all human experience is mediated by ideas. In qualifying certain ideas (and identities) as 'abstract' in the present context, I am intending to signify that they go beyond what is or can be encountered in experience.
24. Clearly overpopulation is also a factor contributing to environmental degradation worldwide. I do not wish to enter into the debate about the relative weightings assignable to these factors. Corporate capitalism is unquestionably at the very least a threat of the highest order.
25. If a major corporation did not wish to pay taxes, nor wished its employees to pay taxes, then the state, being in the pay of, and under the control of, such corporations, would not be in a position to extract the corporation's compliance.
26. Computerisation does not always entail centralisation. The kind of access and responsiveness to specialised markets that computerisation allows also makes small, highly specialised ('boutique') production ventures economically feasible [*Mathews, 1989*]. However these are likely to be co-opted by larger corporations in due course too. Centralised management is of course perfectly compatible with any degree of diversification and specialisation in production.
27. This is presumably not the only route to nationalism, since peoples not traditionally perceived as either individualistic or liberally inclined, such as the Japanese, have demonstrated strong propensities for nationalism. Identification with the nation or the corporation could, perhaps, in the case of the Japanese, have come about as a result of filial sensibility. Confucian-style deference, devotion or loyalty to the father, the executive director, or the Emperor may lead, via a different psychology, to a result convergent with that of abstract holism [*Yamauchi, 1995*].
28. For further elaboration of this idea, see Mathews [*1994b*].
29. An example of a such transnational organization of resistance which exerted considerable political influence on corporations in the late 1980s and early 1990s, is the worldwide Rainforest Action Network.

REFERENCES

Archibugi, Danielle and David Held (1995), *Cosmopolitan Democracy*, Oxford: Blackwell.
Belenky *et al.* (1986), *Women's Ways of Knowing,* New York: Basic Books.
Benhabib, Selya (1992), 'The Generalised and the Concrete Other', in E. Frazer *et al.* (eds.), *Ethics: a Feminist Reader*, Oxford: Blackwell, pp 267-300.
Benjamin, Jessica (1990), *The Bonds of Love*, London: Virago.
Bookchin, Murray (1981), *Towards an Ecological Society*, Montreal: Black Rose.
Buber, Martin (1970), *I and Thou*, New York: Clark.
Callicott, J. Baird (1980), 'Animal Liberation: a Triangular Affair', *Environmental Ethics*, Vol.2, No.4.
Callicott, J. Baird (1986), 'The Metaphysical Implications of Ecology', *Environmental Ethics*, Vol.8, No.4.
Callicott, J. Baird (1989), *In Defense of the Land Ethic*, Albany, NY: State University of New York Press.

Cheney, Jim (1987), 'Ecofeminism and Deep Ecology', *Environmental Ethics*, Vol.9, No.2.

Chodorow, Nancy (1978), *The Reproduction of Mothering*, Berkeley, CA: University of California Press.

Daly, Mary (1979), *Gyn/ecology*, London: The Women's Press.

Devall, Bill (1988), *Simple in Means, Rich in Ends: Practising Deep Ecology*, Salt Lake City, UT: Peregrine Smith.

Eckersley, Robyn (1992), *Environmentalism and Political Theory: Toward an Ecocentric Approach*, Albany, NY: State University of New York Press.

Elshtain, Jean (1981), *Public Man, Private Woman*, Princeton, NJ: Princeton University Press.

Elshtain, Jean (1982), 'Feminism, Family and Community, *Dissent*, Vol.29, No.4.

Elshtain, Jean (1986), *Meditations on Modern Political Thought*, New York: Praeger.

Flax, Jane (1990), *Thinking Fragments: Psychoanalysis, Feminism and Postmodernism in the Contemporary West*, Berkeley, CA: University of California Press.

Fox, Warwick (1984), 'Deep Ecology: A New Philosophy of our Time?', *The Ecologist*, Vol.14, Nos.5/6.

Fox, Warwick (1990), *Towards a Transpersonal Ecology*, Boston, MA: Shambhala.

Gilligan, Carol (1982), *In a Different Voice*, Cambridge, MA: Havard University Press.

Goodin, Robert (1992), *Green Political Theory*, Cambridge: Polity.

Graham, Mary (1992), Interview with Caroline Jones, *The Search for Meaning*, ABC Radio National.

Hartsock (1985), *Money, Sex and Power*, Boston, MA: Northeastern University Press.

Held, Virginia (1987), 'Non-contractual Society: The Post-patriarchal Family as Model', *Canadian Journal of Philosophy*, 13, supp., pp.111–138.

Holler, Linda (1990), 'Thinking with the Weight of the Earth', *Hypatia*, Vol.5, No.1.

Jaggar, Alison (1983), *Feminist Politics and Human Nature*, Totowa, NJ: Rowman & Allanheld.

Keller, Catherine (1986), *From a Broken Web*, Boston, MA: Beacon.

Keller, Evelyn Fox (1985), *Reflections on Gender and Science*, New Haven, CT: Yale University Press.

Kheel, Marti (1990), 'Ecofeminism and Deep Ecology: Reflections on Identity and Difference' in J. Diamond and G. Orenstein (eds.), *Reweaving the World*, San Francisco: Sierra Club Books.

Kymlicka, Will (1993), 'Community' in R. Goodin and P. Pettit (eds.), *A Companion to Contemporary Political Philosophy*, Oxford: Blackwell.

Leguin, Ursula (1988), *Always Coming Home*, London: Grafton.

Mathews, Freya (1991), *The Ecological Self*, London: Routledge.

Mathews, Freya (1994a), 'To Know the World' in Farley, Kelly (ed.), *On the Edge of Discovery: Women in Australian Science*, Melbourne: Text.

Mathews, Freya (1994b), 'Cultural Relativism and Environmental Ethics', *IUCN Ethics Working Group Circular Newsletter*, No.5.

Mathews, John (1989), *Age of Democracy: the Politics of Post-Fordism*, Melbourne: Oxford University Press.

Naess, Arne (1973), 'The Shallow and the Deep, Long-Range Ecology Movement, *Inquiry*, Vol.16, No.1.

Naess, Arne (1979), 'Self-realisation in Mixed Communities of Humans, Bears, Sheep and Wolves, *Inquiry*, Vol.22, Nos.1–2.

Naess, Arne (1989), *Ecology, Community and Lifestyle*, Cambridge: Cambridge University Press, translated by David Rothenberg.

Naess, Arne (1993), 'Beautiful Action. Its Function in the Ecological Crisis', *Environmental Values*, Vol.2, No.1.

Noddings, Nel (1984), *Caring*, Berkeley, CA: University of California Press.

Nye, Andrea (1988), *Feminist Theory and the Philosophy of Man*, London: Routledge.

Pateman, Carol (1988), *The Sexual Contract*, Cambridge: Polity.

Plant, Judith (1989), *Healing the Wounds: the Promise of Ecofeminism*, Philadelphia, PA: New Society.

Plant, Judith (ed.) (1990) *Home! A Bioregional Reader*, Philadelphia, PA: New Society.

Plumwood, Val (1993), *Feminism and the Mastery of Nature*, London: Routledge.

Poole, Ross (1993), *Morality and Modernity*, London: Routledge.
Ritter, Alan (1980), *Anarchism*, Cambridge: Cambridge University Press.
Rose, Deborah Bird (1992), *Dingo Makes Us Human,* Cambridge: Cambridge University Press.
Ruddick, Sara (1984), 'Maternal Thinking' in J. Trebilcot, *Mothering*, Totowa, NJ: Rowman & Allanheld.
Sale, Kirkpatrick (1985), *Dwellers in the Land: the Bioregional Vision,* San Francisco, CA: Sierra Club Books.
Sandel, Michael (1982), *Liberalism and the Limits of Justice*, Cambridge: Cambridge University Press.
Trinh T. Minh-ha (1989), *Woman, Native, Other*, Bloomington, IN: Indiana University Press.
Warren, Karen (1990), 'The Power and Promise of Ecological Feminism', *Environmental Ethics*, Vol.12, No.2.
Weil, Simone (1962), 'Human Personality', in *Collected Essays,* London: Oxford University Press.
Yamauchi, T. (1996), 'Some Traditional Japenese Thoughts – from the Viewpoint of Environmental Ethics', unpublished.
Young, Iris Marion (1990), 'The Ideal of Community and the Politics of Difference' in L. Nicholson (ed), *Feminism/Postmodernism*, London: Routledge.

Environment, Democracy and Community

IAN BARNS

A radical democratic polity might provide a discursive framework more supportive of a green political agenda than that provided by a liberal democracy. Four key themes of a radical democratic project are: the development of a richer public discourse involving a more active, participatory practice of citizenship; the inclusion of group difference within the public domain whilst at the same time maintaining a commitment to working towards 'the common good'; the renewal of those forms of community life that enable the formation of persons with strong moral commitment yet respectful of difference; and the explication of the moral sources of radical democracy through peaceable dialogue between rival versions of the good life. These themes are then applied to the following key issues of green politics: the development of a morally grounded vision of sustainable development; the balancing of green political activities at the 'centre' and the 'periphery' of political life; the recovery of the communitarian basis of an 'ecological self'; and the creation of a 'frame reflexive' dialogue about the moral foundations of both democracy and a respect for the natural world.

Even for the more or less committed, 'staying green' is a demanding moral practice. If you are an urban consumer it means resisting the seductive appeal of television advertising to consume more and to care less, and a willingness to change your habits in relation to energy use, transport, and waste disposal – at a not insignificant cost in time, energy and convenience. If you are a business person it means an ongoing commitment to invest in 'socially useful' and environmentally non-destructive products. If you are 'just' a concerned citizen it implies a persistence in participatory activism in environmental politics, with the hard slog of understanding complex issues, remaining attentive to the spotty records of government, business and unions on conservation issues, and supporting campaigns on diverse environmental issues, ranging from the protection of local wetlands, to matters of national and international policy, such as conventions on

Ian Barns teaches in the Institute for Science and Technology Policy at Murdoch University in Western Australia.

biodiversity and climate change. All this for the long haul, and not just whilst being green is fashionable.

A lifestyle of green practice surely depends upon a deeper motivation than utilitarian self interest or an emotional response to television images of impending ecological disaster. As Freya Mathews suggests, a philosophical vision is needed to sustain patient, inconvenient, time-consuming conservation practice. For Mathews and other ecophilosophers this means a commitment to ecocentrism, in which one's sense of self is rooted in and encompassed by a larger ecocentric social order [*Mathews, 1991a*]. An ecocentric self will persevere in practical and political environmental action, inspired by the vision of forging solidarities with both biotic and human communities.

The trouble is, as Mathews points out [*1991b: 157-9*], an ecocentric self is unlikely to be nourished by the ethos and institutions of a liberal democratic polity and a capitalist economy. To be sure, by virtue of their regard for free speech and relatively open media, liberal democracies have enabled environmental debate and action much more effectively than closed and authoritarian societies. Media dramatisation of environmental issues can be translated into popular awareness, and some measure of political responsiveness by governing elites. For a time during the 1980s, in Australia as elsewhere, 'the environment' became a focus for major policy initiatives and changes in business and consumer practices, as issues of ozone depletion, acid rain, greenhouse and so on grabbed our attention. Yet with the downturn in the economy, we became preoccupied once more by the imperatives of economic growth and employment generation. It seems that our capacities to maintain serious collective attention to what are necessarily long term issues are vitiated by the ethos and institutions of a liberal democratic order: a pervasive possessive individualism, a negative concept of freedom which inhibits purposive collective action, and an eschewal of any shared normative vision beyond the maintenance of personal and property rights. Environmental action in a liberal democracy seems doomed, by and large, to be anthropocentric, selective and short term.

If liberal democracy represented the best achievable form of democracy, we would face a bleak choice between democracy and long-term environmental reform. For all its strengths, however, liberal democracy is a particularly restricted form of democracy. As has often been pointed out, liberalism and democracy are as much competing as complementary, political traditions. 'Liberal democracy' represents a compromise between liberalism's primary concerns with individualistically conceived property rights on the one hand and a vision of democratic representation, participation and accountability on the other.

Liberal democracy is also becoming a more vulnerable form of democracy. The effective practice, if not the formal structure, of liberal democracy in contemporary urban industrial societies is threatened by a number of pressures. These include the concentration and global mobility of transnational corporate power; the dominance of scientific and technical expertise over a wide range of public issues involving a high level of technological complexity; the corrosive effects upon policy development of the ideology of economic rationalism; the weakening of citizenship commitment and capacities by an all-pervasive ethos of consumerism; the questioning of the presumed universalism and neutrality of the liberal state by a range of dissenting voices: feminist, ethnic and alternative life-style; and the undermining of the 'grand narratives' of progress and reason by post-modern critique.

The restrictiveness and vulnerability of liberal democracy has stimulated an active search for an alternative democratic vision which could sustain a more extensive and richer practice of democracy. The common purpose of various alternative theories of democracy, such as Bowles and Gintis's radical democracy, Barber's strong democracy, Dryzek's discursive democracy, Mainsbridge's deliberative democracy and various civic republican accounts of democracy is to identify those discursive conditions which could enable a richer dialogical practice of democratic politics in a wider range of social sites.[1]

The purpose of this essay is to make not only the comparatively modest claim that a radical democracy of this kind would provide a much more favourable discursive context for the promotion of green ideas and practices, but also the stronger claim that the realisation of a green agenda (in both the sense of recognising as well as achieving the goals of environmental reform) is contingent upon the reflexive articulation[2] of the deeper moral sources of a radical democratic polity. I suggest that the flourishing of radical democracy entails not only a 'thicker' form of public dialogue which goes beyond the thin 'proceduralism' of liberal democracy. A commitment to peaceful, democratic dialogism of a radical democracy arises out of some shared, substantive vision of the 'good life'. Thus my claim is that not only does a genuinely green agenda need to be formulated and achieved through the dialogical practices of radical democracy but also that, in the end, the moral sources of radical democracy are the same moral sources that sustain forms of human community and selfhood in which care for the earth and all its creatures are primary commitments.

In a first section I shall identify what I see to be four key discursive challenges raised by a radical democratic agenda (my concern in this study is with the terms of democratic discourse, rather than its institutional arrangements). The first is the challenge of developing a richer discourse of 'public life' which would allow a more active, participatory practice of citizenship, the cultivation of civic virtue and the forging of common public purposes. The second is the challenge of encompassing within such a public domain the plurality or diversity of voices, traditions and associational life of contemporary society in a way that combines a respect for difference with a commitment to working towards 'the common good'. The third is the challenge of renewing those forms of communal life that make possible the formation of selves deeply committed to a vision of 'the good life' and yet also respectful of differences in belief and practice. The fourth is the challenge of seeking to make explicit the moral sources of radical democracy itself through a peaceable dialogue between rival versions of 'the good life' and the meta-narratives that sustain them.

In the second section I sketch some of the ways in which a radical democracy of this kind would provide a discursive space for the moral grounding and outworking of green ideas and practices. I shall consider a 'green agenda' in terms of four broad dimensions which can be linked to the four aspects of a radical democratic agenda discussed in the first section. These are, first, the task of making human material practices, such as the 'extraction' of resources, energy use and consumption, agriculture, manufacturing, urban development, the consumption of goods and services, and the disposal of waste, more ecologically sustainable. This goal has been generally formulated in terms of a project of 'sustainable development' in which economic development and environmental conservation are seen as complementary rather than antithetical values. Whilst the recognition of this conceptual principle has been a major step forward, 'sustainable development' is a highly contested term with many people in the environmental movement suspicious that it ultimately means little more than the co-option of environmental concerns within a continuing commitment to the overriding imperatives of economic development. Neither has it made the political task of modifying unsustainable and exploitative human material practices much easier to achieve. However, at least it has made the preservation of biodiversity, the preservation of natural eco-systems and habitats, and the reform of exploitative and polluting agricultural and industrial activities important economic priorities and not simply environmentalist ideals.

The second dimension of a green agenda is to encourage political and economic reform at both the margins and the centre of modern industrial society, to promote forms of local economic and communal development as alternatives to the centralising forces of a free market economy and bureaucratic state, and at the same time to continue to press for the reform of the environmental practices of government and the business sector. Local eco-communal initiatives involving 'alternative' activities such as permaculture, organic farming, urban forestry and barter economies are flourishing in both rural and urban contexts. Whilst this decentralist orientation arises out of a healthy suspicion of the co-optive powers of a bureaucratic state and an urban consumer society, by itself it runs the risk of weakening environmentalist commitment to and involvement in mainstream political reform.

Thirdly, there is the task, both practical and philosophical, of articulating the kinds of moral practices and virtues that enable the formation of persons and communities who identify with and care for the wider community of living things, at both local and global levels. Finally, the green agenda involves the extended philosophical criticism of the objectivist and mechanistic models of nature which have undergirded the deeply anthropocentric and exploitative use of the world in which we dwell, and the articulation of an alternative green vision of nature.

I suggest that the project of radical democracy provides an appropriate discursive context for framing and articulating these dimensions of a green agenda. The more participative and dialogical public domain of a radical democracy would provide a better discursive environment than that of the dominant discourse of market liberalism for framing the project of sustainable development. The challenge of encompassing associational plurality and difference within the public domain of a radical democracy would provide a better framework for dealing with the tensions between the bureaucratic mainstream and the activist margins in environmental policy-making. A recovery of the communitarian sources of 'the democratic self' would provide the basis for a critical appropriation of eco-philosophical ideas about 'the ecological self'. Finally, a reflexive public discourse about the moral sources of a democratic polity opens up the debates about the limits of western scientific and technological modernity and the need to retrieve a vision of nature which can sustain both the project of democratic emancipation and a deep identification with and care for land and earth.

The Radical Democratic Reconstruction of Liberalism

Samuel Bowles and Herbert Gintis [1986: 6] describe radical democracy as a 'visionary historical' project which is developed in critical opposition to the dominant structures of power rather than as an abstract alternative system of government. Bowles and Gintis thus seek to build on the strengths – as well as to correct the weaknesses – of the enlightenment traditions of liberalism and Marxism which have thus far provided the major discursive frameworks for democratic ideas. By explicating the underlying discursive structure of liberalism (not merely what liberals say but how they say it) they hope to contribute to the further democratisation of a tradition whose emancipatory potential has thus far been limited by its primary concern with the protection of property rights.

Bowles and Gintis's strategy is to re-work the characteristic partitions or boundaries which liberal discourse imposes on social life,[3] in particular those partitions between public and private spheres and between what they call 'choosers' and 'learners' [*1986: 17*]. By blurring these boundaries they hope both to extend and enrich liberal democratic discourse. They want to extend the scope of democracy to include important areas of social life, such as the economy, the workplace, the market, the firm and the family, which in a liberal framework have been regarded as 'off limits' in the private sphere. They also want to enrich democracy by including on the agenda of political discourse questions about what kinds of people we want to be and, by implication, the moral and metaphysical issues that these questions open up.

Strong Democracy, Civic Virtue and the Common Good

In common with other radical democratic theorists, Bowles and Gintis have a vision of the public domain as a discursive space in which a political community is able to develop common interests and forge common purposes through participatory dialogue. A central theme is that of active participatory citizenship, in which citizenship is as much a moral practice as a legal status, and in which the process of participation in the various arenas of public life shapes the development of civic virtue and a more robust public self.[4] It is a political vision in which individual freedom is embedded within and sustained by a stronger sense of political community and of the common good. Ranson and Stewart [*1989*] describe such a vision in the following terms:

> The essential task of the public domain can now be interpreted as enabling authoritative public choice about collective activity and purpose. In short, it is about clarifying, constituting and achieving public purpose. It has the ultimate responsibility for constituting a society as a political community which has the capacity to make public choices. Producing a 'public' which is able to assemble, to enter into dialogue and decide about the needs of the community as a whole is the uniquely demanding challenge facing the public domain.

However, once we begin to talk about a democracy oriented towards developing a more substantive vision of the common good and a public domain in which the practices of democratic participation are recognised as shaping our identities, some troubling questions arise. The first concerns the inclusion of 'difference'. How are we to encompass within a democratic process oriented towards the forging of some substantive 'common good' the diversity of practices, beliefs and voices that constitute our increasingly pluralistic society? Second, given the recognition that democratic participation is also a moral practice, what kinds of selves do we need to be in order to be committed to a particular vision of the good life and yet at the same time live in peaceful harmony with those who are different? What conditions are necessary for the development of such selves? Third, how can we enable productive and peaceful dialogue between communities holding competing and often incommensurable ideological visions?

Including 'the Fact of Difference' in the Public Sphere

In a liberal construction of democratic life, the public/private division is supposed to involve on the one hand a procedural 'thin-ness' in the public sphere, in which the agenda of public life is limited to questions of means rather than ends, and on the other hand the free expression of religious, ethnic, sexual and personal difference within the private sphere (as long as this does not intrude upon the rights of others). However, this liberal partition is becoming increasingly difficult to maintain. The administrative systems of state bureaucracies and the culture of consumer capitalism increasingly pervade and undermine the supposedly autonomous private spaces of family and community life. Conversely public life in liberal democratic societies is increasingly troubled by intense conflicts over life politics: conflicts over gender, lifestyle, ethnicity, religion and community identity. They are disputes that blur the public/private division, and they cannot be easily expressed in terms of the liberal discourses of rights and non-discriminatory due process [*Hunter, 1991*]. Feminists, gays, Muslims, and Christian fundamentalists (to name a few) are claiming more than the right to pursue their different practices in the private sphere. They are also contesting the ostensibly universalist norms of public life with respect to personhood, sexuality, ethnicity and religious belief. In so doing they open up much deeper questions of identity that cut across the public/private division.

Civic republican and communitarian political theorists who want to restore the notion of 'the common good' as a central purpose of public life at least open up public discourse to such expressions of difference. Yet, from a feminist perspective, neither liberal nor civic republican accounts of the public sphere adequately recognise the particularity and difference of various social groups. Both the procedural universalism of liberalism and the thicker citizenship of civic republicans tacitly (and, from a feminist viewpoint, illegitimately) universalise a masculinist particularity [*Young, 1990*]. Chantal Mouffe [*1988*; also *Dietz, 1987*] thus argues for a greater institutional recognition of difference, not by relegation to the private, but by the recognition of different forms of life within a more heterogeneous public sphere. (I note in passing that Mouffe's argument parallels Paul Hirst's [*1992*] advocacy of associational pluralism, in which the state, rather than being the primary agency for achieving social purposes, would function rather to facilitate and regulate a wide diversity of associational activity.)

Mouffe *et al.* do not deny the importance of the public domain as such, or of the need to talk about common interests and the common good. Rather they argue that such public discourse must be based on a much more pluralistic account of citizenship, and the recognition of the essentially contested nature of the common good.[5] Feminist political theorists also want to open up the private sphere to a greater degree of democratic accountability [*Young, 1987; Mouffe, 1988*]. If the private (feminine) sphere of domestic life is incorporated into the domain of democratic politics, then perhaps the distinctive 'ethics of care' of the 'domestic' world can significantly re-shape the practices of the wider public world. Johnson [*1991: 64*] puts this well:

> ... a feminism of difference needs to seek in the intimate sphere traces of an already existing, distinctive interpretation of the principles of liberal humanism. Only by specifying the particular relation of women to these ideals, which liberalism has supposed as only properly ideals of a public sphere, can we give particular content to the demand for a recognition of the distinctive voice of women-as-women in all public discussions over the ends of life.

Restoring the Communal Resources of the Democratic Self

The blurring of the partition between public and private spheres and the inclusion of the expression of difference, particularity and associational pluralism within the public domain in the way suggested by Mouffe, Hirst and others, opens up the deeper question of the nature of the self in a democratic society.

As mentioned previously, Bowles and Gintis suggest that one of the features of liberal discourse is the partition between 'choosers' and 'learners'. We are assumed to be 'choosers' in public life, as more or less mature adults with pre-formed needs and interests. Public life is understood in largely instrumentalist terms. We participate in order to pursue these already formed needs and interests, rather that being engaged in a process of self formation (both individual and collective). The question of what kind of persons we are or choose to be (that is, as 'learners') is thus a matter for the private sphere. The great attraction of this division, of course, is that in terms of our fundamental beliefs and identities, both individual and communal, we are protected from the intrusive or coercive power of the state. However, as Bowles and Gintis [*1986: 17*] point out, it also means that the practices that shape our identities (particularly economic practices) are protected from public, democratic scrutiny:

The walls that liberalism erects do more than create liberties; they also obscure and shelter the citadels of domination. According to its usages, liberty is held to apply to rational agents (choosers) but not to others (learners) and the norms of democracy are held to apply to the actions of choosers in the public realm alone. As a result democratic institutions are held to be merely instrumental to the exercise of choice: democracy facilitates the satisfaction of perceived needs.

From this perspective the question of selfhood should not be excluded from the agenda of public life. Democratic discourse about the processes and priorities of political community necessarily involves dealing with the question of what kind of people we are. It also implies that the core processes of learning within the private sphere – of the becoming of persons in family and community – cannot be 'walled off' from public debate. Moral and personal development within the primary associations of the private sphere – families, communities and so on – becomes a matter of public, democratic discussion.

Bowles and Gintis [*1986: 126*] recognise the troubling implications of their project of blurring the public/private divisions and the claim that participation in public life should be understood in terms of 'becoming' and not merely of 'choosing'.

When individuals are at once choosers and learners, the boundaries between liberty, popular sovereignty, and legitimate authority become blurred. Some simple examples illustrate our point. Ought the producer or consumer determine the nature of a service delivered? If the consumer is considered a chooser, the service is called a commodity, and consumer sovereignty is deemed to hold. If, by contrast, the consumer is considered a learner (for example, a child) the preferences of others count. Schools, for instance, teach what children should know, not what they wish to know. If we reject the learning-choosing dichotomy, however, we must search for new principles to resolve the issue. How do we deal, for example, with the case of the craft that considers not only what consumers want, but what will also contribute to the development of consumers' capacity to appreciate? What about students who fully accept the notion of learning and perhaps even revere the superior wisdom of their teachers, but wish to participate in making educational policy?[6]

What are the terms in which we can talk about 'the democratic self'? Implicit in Bowles and Gintis's radical democratic project is a communitarian understanding of the self. Whilst liberalism – particularly market and economic versions of liberalism – deploys an atomistic view of the self in which the self is assumed to be ontologically prior to and autonomous with respect to community or association [*Arblaster, 1984*], communitarians regard the self as being constituted within and sustained by community: we are persons-in-community.[7]

A major communitarian theme is that the life world of consumer capitalism is deeply corrosive of the integrity of communities and thus of the necessary conditions for the development of virtuous persons. Despite Anthony Giddens's [*1991*] optimism, the difficulties of 'becoming' a morally resilient self in the world of pervasive commodification is a matter of deep concern for many people [*Lasch, 1984; MacIntyre, 1985*]. For example, Jeremy Seabrook has a particularly bleak view of what it means to grow up in a consumer society:

> The child tends to be stripped of all social influences but those of the market place, all sense of place, function and class is weakened, the characteristics of region and clan, neighbourhood or kindred are attenuated. The individual is denuded of everything but appetites, desires and tastes, wrenched from any context of human obligation or commitment. It is a process of mutilation; and once this has been achieved, we are offered the consolation of reconstituting the abbreviated humanity out of the things and the goods around us, and the fantasies and vapours which they emit. A culture becomes the main determinant upon morality, beliefs and purposes, usurping more and more territory that formerly belonged to parents, teachers, community, priests and politics alike.[8]

For Bowles and Gintis [*1986: 139, 145*], this kind of experience, involving as it does the weakening of social bonds and communal identity, undermines our capacities to become active, participatory citizens:

> The instrumentalist conception of politics renders liberalism indifferent or hostile to the formation of those loyalties and social bonds upon which a vibrant democracy must depend. This is nowhere more clear than in its devaluation of decentralized autonomous communities ... In the absence of vital communities standing between the individual and the state, liberalism's cherished political principle, liberty, is experienced more as loneliness than as freedom. And the putative allocative efficiency of the market is challenged by the proliferation of enforcement costs arising from the exercise of instrumental self interest in a conflict-ridden economy inhabited by strangers.

In this view, then, the capacity for democratic participation requires the recovery of a 'social ecology' of strong community. Yet how are we to achieve an appropriate balance between a commitment to community and the protection of the freedom to makes choices and to embrace difference? On the one hand, Michael Sandel [1982] has argued for the notion of the 'encumbered self' – that the communities to which we belong precede us: we do not choose them, but are born into them. On the other hand, Marilyn Friedman [1989: 275], although generally sympathetic to communitarian accounts of the self, fears that Sandel's notion of the encumbered self undermines the possibilities of personal autonomy altogether. She argues instead for 'urban friendship' as the paradigm of the communitarian self: the possibility of rejecting the communities of one's birth and establishing a different self through the choices of friendship.

This issue is significant for the question of what kind of selves we need to be in order to participate in the public sphere of a more radical, participatory democracy. What virtues are needed to engage in a politics of difference, of contestation about opposing accounts of the common good?[9] According to Gutman and Thompson [1990: 76], to go beyond the 'politics of exclusion' (which is the way in which a liberal society deals with insoluble disputes over fundamental issues) requires the special virtue of 'mutual respect':

> Mutual respect manifests a distinctively democratic kind of character – the character of individuals who are morally committed, self-reflective about their commitments, discerning of the difference between respectable and merely tolerable differences of opinion, and open to the possibility of changing their minds or modifying their positions at some time in the future if they confront unanswerable objections to their present point of view.

Could an 'encumbered self' (deeply committed to ideological vision, religious belief or cultural tradition) manifest the sort of 'mutual respect' identified by Gutman and Thompson: 'morally committed, [yet] self-reflexive about their commitments'? Could a more conservative communitarianism, orthodox fundamentalism or tribalism encourage that reflexivity and regard for the other upon which democratic dialogue depends? To deal with these questions we need to consider how a radical democracy project addresses the challenge of conflicts between competing visions of 'the good life'.

Retrieving the Sources of Emancipatory Hope

In liberal democratic discourse there is supposed to be a clear boundary between politics and metaphysics. Public debate is supposed to be neutral with respect to competing accounts of the good life and underlying metaphysical disagreements. Democracy is about procedures rather than goals, rights rather than the good, means rather than metaphysics.

This is not to say that arguments about such issues are formally excluded from public debate. It is rather that the terms of liberal political discourse make it difficult to talk about some of the most pressing ideological conflicts in contemporary politics [*Hunter, 1991*]. We suffer what Charles Taylor [*1991: 18*] calls 'an extraordinary inarticulacy', a lack of a public language in which to debate our different visions of the good life, those visions which ultimately predispose us either to support or oppose (for example) abortion, land rights, progressive taxation, government intervention in the economy, censorship, pollution control and so on.

A central task for a radical democratic project, therefore, should be to facilitate a democratic conversation about rival accounts of the good life: in other words to open up, rather than repress, dialogue between communities representing incommensurable visions of reality [*Rein, 1989*]. This would involve not only ongoing, peaceful dialogue about such differences and the negotiation of an agreed provisional basis for mutual co-operation and co-existence, but also a reflexive public conversation about the moral sources of a democratic polity itself.

An important prerequisite for this is a recognition of the crucial, though increasingly problematic role that liberalism has played in providing the 'meta-narrative'[10] of democratic practice itself. The trouble is that liberal discourse tends to hide its own metaphysical, ideological – and some would say, theological – underpinnings. The 'public square' of a liberal society is supposed to be 'naked' or neutral with respect to ultimate questions. A liberal polity is supposed to be open and pluralistic, allowing a rich diversity of different traditions and practices. In the emerging culture of post-modernity, the rule of 'grand narratives' is supposed to be over.

The liberal disclaimer – that is, with respect to any commitment to any over-arching meta-narrative – comes in two forms. One is the more traditional assertion that public life can be conducted autonomously with respect to questions of ultimate belief. In an older version of this view, metaphysical questions were still regarded as substantive, yet were considered to be best left to the rational deliberation of private individuals guided by conscience. More recently, such issues have come to be regarded as matters of merely subjective or 'life-style' preference, thereby making the instrumentalist and procedural discourse of the liberal public sphere a *de facto* metaphysic.[11] Should the concealed hegemony of secular reason over the public domain be challenged on the basis of an alternative (for example) religious or environmentalist meta-narrative, it is condemned as obscurantist, intolerant, 'ideological', and a threat to the 'universalist' values of freedom and objectivity.[12]

The second form is a more inclusive liberalism which, whilst celebrating the more open expression of difference in public life, nevertheless co-opts such difference within a tacit meta-narrative of cosmopolitan pluralism. The evils of western universalism – particularly in the form of western religion, patriarchy and colonialism – are more readily acknowledged, and the equal validity of different visions of the good life recognised. A more flexible and cosmopolitan pluralism denies attachment to a particular meta-narrative and espouses an open tolerance to all others. Yet as John Milbank [*1990b*] argues, in the very act of embracing diverse particularistic traditions within its own cosmopolitanism, liberalism tacitly reduces these traditions to contingent variations of its own meta-narrative – pluralism. As Milbank points out, this inclusiveness fails to recognise that particular traditions are not merely instances of a broader universalising liberal pluralism, but universalising visions themselves, often incommensurable with each other and with liberalism itself.[13]

A genuinely democratic discourse should thus begin with the recognition – by liberals, socialists, feminists, deep ecologists, neo-pagans, post-modernists, Christians, Muslims, Jews and so on – that it is ultimately not possible to stand outside a particular framework of belief and practice and to appeal to some supposedly objective or autonomous moral principles [*MacIntyre, 1985*]. Genuine dialogue involves a reflexive awareness of one's own 'frame' commitments [*Rein, 1989*] and a capacity to engage in cross-frame dialogue which does not attempt to suppress or ignore fundamental differences coercively whilst at the same time seeking to explicate those moral and metaphysical sources which can sustain a radical democracy as a moral community and not merely as a procedural republic.

It also needs to be recognised that the emancipatory tradition of enlightenment liberalism is not just one vision among many. Rather, it has been that normative framework which has thus far sustained and shaped the conditions of dialogical open-ness and the self-limiting regard for the other which makes any form of democratic life possible.[14] As Charles Taylor [*1992: 62*] observes, liberalism has always been a 'fighting creed'.

In a discussion of Quebec as a polity with a substantive sense of collective moral purpose yet still respectful of difference, Taylor [*1992: 59*] develops an account of liberal society rather different from the 'proceduralist republic':

> On their [Quebeckers] view, a society can be organized around a definition of the good life, without this being seen as a depreciation of

those who do not personally share this definition. Where the nature of the good requires that it be sought in common, this is the reason for it being a matter of public policy. According to this conception, a liberal society singles itself out as such by the way it treats minorities, including those who do not share public definitions of the good, and above all by the rights it accords to all its members ... . A society with strong collective goals can be liberal, on this view, provided it is also capable of respecting diversity, especially when dealing with those who do not share its common goals; and provided it can offer safeguards for fundamental rights.

Yet the emancipatory character of liberal, enlightenment reason is under serious challenge. It is being questioned, deconstructed and rejected by a chorus of post-modernist, feminist, Tory radical, conservationist or religious voices, as well as undermined by techno-economic developments. If a frame-reflexive dialogue is to contribute to the retrieval of the deeper sources of the emancipatory hope of which liberalism has been an expression, a major task will be to develop a constructive response to the various critiques of liberalism, and in particular, the claims that rather than being the source of emancipation, liberal reason is ultimately an instrumental rationality which embodies a project of domination (either anthropocentric and/or patriarchal) ultimately destroying the very intelligibility of moral discourse [*MacIntyre, 1985; Poole, 1991*].

This task of reconstruction has, of course, been tackled by a wide diversity of social theorists. I shall briefly mention three significant exemplars: Jurgen Habermas, Alasdair MacIntyre and John Milbank. For Habermas, the problem is not with instrumental rationality as such, but with the distorted nature of modernisation. Rather than rejecting modernity, Habermas [*1984*] argues that we need to complete the communicative rationalisation of society. The destructive effects of instrumental reason can be resisted by limiting it to the domain of the 'steering systems' of the economy and the formal political system and recovering the integrity of practical reason or 'communicative rationality' within the 'life world'.

This response does not, however, deal with the pervasive instrumentalising of social life resulting from the continuing development of the techno-sciences [*Aranowitz, 1988*], a process which Jacques Ellul [*1964; also Hill, 1988*] has explored intensively in terms of the dominance of *la technique*. Habermas does not adequately recognise the problematic nature of science in its own domain, either at the level of the powerful mechanistic models of nature, or at the level of the astonishing technologies through which our human experience is being progressively reconstructed in instrumentalist terms – particularly the new communications and information technologies [*Haraway, 1987*]. Within the expansionary logic of late capitalism these technologies threaten an even more pervasive instrumental dominance over human life [*Harvey, 1989*]. Through the new worlds of the global internet and the human genome project we can glimpse the ways in which modern techno-science mediates the reconstruction of the life world [*Aranowitz, 1988*].

Alasdair MacIntyre, on the other hand, is so deeply critical of the destructive and nihilistic consequences of the enlightenment project that it is difficult to imagine any possibility of reconstruction.[15] Yet despite his hostility to modernity, MacIntyre does identify the key issue of *teleology* in relation to our underlying models of persons and nature. MacIntyre himself argues that it is necessary to return to some kind of neo-Aristotelian account of persons as the basis for any defensible moral theory – an argument that is difficult to reconcile with modern science. There are many others, however, who argue that a post-positivistic understanding of science and the world opens up the possibility that moral purpose is a primary rather than a secondary quality of nature [*Sheldrake, 1990*].

For John Milbank [*1990a*] the root problem with instrumental rationality lies more deeply in the presumption of the natural 'secularity' of the world. Milbank argues [*1990a: 9*] that from the perspective of secular reason 'desacralisation' involves 'a metaphor of the removal of the superfluous and additional to leave a residue of the human, the natural and the self-sufficient'. Because of this the usual response to the unexpected contemporary flourishing of religious belief and practice (what Daniel Bell [*1977; also Casanova, 1984*] has called 'the return of the sacred') is to explain away such religiosity as a reactive response to the disorders of modernity. Religious practice is a phenomenon to be encompassed within a multicultural pluralism or feared as a reactionary threat to human freedom. Milbank [*1990a: 9*] implies (without at all endorsing a 're-enchantment of the world') that it is possible that the sacred is primary and that the secularity of the world is a positive construction: 'a domain that had to be instituted or imagined',[16] and that the deeper sources of emancipation lie in a Christian, trinitarian ontology.[17]

It is beyond the scope of this study to explore in any detail the contours of a post-instrumentalist and post-secular moral tradition which can sustain the practice of radical democracy. Certainly, a democratic discourse cannot dismiss the challenges of post-modern, communitarian, feminist, religious and environmentalist criticisms of enlightenment reason out of hand [*Frankel, 1992*]. The agenda of radical democracy should include, as an essential aspect of 'frame-reflexive' dialogue between competing ideological visions, the task of arguing about those central narratives of human existence, narratives which make possible the development of selves and communities sustained by a vision of hope and yet able to live in peaceable democratic harmony with those who are different. It should seek to recover that substantive vision of the good life which enables the virtues of peaceable difference. In my view, a view which I readily recognise as being an increasingly deviant one, central to the task of reflexively retrieving the sources of a radical democratic polity is a constructive interrogation of the connections between Christian theology and the enlightenment emancipatory project of the sort exemplified by Milbank's *Theology and Social Theory,* and Colin Gunton's *The One, The Three and the Many.* In the end, like Milbank and Gunton, I believe that the sources of emancipation are to be found, not in the negation of Christianity but in and through the renewal of its central vision of trinitarian sociality [*Moltmann, 1985*].

Radical Democracy and a Green Agenda

Thus far, I have argued that the central task for a radical democracy project should be to create a public domain which would enable the active participation of citizens in the forging of common public purposes. It should also deal with the questions that this raises: how such a domain can best encompass the many different voices of contemporary social life, what forms of community life are needed to foster democratic virtues and persons, and how to develop a 'frame-reflective discourse' which would enable productive and peaceful conversation between incommensurable ideological visions about the moral sources of a democratic polity.

In this section I want to illustrate the claim that this kind of discursive framework (assuming its effective institutionalisation) is integral to the expression and critical development of green ideas and practices. I shall try to show this by considering how the four dimensions of the green agenda outlined earlier might be productively developed in terms of the four themes of radical democracy. First, the notion of a public domain oriented towards the forging of common purposes would provide a better framework for dealing with environmental 'commons' issues, such as, for example, the challenge of the 1987 report of the World Commission on Environment and Development, *Our Common Future.* Second, encompassing the diversity of associational life, particularly through the development of a more facilitative mode of state administration, would help to resolve a major dilemma faced by environmental activists, namely, that of choosing between effective action at the centre which runs the risk of bureaucratic co-option, and creative decentralised eco-communal practice which runs the risk of being politically irrelevant and/or undermining the capacity of the state to generate progressive environmental reform. Third, a concern for restoring the conditions for the formation of the democratic self enables a better appreciation of the political importance of notions of the 'ecological self'. Fourth, the encouragement of frame-reflective discourse between competing visions of the good life would make the environmentalist critique of Western anthropocentrism and the search for an alternative meta-narrative central to public democratic debate.

Dialogical Political Community and Responding to 'Commons' Issues

In the first section I argued that from a radical democratic perspective the purpose of the public domain was to forge political community and common purpose through active participatory dialogue: a vision quite different from that of the individualistically conceived market place of exchange and competition promoted by contemporary market liberalism. This alternative vision of public life is essential for global environmental problems to be dealt with effectively. As the title of the Brundtland report, *Our Common Future*, suggests, many of the most pressing environmental problems facing communities, nations and the world are 'commons' problems. Issues such as enhanced global warming, acid rain, the depletion of the ozone layer, de-forestation, desertification and the loss of biodiversity are problems which transcend the particular interests of individuals and nations and need to be addressed co-operatively.

From the perspective of liberal individualism therein lies what Garrett Hardin [*1971*] called the 'tragedy of the commons': the disinclination of rational self-maximising individuals to act altruistically in order to deal with common problems. Writing in the 1970s, Hardin advocated a draconian, interventionist response to the particular 'commons' tragedy he was concerned about: that of over-population. In its report *Our Common Future* [*World Commission on Environment and Development, 1987: 71*] the Brundtland Commission also lamented the incapacity of nations, regions and communities to work together for a 'common future': 'The Earth is one but the world is not. We all depend on one biosphere for sustaining our lives. Yet each community, each country, strives for survival and prosperity with little regard for its impact on others ... .' Despite this, the Brundtland Commission approached the challenge of integrating environmental and economic goals from within an implicit social democratic political framework, based on a vague 'communitarian' ethos. It was hopeful 'that people can cooperate to build a future that is more prosperous, more just, and more secure' [*1987: 72*].

Our Common Future argued for a key role for government coordination and planning in the effective management of the environment.[18] However, when introduced into Australia, the project of 'sustainable development' advocated by the Brundtland Commission was effectively re-framed within the discourse of market liberalism. The key discussion papers [*Barns, 1992*] which set the agenda for the debate about sustainable development in Australia in 1990 adopted the neo-classical, free market perspective of environmental economist David Pearce [*1990*] rather than the social democracy of the Brundtland Commission.

Pearce's approach to environmental economics of course identifies many valuable policy instruments by which individual actors within a market context can be guided into more environmentally acceptable behaviour. What is more problematic, however, is the framework of market liberalism which is taken for granted. It assumes a society of atomistic individuals, pursuing their individualistically defined interests with little sense of 'moral community' and thus without the conceptual resources to forge common interests and purposes. This is not to say that we do not need to deal with conflict or competition between sectional interests. It is rather to say that the frame of economic liberalism occludes the underlying, taken-for-granted common purposes and shared identities which have provided in the past, and will continue to provide in the future, the resources to deal with commons problems. Ironically, the danger is that the successful extension of the frame of market liberalism into the domain of environmentally problematic practices can itself become a self-fulfilling prophecy. Policies based on the assumption that we can only think and act as self-interested consumers will tend to produce self-interested consumers.

The displacement of the communitarian rhetoric of *Our Common Future* by the discourse of neo-liberalism parallels what has happened to the discourse of the welfare state in general. As David Marquand has argued in *The Unprincipled Society* [*1988*], the vulnerability of the British social democratic welfare state to the alternative new right policies of the Thatcher government was ultimately due to its failure to develop a language of communal purpose and solidarity, over and above that of atomistic individualism. According to Marquand, the vision of a British welfare state remained grounded in an individualist social ontology, and thus lacked the language of communal identity and common interests needed to sustain the redistributive and welfare goals of the welfare state.

Both the re-theorising of the welfare state and the framing of environmental policy thus need to draw upon those older communitarian and civic republican traditions which enable the development of common purpose and civic identity without collapsing into bureaucratic statism [*Dryzek, 1990*]. The problems of the commons can only be dealt with within the larger discursive framework of public dialogism committed to participatory engagement in the development of common purposes. As Mark Sagoff [*1990*] has argued, environmental issues are irreducibly moral, civic and communal problems, requiring the discourse of citizenship which is irreducible to that of consumer preferences.

Linking the Centre and the Periphery

The second theme in the radical democratic agenda outlined above was the need to encompass the pluralistic diversity of social life within a larger framework of some shared vision of the public good. An implication of this is a different understanding of the purpose of the state: that rather than the state being the central active agency or provider *vis-à-vis* passive consumers (in terms of the consumption of economic, political or social services), its primary role should be to facilitate the plurality of associational life in civil society. This notion of a facilitative state within a more heterogeneous public sphere can contribute, I suggest, to a resolution of the central eco-political problem of linking the bureaucratic centre to the eco-communalist periphery.

Environmental activists are routinely faced with a dilemma with respect to the role of the liberal state in conservation and environmental management. On the one hand, coordinated state action is necessary for long term environmental reform, and lobbying by activists and involvement in bureaucratic policy development by committed environmentalists is vital. Indeed, much has been achieved in recent years in terms of legislation and policy development. The 'environment' has been recognised as a major public issue, resulting in substantial government expenditure and the creation of environmental bureaucracies.

Yet, despite all the rhetoric, environmental action by governments often turns out to be limited and ineffective. What begins as community action is soon taken over by government and experts thus absorbing and neutralising its distinctive 'voluntary' and participatory character. Active participation by conservationists in the mainstream ends up being co-opted by the bureaucracy.[19] This pattern of co-option was particularly evident in the recent 'ecologically sustainable development' process in Australia. Whilst groups such as the Australian Conservation Foundation actively participated in the Federal Government's ESD process and were able to achieve a degree of influence, in retrospect adopting the language of 'economic responsibility' both alienated mainstream conservationists from their eco-communalist supporters and also expedited the displacement of 'ecologically sustainable development' from the public agenda after 1991–92.

Many eco-activists argue that the most effective and impressive forms of environmental practice have been at the margins, independent of the state, in a rich diversity of traditional agrarian practices and newer self-help eco-communal experiments [*Durning, 1989*]. Michael Redclift [*1987*] has argued that the real hope for long term sustainable development lies in the diverse local knowledges of small communities around the world, knowledges which are in danger of being destroyed by the emerging regime of global environmental management.

Yet the problem with such green wisdom and green experiments is that they remain marginal to the mainstream, having little obvious relevance to the larger task of re-directing national and global economies [*Frankel, 1987*]. Furthermore, by 'opting out' 'eco-communalists' or 'bio-regionalists' exacerbate rather than ameliorate environmental problems. As Robyn Eckersley [*1992a: 36*] observes, 'opting out' can jeopardise the urban democratic and liberal cultural values which have sustained most environmental reformist activity. Whilst the idea of a totally decentralised 'bio-regionalism' seems to offer the freedom for green communities to flourish, it would also allow anti-environmental practices to flourish, unchecked by effective government regulation and reform activity:

> ... ceding complete political and economic autonomy to the local communities inhabiting bioregions determined say, in terms of watersheds, will provide no guarantee that local development will be ecologically benign or cooperative ... Nor will such a devolution of power provide any guarantee that local communities will form a confederation with their neighbours so as to enable proper bioregional management. The maxim 'leave it to the locals who are affected' only makes sense when the locals possess an appropriate social and ecological consciousness.

The kind of radical democracy outlined above offers a discursive framework within which the centre and the periphery could be more productively connected. The problem with the discourse of liberal instrumentalism, in which the administrative state becomes the central agency of public life, is that community agency, as well as the diversity and particularities of community and regional concerns or experience, are effectively suppressed. An associational conception of civil society involving a more heterogeneous public sphere and a facilitative state would enable the contribution of such groups to be recognised as central and constitutive [*Hirst, 1991; 1992*]. It would be much more conducive to the development of genuine and diverse environmental practices. It would enable the flourishing of the languages of 'the life world', giving voice to a diversity of communal stories and places, rather than their suppression by the ostensibly universalising language of bureaucratic management. At the same time, associationalism, unlike bio-regionalism, does not under-estimate the importance of state agency at the centre. The state continues to play an important role, not only facilitating the diverse activities of civil society but also providing the regulatory framework through which the balance between common purpose and plural diversity can be maintained [*Hirst, 1991*].

The 'Ecological' Self: Ecocentric and Communitarian Perspectives

The third theme was that the blurring of the division between public and private spheres (and, in Bowles and Gintis's terms, between 'choosers' and 'learners') brings the question of the nature and conditions of the democratic self on to the agenda of democratic politics. The nature and conditions of the self are also a central concern of environmental philosophers. A common theme of deep ecologists, eco-feminists and transpersonal ecologists has been that environmentalism has to go beyond an instrumentally construed restoration of degraded environments and the preservation of biodiversity. It must also re-define the nature of the self, and overcome the taken-for-granted instrumentalism and anthropocentrism of Western views of the self [*Mathews, 1991a*]. It must develop an 'ecological self'.

In the view of Robyn Eckersley [*1992b: 28*] the establishment of an ecocentric framework (which would nourish the formation of the ecological self) should take priority over the maintenance of western anthropocentric political traditions: liberalism, socialism, or radical democracy:

> In terms of fundamental priorities, an ecocentric approach regards the question of our proper place in nature as logically prior to the question of what are the most appropriate social and political arrangements for human communities. That is, the determination of social and political questions must proceed from, or at least be consistent with, an adequate determination of this more fundamental question.

This claim raises the crucial question: would an ecological self necessarily be a democratic self? Eckersley suggests that in fact it is the larger framework of ecocentrism that ultimately nourishes the virtues and practices of the democratic – or socialist – self. Ecocentrism overcomes the anthropocentrism of liberalism and socialism (or communitarianism) whilst at the same time preserving the regard for autonomy and self-in-community respectively: 'In lieu of the atomistic and individualistic self of liberalism or the more social self of socialism, ecocentric theorists have introduced a broader, ecological notion of the self that incorporates these individual and social aspects in a more encompassing framework' [*1992b: 55*].

In this and the following section I want to question this claim that ecocentrism introduces a 'broader, ecological notion of the self' which can encompass a deeper identification with nature as well as the central virtues of an emancipatory democratic tradition. In this section, I question the claim that the development of an ecocentric world view is logically prior to 'questions of social and political arrangements for human communities'. On the contrary, I suggest that for both theoretical and practical reasons, the development of an ecological self is a possible (and certainly desirable) outcome of a process of self development that should be understood in communitarian terms. In the next section, I shall question Eckersley's claim that ecocentrism belongs to and provides the deeper metaphysical grounding for the Western emancipatory tradition.

I wish to argue that rather than ecocentrism having a logical priority over questions of social and political arrangements, it is better understood in terms of an articulation of a communitarian perspective of the self as self-in-community. At a theoretical level, communitarians remind us that the self is not given by nature but constructed out of the possibilities opened up by the complexity of living things. One of the weaknesses of a strong ecocentrism is that in a desire to overcome the sharp human/nature division of anthropocentrism, it risks dissolving human difference within the 'internal relations' of nature. It can forget that whilst humans are part of the web of living things, the human self is not merely an emergent property of nature but is, as Freya Mathews [*1991a: 135–6*] observes, a cultural or linguistic construction.[20]

This observation does not imply a sharp ontological division between the human self and the wider natural world. It is rather to say that any cultural unity between humans and 'nature' is not 'natural' or given, but must be constructed linguistically, mediated through material practices, and sustained in communal narratives. It is this very 'social constructedness' which makes us different. An ecocentric account of the self is itself not an unmediated embracing of identity with nature. Even as we tell ecocentric stories that proclaim this identity, we constitute our difference from nature.[21]

Neither does an abstract ecocentrism adequately conceptualise the processes of self-formation through communal practice. Ironically, with abstract notions of 'internal relations', ecophilosophy still retains something of the 'mid-air' stance of liberal moral theory [*Hauerwas, 1983: 17*]. By contrast, a communitarian approach gives greater recognition to the importance of the symbolic and semiotic density of the 'life world' in the formation of the self. It is the *practice* of ecological relatedness – made intelligible in terms of particularistic communal narratives – that is vital for the development of those sensibilities of care for the environment. The identification with nature central to ecocentrism is mediated through specific practices – practices by which one includes the world of 'things' – both constructed and natural – as part of a wider world of enduring community [*Lasch, 1984; Borgmann, 1984*].[22] It is particularly through childhood experiences of particular places and relationships, that we learn to care (or not to care) about the natural and social environment in which we live. George Eliot [*1970: 20*] puts it thus in *Daniel Deronda*:

> A human life, I think, should be well rooted in some spot of native land, where it may get the love of tender kinship for the face of the earth, for the labours men go forth to, for the sounds and accents that haunt it, for whatever will give that early home a familiar unmistakable difference amid the future widening of knowledge, a spot where the definiteness of early memories may be inwrought with affection, and kindly acquaintance with all neighbours, even to the dogs and the donkeys, may spread not by sentimental effort and reflection, but as a sweet habit of the blood. At five years old, mortals are not prepared to be citizens of the world, to be stimulated by abstract nouns, to soar above preference into impartiality; and that prejudice in favour of milk with which we blindly begin is a type of the way body and soul must get nourished at least for a time. The best introduction to astronomy is to think of the mighty heavens as a little lot of stars belonging to one's own homestead.

Ecocentrism and the Emancipatory Project

The final theme was that the practice of democracy also entails a 'frame-reflexive dialogue' through which differences with respect to the fundamental sources of 'the good life' can be productively and peaceably debated, and that the creation of such a dialogical space entailed a reconstruction of the emancipatory tradition itself. In this section I suggest that this kind of frame-reflexive public dialogue would, on the one hand, enable a clearer recognition of the importance of metaphysical and spiritual concerns of environmentalists within the domain of political life, and on the other hand encourage the articulation of the political implications of eco-philosophical visions.

In the context of the 'conversation' of this collection, I shall again focus on Robyn Eckersley's exploration of the relationship between environmentalism and political theory as an exemplar of ecophilosophical frame-reflexive discourse. Eckersley [*1992b*] rightly argues that the ecological crisis reflects a larger 'crisis of culture and character' (of modernity) and environmental reform thus requires a fundamental re-working of the emancipatory tradition itself. Her central claim is that ecocentrism, which belongs to the tradition of emancipatory social and political movements and not that of scientistic 'survivalism', provides the necessary ideological vision which can both renew emancipatory hope and also deal with the deeper causes of the environmental crisis:

> I have argued that only a thoroughgoing ecocentric Green political

theory is capable of providing the kind of comprehensive framework we need to usher in a lasting resolution to the ecological crisis. When compared to other ecophilosophical approaches examined in this inquiry, an ecocentric approach has been shown to be more consistent with ecological reality, more likely to lead us toward psychological maturity, and more likely to allow the diversity of beings (human and nonhuman) to unfold in their own ways [*1992b: 179*].

Yet, despite her observations about a crisis of culture and character, Eckersley does not, in my view, adequately address the crisis of enlightenment reason resulting from the dominance of instrumental rationality and the pervasive instrumentalising of social life by contemporary techno-science. Certainly, like many other ecophilosophers, she is highly critical of classical atomistic and reductionist science. However, there is a tendency to regard recent developments in twentieth-century science, particularly in ecology, evolutionary biology and quantum physics, as expressing a more holistic vision of nature, with a central motif of inter-connectedness, and an underlying metaphysic of 'internal relations', which render it convergent with ecocentrism.

As suggested above, what needs to be more strongly challenged is the enduring positivistic self understandings of scientific practice. The official view (despite Kuhn *et al.*) is still that science provides some objective, disinterested account of reality. It is a model of science that obscures the primacy of 'life world' meta-narrative in the elaboration of particular models of nature. In an alternative social constructivist account of scientific practice, it is recognised that the specific models of nature elaborate the practical interests expressed in and sustained by a larger meta-narrative of science. Modern, positivistic scientific practice embodies a practical interest of technological control.[23]

From this perspective, whilst the models of nature of post-Darwinian science might, at a purely cognitive level, be regarded as holistic and non-anthropocentric, in fact they also elaborate an intensely anthropocentric meta-narrative of the domination and appropriation of nature [*Merchant, 1980*]. Although it is possible to claim that the new models of nature, in as much as they are non-reductionist and involve ideas of inter-connectedness, provide support for ecocentrism, it can be equally argued that, at a deeper level, such models embody the technological project of a globalising, systems-oriented capitalism. The world of complex communication and cybernetics is indeed a world of increasing inter-connectedness, involving the dissolution of older atomistic boundaries. Yet such a world is experienced more often than not as eroding stable self-hood and spiritual inter-connectedness. Rather than providing genuinely new kinds of spirituality, the new sciences may merely contribute to the 'simulation' of spiritual experience in the commodified world of global capitalism.

If the emancipatory potential of the natural sciences is to be salvaged, there will need to be a displacement of that positivistic positioning of scientific practice as instrumental control and a re-opening of a reflexive consideration of the practical interests of scientific inquiry and the nature of scientific meta-narrative [*Milbank, 1990a*]. That means taking much further Kuhn's key insight that science is a moral and social practice [*Aranowitz, 1988; Jacob, 1992*]. What virtues, what vision of life and what engagement with the world should frame the practice of science?

In addition, in her identification of ecocentrism with the enlightenment emancipatory tradition, Eckersley also uncritically accepts its presumption of the natural secularity of the world, and thus does not take seriously the problems which a re-sacralisation of society might create. It is surely necessary for a reflexive ecophilosophy to take seriously the implications of a return of the sacred for public life. It is possible that an ecocentrism might have a deeper affinity with a pagan rather than a secular vision of the world. It is also possible that a renewed sacral vision would be antithetical to a Western emancipatory tradition. Historically, a central theme of modernity has been its promise of freedom from the constraints of and domination by nature [*Hogan, 1994*]. In opposition to this, ecofeminism and deep ecology have been for many people pathways to a recovery of the sacredness of life and nature [*Ross, 1992*]. It is by no means obvious that a return of the sacred would mean a retention of a culture of personal freedom of the sort so highly valued in secular democratic life. An ecocentric regrounding of social life might mean the re-emergence of an 'interpretive priesthood' whose authority is systematically imposed on all aspects of social and political life. I am not, of course making the claim that ecocentrism would necessarily entail a re-sacralising view of the world. However, I do suggest that, even as she proclaims ecocentrism as a radically different ideological vision, Eckersley still takes for granted a framework of enlightenment reason, and does not take seriously the possibility of the displacement of the secular through a restoration of a sacralising mode of life, and of its possible implications for politics.

Eckersley is right, I believe, to focus on the 'crisis of culture and character' of our late modern society, as a point of departure for the renewal of the emancipatory tradition in a way that recovers an ethic of ecological relatedness and inter-dependence, and overcomes the ethic of anthropocentric domination. Renewing the tradition requires not only the critique of instrumentalism, anthropocentrism and secularity. It also requires the establishment of resilient forms of life which are ultimately sustained by meta-narratives which connect our world of material practice

and politics to the wider ecology of living things and which can somehow
resist the pervasive commodifying power of global capitalism.

Conclusion

In this contribution I have argued that it is through the development of the
discursive conditions of a radical democratic polity that a green agenda
might be best formulated and achieved. An important question which has
been raised in relation to this argument is whether a radical democracy
would be necessarily green, or only contingently so. In other words, could
the development of the kind of extended and enriched democratic discourse
outlined above still lead – through open dialogical debate – to a society
which was hostile or indifferent to green ideas? Could frame-reflexive
dialogue about the larger questions of 'the good life' still result in agreed
collective purposes which made care for the earth a secondary and still
utilitarian value? Would the greenness of a radical democracy thus
ultimately depend on the abilities of ecophilosophers and eco-activists to
persuade others through dialogue and practice of the wisdom of adopting
green policies and promoting green practices for the common good in an
otherwise 'neutral' polity (that is, neutral with respect to green values)?

I have claimed, although without developing the claim in detail, that
there is a stronger and more 'necessary' connection between a green agenda
and the flourishing of a radical democracy. First, I have suggested that the
detailed development of a richer or 'thicker' greenness of the sort that deep
ecologists and eco-feminists have in mind is contingent upon the
development of the discursive practices of a radical democracy. What a
green agenda (which it might be possible to sketch in abstract philosophical
or techno-scientific terms) actually means in terms of communal and
political particularity is only possible to discover through processes of civic
dialogue. As John Milbank [1993] comments, 'knowing what to do' in
relation to complex issues of land use, resource development, and
environmental management is necessarily a civic process, and not simply a
matter of the application of scientific expertise or eco-spiritual wisdom.[24]
Thus, a green polity cannot be developed instrumentally (surely a
temptation of green activists, eco-scientists and green parties) but only
dialogically. Intrinsic to a genuinely green society is the kind of frame-
reflexive discourse advocated above, in which different communities of
discourse – liberal, socialist, feminist, environmentalist, Christian, new-age,
neo-pagan – are able to engage in a more open dialogue about competing
visions of selfhood, community and public life. As argued above, this
thicker dialogue entails overcoming the constraints of instrumental
rationality, and creating a more effective public conversation about the

moral sources of emancipatory hope.

However, there is a second and rather stronger sense in which I claim that there is a necessary connection between a radical democratic polity and a green agenda. I have argued, following Taylor, that the development of a radical democracy involves overcoming the fiction of contemporary liberalism that a neutral public sphere or a merely 'procedural republic' is the necessary condition of liberty and plurality. Instead, even the liberty and plurality beloved by liberals depends upon a reflexive public dialogue aimed at recovering the deeper sources of moral community which sustains dialogism, pluralism and the respect for individual rights [*Skinner, 1992*]. I argued that this task involves a critique of the instrumentalism and secularity which have been central to the emancipatory tradition and which have nurtured the confident, masculine, enlightenment self supposedly able to transcend the limits of tradition, community and nature. In the context of late modernity, in which the modern self becomes increasingly fragmented and ungrounded as a result of the pervasive impact of instrumentalism and secularity, the public, dialogical retrieval of the sources of the self becomes a vital democratic task. At the very least, this is a task which would bring the philosophical concerns of the green movement to the centre of the public agenda of a radical democracy. Ecophilosophers would surely make a major contribution to the development of a vision of moral community that would overcome the limits of instrumentalism and hence the formation of a public philosophical basis for a green, democratic polity.

Yet how eco-philosophers deal with the question of the secularity of modernity is of critical importance for the possibility of a green democracy. I suggested above that whilst within the green movement there is a strong movement towards the recovery of the sacredness of nature, philosophers such as Eckersley display their enlightenment commitments by continuing to take the natural secularity of the world for granted and by not taking seriously the implications of the re-sacralising of nature which has become an important theme in the wider green movement. In my view, it is not sufficient merely to assert that 'ecocentrism' can provide an adequate grounding for a renewed emancipatory tradition which is both green and democratic. To do so fails to deal with the possibility that a re-sacralisation of nature would undermine rather than strengthen the moral sources of the Western emancipatory tradition. How we deal with the question of secularity and, in particular, how we deal with the connections between Western secularity and Christian theology, is critical to the possibility of a convergence between radical democracy and a green agenda. In my view, as noted above, *contra* the self-understanding of secular liberalism, the deeper sources of both human freedom and a deep connectedness with nature are to be found in a Christian, social trinitarian vision and way of life. This is undoubtedly a deviant view, and to be made plausible to a post-Christian audience would require a good deal of self-criticism by contemporary Christians of the evils of Christendom and a demonstration that the coercive imposition of Christianity was in fact a betrayal of the 'peaceable kingdom' displayed in the central narrative of Christianity [*Hauerwas, 1991*]. Yet it can be argued more generally that addressing the problematic connection between secular reason and Christian theology is central to the possibility of a polity which is both green and democratic.

NOTES

1. See Barber [*1984*]; Dryzek [*1990*]; Mansbridge (1983) and Bowles and Gintus [*1986*]. For discussions of civic republicanism see Mouffe [*1988*]; Oldfield, [*1990*]; Jordan [*1989*]; Marquand [*1988*]; Bellah et al., [*1986*]; see also Arendt [*1959*].
2. The notion of 'reflexivity' is a central concern in Giddens[*1991*].
3. See also Walzer [*1984: 314–30*].
4. See Oldfield [*1990*].
5. As Mouffe [*1988: 30*] comments: 'The common good can never be actualised. There will always be a debate over the exact nature of citizenship. No final agreement can ever be reached. Politics in a modern democracy must accept division and conflict as unavoidable. The reconciliation of rival claims and conflicting interests can only be partial and provisional.'
6. This implies not only the legitimacy of the 'intrusion' of questions of cultural politics, gender and spirituality into the sphere of political discussion, but also conversely the appropriateness of public discourse about the moral meanings of diverse sexual, religious and other social practices. The inclusion of issues of identity as part of political discussion thus raises in a sharper way the question of how 'the private sphere' is to be defined. It suggests that rather than 'privacy' being defined in terms of a separate 'private sphere' or a class of activities, it is better understood as that condition or space for free and autonomous action by persons or citizens. This notion of privacy – which is applicable in all social sites – is expressed in terms of social, civil and political rights, and concepts of human dignity, of freedom of association. Yet, in so far as it construes personal freedom as that space within which moral agency is formed it is not a position which is indifferent to the moral character of that agency.
7. In Benhabib's [*1987*] words: 'Identity does not refer to my potential for choice alone, but for the actuality of my choices, namely how I as a finite, concrete, embodied individual, shape and fashion the circumstances of my birth and family, linguistic, cultural and gender identity into a coherent narrative that stands as my life's story.'
8. Jeremy Seabrook, *What Went Wrong? Why Hasn't Having Made More People Happier?* [*1978: 95–6*], quoted by Daly and Cobb [*1989: 163*]; see also Cornell West: 'We have created a rootless dangling people with little link to the supportive networks – family, friends, school – that sustain some sense of purpose in life. We have witnessed the collapse of the spiritual communities that help us face despair, disease and death and that transmit through the generations dignity and decency, excellence and elegance', *New York Times Magazine*, 2 Aug. 1992 (quoted by R. Westbrook [*1993: 13*]).
9. See Christopher Lasch's [*1991*] comment that one of the key elements of liberalism has been the belief that a good society did not depend on the civic virtue (or otherwise) of its citizens.
10. The term 'meta-narrative' is used by John Milbank [*1990a*] to refer to the basic categories within which particular communal accounts of the world are framed.
11. See for example, Charles Frankel [*1962: 28*], 'In the end, the plurality of ultimate beliefs in a democracy produces a climate in which ultimate beliefs are seen to be what they are –

choices and commitments.'

12. Stanley Hauerwas [*1992*] provides an example of this when he quotes Michiko Kakutani's review of *Debating P.C.: A Controversy Over Political Correctness on College Campuses*. Whilst generally praising the book, Kakautani stated:

> 'most disturbing in this volume are a few essays by radicals who shamelessly put their ideological concerns before the basic principles of democratic freedom and liberal education. Stanley Fish, a Professor of English and Law at Duke University, goes so far as to attack the First Amendment. 'Speech, in short, is never and could not be an independent value', he writes, 'but is always asserted against the background of some assumed conception of the good to which it must yield in the event of conflict'. Such statements can only leave the reader with the conviction that some of the traditionalist fears about political correctness are very real.

13. An example of the way in which an uncritical acceptance of the meta-narrative of secular reason undercuts religious belief and practice, even as it celebrates them, is provided by Jeffrey Isaacs' [*1991*] account of his Jewish identity:

> Thus as a Jew, someone born into the Jewish tradition and raised as a Jew in a secular multi-cultural environment, who has chosen to identify as Jewish, my views about how I should live my life will differ from those of most Protestants. In a modern democratic society it becomes possible for me to appreciate the contingency of my Jewish identity, and to prize it all the more as I respect the existence of the equally contingent ethnic and religious identities. Democratic secularism and universalism allow particular traditions to thrive, but they also set limits upon them in criminal and civil matters, prohibiting certain forms of physical abuse and allowing such procedures as civil divorce and geographical mobility. And democratic freedom of association, in allowing us to identify with the range of existing communities, also allows us to forge our own alternative lifestyles and communities. There is nothing in a democratic ethos that requires us to live our lives in the same ways. But there is a commitment to mutual respect, and to participation in a larger common world that makes the retreat into insularity difficult if not impossible. Ideally we can learn to respect our differences and robustly join together as citizens in order to shape broader forms of public identity.

See also Jonathan Sachs [*1990: 16*].

14. As MacIntyre [*1988: 347*], writes:

> In what Dahl calls pluralist democracies, which are very much what I have called liberal political orders, individuals pursue a variety of goods, associating in groups to achieve particular ends and to promote particular forms of activity. None of the goods thus pursued can be treated as overriding the claims of any other. Yet if the good of liberalism itself, the good of the pluralist democratic polity rather than the goods of its constituent parts, is to be achieved, it will have to be able to claim an overriding and even a coerced allegiance.

15. See, for example, MacIntyre's concluding comments in *After Virtue* [*1985*].

16. Milbank argues that whilst a post-modern deconstruction of secular reason can result in a nihilistic destruction of moral meaning, it can also open into a new paganism, a re-sacralisation of the world:

> ... those 'post-modernist' thinkers broadly influenced by Nietzsche have tended to dismantle the claims both of sociology and the Marxist-Hegelian tradition to uncover the governing factors of human association and to tell naturalistic, evolutionary stories about the whole of human history. While the Nietzschean tracing of cultural formations to the will-to-power still results in a 'suspicion' of religion, it also tends to assert the inevitably religious or mythic-ritual shape that these formations must take. In this mode of suspicion, therefore, there ceases to be any social or economic reality that is permanently more 'basic' than the religious ... Moreover, the question has now arisen for social theory as to whether Nietzschean suspicion is the final and truly non-metaphysical mode of

secular reason, or else itself embodies an ontology of power and conflict which is simply another mythos, a kind of re-invented paganism.

Milbank's essential point is that religion cannot be dismissed as part of the discarded 'childhood of the race', but that the question of the sacred is ultimately foundational to political life. As Christian social theorists, neither Ellul nor Milbank want to see the re-sacralisation of society. Rather, their view is that it has been the secularisation of the world by Christianity which has created the space of the secular within which an emancipatory politics can develop.

17. The Christian sources of Western secular reason and liberalism in particular are as obvious as they are neglected by social theorists who take 'secularity' for granted. Yet as Taylor [1992: 62] observes,

> ... as many Muslims are well aware, Western liberalism is not so much a expression of the secular, postreligious outlook that happens to be popular among liberal *intellectuals* as a more organic outgrowth of Christianity – at least seen from the alternative vantage of Islam. The division of church and state goes back to the earliest days of Christian civilisation. The early forms of the separation were very different from ours, but the basis was laid for modern developments. The very term *secular* was originally part of the Christian vocabulary.

18. See, for example, Chapter 10: 'Managing the Commons'.
19. See also the discussions on 'populism' by Paul Piccone [1990; 7].
20. Mathews' [1991a: 135–6] account of 'the ecological self' clearly recognises the discontinuity that language interposes. But as she points out, the 'representational freedom' of culture is not freedom at all, but only becomes so as it truly represents the spiritual principle of nature:

> Assuming that Nature does indeed embody a spiritual principle – that it is a self, possessed of conatus and imbued with intrinsic value – then we can say that, in order to be viable, any culture must include a representation, at whatever level of abstractness, of this conative aspect of Nature. Such a representation will in turn entail attitudes to the environment which will ensure that culture is an instrument of Nature, and that we are fully inter-connected with the whole. If our culture misrepresents Nature as being dead, blind, without purpose or spiritual principle, then it does indeed cut the cord to Nature – but through malfunction, not through transcendence. We are in this case in the same position as the organism whose genes have betrayed it so that it can no longer function as a self-realising system integrated with the wider systems of Nature. The price of this failure is ultimately of course extinction.

21. See Christopher Lasch's discussion of the attempt to collapse the differentiation between the self and the world in Chapter 7 ('The Ideological Assault on the Ego') in *The Minimal Self: Psychic Survival in Troubled Times* [1984].
22. See Lasch [1984] and Borgmann [1984] for discussions of the distinction between ephemeral commodities and the enduring world of things.
23. See Marcuse's notion of modern views of nature being governed by a 'technological a priori' in Marcuse [1964]; see also Stanley Aranowitz [1988].
24. Milbank [1993] comments:

> But we don't know what to do. That's the problem, and that's what's being evaded by green consciousness and eco-theology. Since we can't take decisions that are genuinely in common, we can't produce physical environments of convenience and beauty, because these reflect and embody a common civic life; constitute, materially, a mode of human reciprocity collectively affirmed. It's here that the real 'religious' problem arises. The question of 'what binds us together', a something that nature cannot supply – the 'Spirit' which speaks to us after all subjectively, enthusiastically (but not before/without our public discourse). If we knew what rule was for, if we could somehow reconcile democracy (and so renew it)with *paideia*, if we knew whom to encourage and whom to restrain, what to produce and why; the just measures in exchange between diverse

products ... then we could inhibit our economism and technologism and protect our environment. However much more urgent such protection may daily become, this still does not alter the necessarily indirect path to the healing of our environmental woe ... [*1993: 13*].

REFERENCES

Aranowitz, Stanley (1988), *Science as Power: Discourse and Ideology in Modern Society*, Hampshire: Macmillan.

Arblaster, Anthony (1984), *The Rise and Decline of Western Liberalism*, London: Blackwell.

Arendt, H. (1959.), *The Human Condition*, New York, Doubleday.

Barber, Benjamin (1984), *Strong Democracy: Participatory Politics for a New Age*, Berkeley, CA: University of California Press.

Barns, I. (1992), 'Value Frameworks in the Sustainable Development Debate', in Ronnie Harding (ed.), *Ecopolitics V: Proceedings*, Sydney: University of New South Wales.

Bell, Daniel (1977), 'The Return of the Sacred', *British Journal of Sociology*, Vol.28, No.4.

Bellah, Robert *et al.* (1986), *Habits of the Heart*, New York: Harper & Row.

Benhabib, Selya (1987), 'The Generalised and the Concrete Other: The Kohlberg–Gilligan Controversy and Feminist Theory', in Benhabib & Cornell [*1987*].

Benhabib, S. and D. Cornell (eds.) (1987), *Feminism as Critique*, Cambridge: Polity.

Borgmann, Albert, (1984), *Technology and the Character of Contemporary Life*, Chicag, IL: University of Chicago Press.

Bowles, Samuel and Herbert Gintis, (1986), *Democracy and Capitalism: Property, Community and the Contradictions of Modern Social Thought*, New York: Routledge & Kegan Paul.

Casanova, J. (1984), 'The Politics of Religious Revival', *Telos*, 59.

Daly, Herman and John Cobb (1989), *For the Common Good*, Boston, MA: Beacon Press.

Dietz, Mary (1987), 'Context is All: Feminism and Theories of Citizenship', *Daedalus* Vol.116, No.4.

Dryzek, John (1990), 'Designs for Environmental Discourse: The Greening of the Administrative State?', in R. Pahlke and D. Torgerson (eds.), *Managing Leviathan: Environmental Politics and the Administrative State*, London: Belhaven Press.

Dryzek, John (1990), *Discursive Democracy*, Cambridge: Cambridge University Press.

Durning, Alan (1989), 'Mobilising at the Grassroots', in Lester Brown (ed.), *State of the World 1989*, Worldwatch Institute Report, New York: Norton.

Eckersley, Robyn (1992a), *Environmentalism and Political Theory: Towards an Ecocentric Approach*, New York: State University of New York Press.

Eckersley, Robyn, (1992b), 'Linking the Parts to the Whole: Bioregionalism in Context', *Habitat Australia*, 36, Feb.

Eliot, George (1970), *Daniel Deronda*, London: Zodiac Press.

Ellul, Jacques (1964), *The Technological Society*, New York: Vintage Books.

Frankel, Boris (1987), *The Post-Industrial Utopians*, Cambridge: Polity Press.

Frankel, Boris (1992), *From the Prophets Deserts Come: The Struggle to Reshape Australian Political Culture*, Melbourne: Arena Publishing.

Frankel, Charles (1962), *The Democratic Prospect*, New York: Harper & Row.

Friedman, Marilyn, (1989), 'Feminism and Modern Friendship: Dislocating the Community', *Ethics*, 99, Jan.

Giddens, Anthony (1991), *Modernity and Self Identity: Self and Society in the Late Modern Age*, Stanford, CA: Stanford University Press.

Giddens, Anthony (1991), *Modernity and Self-Identity*, Stanford, CA: Stanford University Press.

Gunton, Colin (1993), *The One, The Three and the Many: God, Creation and the Culture of Modernity*, Cambridge: Cambridge University Press.

Gutmann, Amy and Dennis Thompson, (1990), 'Moral Conflict and Political Consensus', *Ethics*, 101, Oct.

Habermas, J. (1984), *The Theory of Communicative Action*, Boston, MA: Beacon Press.

Haraway, Donna (1987), 'A Manifesto for Cyborgs: Science, Technology and Socialist Feminism in the 1980s', *Australian Feminist Studies*, Vol.4, No.4.

Hardin, Garrett (1971), 'The Tragedy of the Commons' in J. Holdren and P. Ehrlich (eds.), *Global Ecology*, New York: Harcourt Brace, Jovanovitch.

Harvey, David (1989), *The Condition of Postmodernity*, Oxford: Blackwell.

Hauerwas, Stanley (1992), 'A Non-Violent Proposal for Christian Participation in the Culture Wars', *Soundings,* Vol.75, No.4.

Hauerwas, Stanley (1983), *The Peaceable Kingdom*, Notre Dame, IN: University of Notre Dame Press.

Hauerwas, Stanley (1991), *After Christendom?*, Nashville, IN: Abingdon Press.

Hill, Stephen (1988), *The Tragedy of Technology*, London: Pluto Press.

Hirst, Paul (1991), 'Plural Prospects', Australian Left Review, April.

Hirst, Paul (1992), 'Sidestepping the State', *Australian Left Review,* Sept.

Hogan, Trevor (1994), 'Feeling Green?: Eco-centric Politics in Australia', *Thesis Eleven,* 38.

Hunter, James D. (1991), *The Culture Wars: The Struggle to Define America*, New York: Basic Books.

Isaacs, Jeffrey (1991), 'On Christopher Lasch', *Salmagundi*, Vol.92, Autumn.

Jacob, Margaret (1992), 'Science and Politics in the Late Twentieth Century', *Social Research,* Vol.59, No.3.

Johnson, Pauline (1991), 'Feminism and Liberalism', *Australian Feminist Studies*, Vol.14, Summer.

Jordan, Bill (1989), *The Common Good*, Oxford: Blackwell.

Lasch, C. (1991), 'Liberalism and Civic Virtue', *Telos,* 88, Summer.

Lasch, C., (1984), *The Minimal Self: Psychic Survival in Troubled Times*, New York: Norton.

MacIntyre, Alasdair (1985), *After Virtue*, London: Duckworth.

MacIntyre, Alisdair (1988), *Whose Justice? Which Rationality?*, Notre Dame, IN: University of Notre Dame Press.

Mansbridge, Jane (1983), Beyond Adversary Democracy, Chicago, IL: University of Chicago Press.

Marcuse, H., (1964), *One Dimensional Man*, Boston, MA: Beacon Press.

Marquand, David (1988), *The Unprincipled Society: New Demands and Old Politics*, London: Fontana.

Mathews, Freya (1991a), *The Ecological Self*, London: Routledge.

Mathews, Freya (1991b), 'Democracy and the Ecological Crisis', *Legal Services Bulletin,* Vol.156, No.4.

Merchant, Carolyn (1980), *The Death of Nature: Women, Ecology and the Scientific Revolution*, San Francisco, CA: Harper & Rowe.

Milbank, John, (1990a), *Theology and Social Theory: Beyond Secular Reason*, Oxford: Blackwell.

Milbank, John (1990b), 'The End of Dialogue', in G. D'Costa (ed.), *Christian Uniqueness Reconsidered: The Myth of a Pluralistic Theology of Religions*, New York: Orbis Books.

Milbank, John (1993), 'Out of the Greenhouse', *New Blackfriars* Vol.74, Jan.

Moltmann, Jurgen (1985), *God in Creation: An Ecological Doctrine of Creation*, London: SCM Press.

Mouffe, Chantal (1988), 'The Civics Lesson', *New Statesman and Society*, Oct.

Oldfield, Andrew, (1990) *Citizenship and Community: Civic Republicanism and the Modern World*, London and New York: Routledge.

Pearce, David (1990), *Blueprint for a Green Economy*, London: Earthscan Publications.

Piccone, Paul (1990), 'The Crisis of Liberalism and the Emergence of Federal Populism', *Telos,* Vol.89, Autumn.

Poole, Ross (1991), *Morality and Modernity*, London: Routledge.

Ranson, S. and J. Stewart (1989), 'Citizenship and Government: The Challenge for Management in the Public Domain', *Political Studies,* Vol.37, No.1.

Redclift, Michael (1987), *Sustainable Development: Exploring the Contradictions*, London: Methuen.

Rein, Martin (1989), 'Frame Reflective Policy', in L. Orchard (ed.), *Markets, Morals and Public Policy*, Annandale: The Federation Press.

Ross, Andrew, (1992) , 'Wet, Dark and Low, Eco-Man Evolves from Eco-Woman', *Boundary* Vol. 2 (Summer).

Sachs, Jonathan (1990), 'Paradoxes of Pluralism', *The Listener*, 6 Dec.

Sagoff, Mark (1990), *The Economy of the Earth,* Cambridge: Cambridge University Press.

Sandel, Michael (1982), *Liberalism and the Limits of Justice*, Cambridge: Cambridge University Press.

Sheldrake, Rupert (1990), *The Rebirth of Nature: The Greening of Science and God*, London: Random Century.

Skinner, Quentin (1992), 'On Justice, the Common Good and the Priority of Liberty', in Chantal Mouffe (ed.), *Dimensions of Radical Democracy: Pluralism, Citizenship, Community*, London: Verso.

Taylor, Charles (1991), *The Ethics of Authenticity*, Cambridge, MA: Harvard University Press.

Taylor, Charles (1992), *Multiculturalism and 'The Politics of Recognition'*, Princeton, NJ: Princeton University Press.

Walzer, Michael (1984), 'Liberalism and the Art of Separation', *Political Theory*, Vol.12, No.3.

Westbrook, R. (1993), 'Democratic Evasions: Cornell West and the Politics of Pragmatism', *Praxis International*, Vol.13, No.1.

World Commission on Environment and Development (1987), *Our Common Future*, Oxford: Oxford University Press.

Young, Iris Marion (1987), 'Impartiality and the Civic Public: Some Implications of Feminist Critiques of Moral and Political Theory', in Benhabib and Cornell [*1987a*].

Young, Iris Marion (1990), *Justice and the Politics of Difference*, Princeton, NJ: Princeton University Press.

Has Democracy Failed Ecology?
An Ecofeminist Perspective

VAL PLUMWOOD

The superiority of democracy over other political systems in detecting and responding to ecological problems lies in its capacity for correctiveness. That this correctiveness is not operating well in liberal democracy is a further reason for questioning its identification with democracy. The radical inequality that increasingly thrives in liberal democracy is an indicator not only of the capacity of its privileged groups to distribute social goods upwards and to create rigidities which hinder the democratic correctiveness of social institutions, but is also an indicator of their ability to redistribute many ecological ills downwards and to create similar rigidities in dealing with ecological ills. It is therefore not democracy that has failed ecology, but liberal democracy that has failed both democracy and ecology. Ecological denial is structured into liberalism in multiple ways, particularly through its reason/nature dualism, its limitation of democracy, its disposition of public and private spaces, and its marginalisation of collective forms of life. A radical democratic alternative would reshape the public/private distinction to open the way for a public as well as a private ethics of environmental responsibility, for the diffusion of practices of responsibility and care through crucial areas from which liberalism strips them, and for the development of a democratic culture which displaces reason/nature dualism.

Ecological Consciousness and the Persistence of Ecological Degradation

As we approach the fourth decade of ecological consciousness and scientific concern about the degradation of the earth's life support systems, the evidence is mounting that the unprecedented level of public concern and activist effort which these decades have seen is not being reflected in adequate, effective or stable forms of change at the political level. Although

Val Plumwood has taught Philosophy in a number of Australian universities, and is currently teaching in the Division of Multidisciplinary Studies at the State University of North Carolina, USA.

ecological consciousness has some successes to its credit in the form of better standards and regulations, and even in some areas better practices, these are themselves under constant threat. What is more significant, however, is that even these hard-earned measures have done little to arrest the ever-accelerating progress of environmental degradation. David Orr outlines this progress:

> If today is a typical day on planet earth, we will lose 116 square miles of rainforest, or about an acre a second. We will lose another 72 square miles to encroaching deserts, the results of human mismanagement and overpopulation. We will lose 40 to 250 species, and no one knows whether the number is 40 or 250. Today the human population will increase by 250,000. And today we will add 2,700 tons of chlorofluorocarbons and 15 million tons of carbon dioxide to the atmosphere. Tonight the earth will be a little hotter, its waters more acidic, and the fabric of life more threadbare.

Even in the area where ecological consciousness appears to have had some success, in recycling and consumer education, the results have been disappointing. As Timothy Luke states:

> After twenty years of ecological consciousness ... the average per capita daily discard rate of garbage has risen from 2.5 pounds in 1960 to 3.3 pounds in 1970 to 3.6 pounds in 1986. By 2000, despite the impact of two decades of recycling, this figure is expected to rise to 6 pounds a day. Similarly, even though ecological concern is rising, the average gas mileage of new cars declined 4 per cent from 1988 to 1990, and the number of miles driven annually continues to rise by 2 per cent by year.

In the sphere of international politics, the message that has emerged most clearly from the Rio Conference and from recent reversals in environmental regulation is the disturbing one of the extreme difficulty of mobilising our present systems of national and international governance to stem escalating ecological damage.

Any civilisation that sets in motion massive processes of biospheric degradation which it cannot respond to and correct will plainly not survive. The escalation of the processes responsible for ecological degradation, despite the great citizen effort which has gone into challenging them in democratic polities, therefore represents an alarming failure. It is not primarily a failure of knowledge or of technology, for we largely possess the scientific and technological means to live upon the earth without destroying its capacity to support life, even if our present numbers compound the problem. The failure is primarily a failure of our political systems and systems of morality and rationality and, what is especially alarming, it includes those systems that many of us have seen as among our finest achievements – systems of political democracy, especially liberal democracy. Although confronting this failure is not popular with the eco-establishment, it is imperative that we do confront it fully and trace the reasons for failure.[1] The evidence of the last two decades suggests that serving up the same recipe for reform will not be effective, and that we will not turn the processes of environmental degradation around without accepting many more major kinds of change in our political systems. In this paper I draw on recent democratic and feminist theory and other critical resources to reflect on the implications of this failure for democracy and to outline some of the systemic change necessary to stop the escalation of environmental damage.

Responsive Democracy and Ecological Failure

The main focus for our investigation must be the failure of liberal democratic systems. It is no real surprise that authoritarian political systems, especially the military systems organised around protecting privilege which control so much of the planet, fail to protect nature. Military systems are neither responsive nor accountable, and have a record of gross environmental destructiveness which parallels their record of gross human destructiveness [*Seager, 1993*]. Regimes based on authoritarian, military thinking and coercion usually fail systematically to consider the lives and rights of most of their human citizens, so that it is hardly to be expected that they will protect what is even lower in the usual scale of consideration – nature and animals.[2] Both political argument and political observation suggest that we should rule authoritarian and military-coercive systems out as possible routes to solving environmental problems, despite the arguments of the authoritarian school of environmental thinkers who pin their hopes on environmental and scientific oligarchy. Even if we grant regimes of environmental oligarchy possession of powerful means to enforce compliance with environmental regulation (Thompson, this collection), what is unexplained is how they can develop or maintain the political conditions that will guarantee the oligarchy's motivation to use these powerful means for the purpose of protecting nature, rather than for other ends which buttress their own power.[3] Such regimes must be fatally lacking in capacities for correcting such tendencies and soon must come to suffer, like the normal authoritarian regime, from severe informational distortion.

The environmental disasters and rigidities of the Soviet Union and satellite Marxist systems lend support to the view that political democracy, if not a sufficient condition for adequate environmental action, is at least a necessary condition. Thus it is primarily democracies that have been able to sustain vocal environment movements able to raise and pursue ecological issues in ways that would bring repression elsewhere. An elite-dominated polity which silences messages that those in power do not wish to hear and pushes on regardless with elite-benefiting projects will come to possess a dysfunctional rigidity and informational distortion regarding the degradation of nature which render it resistant to an important range of changes, unable to detect or correct its blindspots, as indifferent to gross damage to the surrounding natural world as it is to gross damage to the social world. In contrast, a polity that is open to reshaping institutions in response to the views and needs of a wide range of social groupings, especially those at greatest risk of ecological damage, is likely to be able to respond reflectively and usefully to a crisis in its ecological, as in its social, world. It is at any rate more likely to be able to do so than a polity caught in structures that are responsive mainly to the needs of a small elite, an elite that derives much of its privilege from the institutions that bring about ecological destruction and is able to buy relief from many of its ill effects.

The superiority of democracy to other systems in detecting and responding to ecological problems would seem to lie largely, then, in its capacity for adaptation and correction. So in order to discover why democracy is failing, we must now ask which political features of democracy contribute to and what forms hinder its capacity for correction? I shall argue that an important feature that hinders this capacity is radical inequality within democratic polities. There is a rather persuasive set of political arguments confirming the thesis that democracy is essential, but these same arguments encourage us to a critical and differentiated approach to what passes for democracy. They suggest that those responsive democratic forms that open communication and spread decision-making processes most equally should offer the best protection for nature. Thus systems that are able to articulate and respond to the needs of the least privileged should be better than less democratic systems that reserve participation in decision-making for privileged groups. This is because radical inequality is both itself a hindrance to correctiveness and a key indicator of other hindrances to societal correctiveness.

Much of the politics of ecological conflict, as Ulrich Beck [1995] notes, takes the form of 'distributing exposure to undesirable things' [1995: 9], in contrast to the politics of class conflict, which mainly concerns the distribution of societal rewards. Beck assumes that ecological ills, in contrast to societal goods, are distributed equitably in liberal democracy, cutting across boundaries of class and power: 'poverty is hierarchical', writes Beck, 'while smog is democratic' [1995: 60]. The assumption of equality of impact, however, holds good only for a certain range of environmental harms – those forms of degradation which have highly diffused or unpredictable effects not amenable to redistribution – and then only partially. For those kinds of environmental degradation that are more local and particularised in their impacts, such as exposure to toxins through residential and occupational area, the same kind of politics of distribution can be played out as in the case of societal goods: the powerful will strive to redistribute these ills, just as they distribute the goods, in their own favour, with varying success depending on the extent to which the social system is susceptible to their influence. Such forms can and do impact differentially in terms mediated by privilege.

For a considerable range of environmental ills resulting from the institutions of accumulation, then, some redistribution and insulation is possible. It is the privileged members of a society who can most easily insulate themselves from these forms of environmental degradation; toxic wastes and occupations can be directed to poorer residential areas (including Third World destinations), and if privileged suburbs, regions or territories become noisy, degraded or polluted, the privileged can buy places in more salubrious environments. When local resources (including amenity resources) become depleted, they will be best placed to take advantage of wider supply sources and markets; often these will continue to deplete poorer distant communities in ways that elude knowledge and responsibility. The privileged can buy expert help and remedies for environmental health and for other problems, and their working life is likely to involve a minimum of environmental pollution and disease compared to other groups [*Jennings and Jennings, 1993*].

At the same time, they are the group who consume (both directly for their own use and indirectly through income generation) the greatest proportion of resources, who are likely overall to be creating the most pollution and to have the strongest economic stake in maintaining forms of accumulation which exploit nature. Since the privileged can most easily purchase alternative private resources, they have the least interest in maintaining in good condition collective goods and services of the sort typically provided by nature, and are most distanced from awareness of their limits. So they are normally the group with the strongest interest in maintaining the nature-destroying processes of accumulation from which they benefit and the group with the least motivation to support any fundamental challenge to these institutions that might be needed.[4] For the highly diffused forms of environmental ills, the ability of the privileged to buy relief from vulnerability to environmental ills is ultimately an illusion,[5] but it may still be a long-lasting and influential illusion which affects political decision-making.[6] Thus in a polity in which the privileged have the sole or central role in decision-making, decisions are likely to reflect their especially strong interest in maintaining processes destructive of nature.

If the privileged have the key role in determining culture and information flows, news about the degradation of nature and its impact on less privileged human lives is likely to be obstructed or given little weight in their media, which may be weighted to consider mainly the kinds of problems that impact on the powerful. The wider culture may be distorted in ways that make the 'losers' inferior – for example, in the West, those associated with bodily labour, materiality and nature – and give little attention to their ills. Cultural ideals will often tend to idealise the rich and successful, and reflect their styles and standards of resource overconsumption, while portraying low consumption, satisficing lifestyles in negative or contemptuous terms [*hooks, 1995*]. To the extent that the privileged are able to exert control over cultural and political processes then, these are more likely to be distorted in ways that resist response, deny ecological problems and push exploitation past sustainable limits. Note that these considerations apply equally to those privileged through market systems and those privileged through bureaucratic and authoritarian/ military systems. They apply not only to those privileged by economic class but also to those privileged by race and gender. We can see these insulating and information-distorting features of privilege clearly at work in many parts of the world where environmental destruction has been at its worst, in the decisions of class elites from Sarawak and Brazil to eastern Europe where political systems have lacked most of the corrective measures created in more democratic systems. We can see similar insulating features of gender privilege at work in the association between the destruction of subsistence agricultures and the dispossession of women agriculturalists in the processes of development in India and Africa [*Shiva, 1988; 1994*]. Here, as a number of Third World theorists have argued, the intentional connection is often even closer: impoverishment and environmental degradation are produced as twin offspring of the same processes of development [*Shiva, 1988*].

The most oppressed and dispossessed people in a society are those who are made closest to the condition of nature, who are made to share the same expendable condition as nature. The logic of the market is one factor that ensures that the least privileged are likely to feel the first and worst impacts of environmental degradation, as in the case of much deforestation, pollution, waste dumping in poor and coloured communities, and environmentally hazardous working and living conditions for the poor. This logic treats the least privileged as the most expendable, defining them as having 'least to lose' in terms of the low value of their health, land and assets and, by implication, of their lives.[7] The fact that they feel the first and worst impacts does not mean that, in highly hierarchical or repressive contexts, they will necessarily be in a good position to observe or contest such degradation, any more than to contest their own fate. It is a sad irony of present forms counted as democratic that those most oppressed are usually least able to contest their oppression [Green, 1985]. However, groups at the margins who are able to observe and contest the degradation of their local environments, such as those women who must attend to them as agricultural workers, household managers or carers for the bodily needs of vulnerable others, often make up the bulk of those active in grassroots movements and citizen activism [Seager, 1993].

If the flows of power and information in a society are such that the needs of the least privileged cannot be articulated or considered, then key sources of ecological information and correction are also blocked. The occupational health hazards of minority workers, the systematic poisoning of millions of migrant agricultural workers (the immediate life-expectancy of US farmers is estimated to be twenty years below the national average), and the dumping of toxic wastes on poor communities can pass unremarked while environmental attention is focussed on green consumer issues which impact on more privileged groups [Jennings and Jennings, 1993]. Radical inequality is a major factor that hinders the ability to respond to many collective forms of ecological degradation and especially to those forms which impact differentially in terms mediated by privilege (ecojustice issues), because inequality acts both as a barrier to information and feedback on degradation and its human impacts, and to responsiveness to this information. These points provide a theoretical basis for understanding the ecojustice issues known (too narrowly) as 'environmental racism', for the well-attested convergence between activism on environmental and activism on social justice issues [Seager, 1993], and for linking the persistence of ecological degradation with the persistence of radical inequality.

If social forms that can express and heed the needs of the least privileged are also more likely to be responsive to the needs of the biosphere and those who articulate them, and subject to fewer systematic and disabling distortions of knowledge and perception, then an ecologically responsive democracy should be one which minimises such information blocks, spreads as widely and as equally as possible the means to act politically and articulate needs, and has the capacity to change institutions in response. However, a good deal of empirical work shows that the responsiveness in the dominant form of democracy, liberal democracy, is mainly directed to privileged and upper income groups, that it is these groups who are selected as politically active and are able to have their needs considered in the liberal political structure [Pateman, 1989].[8] That is, liberal democracy selects as politically active primarily that group who are most likely to react to ecological crisis by supporting cosmetic change and by redistributing ecological ills downwards rather than by supporting fundamental and effective ecological change.

The radical inequality of liberal democracy is an indicator not only of the capacity of its privileged groups to distribute social goods upwards and to create rigidities which hinder the corrective, democratic reshaping of social institutions, but also an indicator of their capacity to redistribute ecological ills downwards and to create similar rigidities in dealing with ecological ills. If the capacity to correct and reshape ecologically destructive institutions is thus hindered in liberal democracy by the rigidities resulting from its protection of privilege, the elements of an ecologically responsive democracy will never be sufficiently available in liberal democracy. They are most likely to be found elsewhere, within the alternative democratic tradition that interprets democracy as widespread popular participation, choice and involvement in decision-making, that stresses the shaping of institutions in communicative structures which enable all citizens to be equally consulted and responsible.

This argument suggests that we might view ecological responsiveness on ecojustice issues as a criterion of adequacy for democracy. Like the severe forms of inequality which now proliferate in liberal democracies, the failure of ecological responsiveness where there is widespread citizen concern and support for change,[9] can be taken as an indication that something is rotten, that communication and participation are somehow blocked or skewed. We can employ the framework suggested by John Rawls to conclude that such a democracy is not what it pretends to be, the result of universal and equal choice opportunities, because if people really had the equal opportunities for communication, participation and choice they are said to have in such a structure, such outcomes could not emerge.[10] The responsiveness of the apparatus of democracy to persistent violations of ecojustice which create severe costs for groups of non-privileged citizens, can be viewed then as a key test for whether or not a system is genuinely democratic in its operation. But this test is one that actually existing liberal democracy, as well as several other proposed forms, largely fails, in practice as well as in theory.

If liberal democracy (by which I mean the attempt to combine liberal principles of free speech and representative democracy with a system of liberal market economics) is, as is now often claimed, the best of our political systems and the final victor in the contest of systems and ideologies, its inadequacies in ecological matters give us good reason to be very concerned about our prospects for survival. It is a matter of widespread observation that actually-existing liberal-democratic political systems are not responding in more than superficial ways to a state of ecological crisis which everyday grows more severe but which everyday is perceived more and more as normality. To be sure, liberal democracy has enabled a certain range of environmental concerns to be voiced, even at government level, but it has not enabled a correspondingly adequate response.[11]

The grassroots environment movement has put a major effort into articulating and raising public awareness of ecological problems, and such an awareness is clearly a necessary condition for any democratic ecological progress. But such a strategy assumes the democratic ideal, and can only be effective in the presence of a genuinely responsive democracy; it is insufficient for effective change in the presence of the major structural barriers to ecological responsiveness present in actually existing liberal democracy. In actually existing liberal democracy, not only is systematic action on the crucial issues in most places stalled by these barriers, but there is an increasingly successful effort to erode the gains environmental groups have struggled for over decades [Dowie, 1995]. It is increasingly apparent that the 'interest group' politics of actually existing liberal democracy is inadequate for ecological protection: it cannot create stable measures for the protection of nature and is unable to recognise that nature is not just another interest group or another speaker, but the condition for all our interests and for all our speech.[12]

Green Consumerism and the Ecological Failure of Existing Liberal Democracy

That liberal democracy is failing to deal effectively with environmental problems is an observation to which both liberal and radical environmentalists might in principle agree. They would tend, however, to give very different interpretations and accounts of what this means and of the reasons for it, their explanations falling basically into two broad classes, which I shall designate liberal and critical. The first, liberal, type of explanation takes ecological failure to be due to the lack of concern for future survival or for the needs of the biosphere among the bulk of the population, who are thought to be preoccupied, rightly or wrongly, with personal or consumerist goals. This liberal avenue of explanation, according to which 'the enemy is us', treats change in liberal terms as a matter of consumer willpower and argues back from the absence of change to the absence of consumer concern. If responsibility for change in democracy is framed in liberal terms, as resting primarily with consumers, the democratic route to change can only lie in overcoming their resistance through intensifying education or ecological consciousness-raising efforts. Explanatory frameworks of this consumerist type tend, as Timothy Luke points out, to be favoured because they fall in with the liberal imperative of saving the political structure of liberalism from criticism and preserving the fiction that liberalism is democracy.

There has been a tendency for this consumerist type of explanation to be adopted in default by much of the conventional environment movement, precisely because it appears to absolve liberal democracy from responsibility and remove the need for any larger and bolder challenges to liberal rationality. In fact it does so only if it makes the self-defeating assumption that ecologically harmful, self-maximising 'consumerist' behaviour is a natural, invariant aspect of 'human nature', rather than one itself institutionally constructed and specified as rational within the framework of liberal capitalism. It assumes a commodified model of nature, and overlooks the crucial importance for nature of collective forms of life which cannot be properly commodified and opened to individual consumer influence. The central point however against the consumerist explanation and green consumer strategy invoking consumer responsibility as the solution is that it involves a mistaken view about the nature of liberalism and about the effectiveness of its chosen area of leverage. There is something right about the green consumer strategy, as we will see, but also something badly wrong about it.

The inevitable outcome of attempting to give priority to saving the conventional identification of liberalism with democracy is to cast the ecological failure of liberalism as a conflict between environment and democracy, and thus ultimately to force a reluctant construction of ecological failure as lending support to authoritarian strategies and regimes oriented to coercion of this recalcitrant 'human nature'. This is another source of movement inability to confront liberal failure and the need for systemic change. But this conflictual explanatory strategy is flawed for several reasons. It ignores the crucial and continuing role that grassroots democracy plays in contesting environmental issues, and at the level of political theory overlooks the severe limitations in the power for change citizens are allowed in the roles liberalism defines for them as consumers and as voters. It leaves unchallenged those further major kinds of power which structure the frameworks of consumer choice and bear on the continuance of environmental degradation, but which are not subject to any effective democratic control, such as decision-making about production and about technology. It thus locates the major sources of responsibility in the wrong places [*Luke, 1993*] and promotes a strategy whose failure invites an explanatory and activist impasse, a choice between two unacceptable alternatives – that of sacrificing either democracy or the environment. In the name of taking successful and effective action for change within the system, the movement has focused increasingly on ineffective action which defines success as compatibility with the system. Although activists are enticed into accepting the 'insider' liberal strategy by the promise of quick results, the promise is a fraud: accepting the larger, critical challenge is, in the long run, the only source of hope for real improvement.

The alternative, critical type of explanation opens up the possibility that it is not primarily the democratic aspect of liberal democracy that creates these problematic structures of resistance to ecological action, but rather its democratic failures, its steadfast commitment to an alliance with privilege and economic power and the contradictions between its rhetorical assertion of democratic principles and the crippling limitations it imposes on their application [*Green, 1985*]. If we follow the second avenue of explanation for failure, we do not need to posit a fundamental conflict between environmentalism and democracy. Rather, such a critical explanatory framework opens space for exploring the ecological virtues of more thoroughgoing forms of democracy. This second, critical strategy for explaining the failure of liberal democracy has much independent support. If the degree to which democratic principles determine the structures in which most people live their daily lives is a measure of the success of the democratic project, this project has clearly been railroaded in current forms of liberal democracy by the absence of economic, household and workplace democracy as well as by other relations of domination. Thus it is open to us to take the ecological failure of liberal democracy as an indicator of the extent to which effective and responsive democracy has been subverted and rendered docile in the current liberal forms of government which are conventionally called democratic.

Accordingly, the poor ecological performance of those states termed 'liberal democracies' hardly provides a test of the ecological responsiveness of democracy in more meaningful and responsive senses. We can draw few negative conclusions from actual liberal performance about the ecological satisfactoriness of more radical forms of democracy; rather it remains open to us to interpret current ecological failure as a gauge of the extent to which dominant concepts of democracy have weakened almost beyond recognition the original meaning of democracy as popular control and decision-making in areas of common life. Thus green consumerism may be on the right track in wanting to diffuse a sense of responsibility for nature into the structures of the economy and of everyday life, but is astray in its uncritical understanding of existing liberal structures and their capacity to support practices which take responsibility for impacts on nature.

A Critical Explanatory Strategy

An alternative critical strategy which abandons the imperative to maintain faith in liberalism can begin to explore the hypothesis that liberalism has failed ecology primarily because it builds in, systematically, features that severely limit democracy and hence ecological adaptation. The concept of responsive democracy suggests a way to explain the persistence of ecological abuse by showing how it is connected to the betrayal of democracy and the persistence of radical inequality and oppression in liberal polities. The incompleteness and subversion of democracy in liberalism helps explain both ecological failure and also why formal democratic political structures do not eliminate, but rather cohabit with, major forms of oppression and domination, which concepts must still have a major place in any analysis of liberal democratic societies [*Young, 1990*].

I have argued in general terms that to the extent that liberal democracy removes major areas of ecological impact from democratic reshaping and allows privilege and inequality to govern its political, informational and cultural systems, its capacity for crisis adaptability and ecological responsiveness is reduced or defeated. To see how many of the same rigidities operate in both cases, we can begin by noticing some of the barriers that liberal inequality generates for information flows, the area where liberal democracy appears strongest. Even here, the openness and responsiveness of liberal political democracy and its information systems are only relatively good when compared to more authoritarian systems.

We have already noted one of the generalised informational impacts of inequality, that for educational and participative reasons the greatest obstacles to effective communication tend to fall on those citizens liable to suffer most from ecological damage, but there are many others. The existence of normalised forms of censorship fostered by hierarchy within liberal academic, scientific and bureaucratic institutions, and their role in obstructing the flow of information about environmental degradation, have been well documented [*Plumwood, 1994a; Martin et al., 1986*]. This also applies more widely: in a polarised society where work structures create grave insecurity, hierarchy and dependency [*Schor, 1991; Green, 1985*], liberal citizens often find difficulty in exercising ecological and social responsibility in making public information deriving from their workplaces about harms, toxicity and ecological damage. The control of information in liberal democracy by those, especially governments and corporations, with an interest in hindering social and environmental change is also well documented.[13] In the process of 'manufacturing consent' through collusion with policy-makers [*Parry, 1992; Alterman, 1992; Chomsky, 1991; Lindsay, 1943*], the liberal media are at least as much engaged in shaping 'public opinion' as liberal democracy is in receiving popular input, thus removing a major basis for responsiveness to citizen input and reversing its direction. These are only a few of the barriers that privilege creates to change in the crucial process of informing citizens. In the equally crucial process of transforming any citizen choice thus formed into action by elected representatives there are very many more such obstacles.[14]

Liberal democracy also creates major barriers to corrective ecological action by placing crucial areas of environmental impact beyond the range of democratic correction and reshaping, especially the institutions of accumulation and property. This characteristic is becoming more marked, in what gives signs of being a positive feedback process. The democratic component of liberal capitalism has always been in conflict with the undemocratic control of economic life and of technology, but this antagonism grows more acute as the nation state, the chief arena of democratic decision-making, becomes itself increasingly inadequate to direct economic life. As the economy is globalised without the likelihood of corresponding political structures, the area of life accountable to democratic decision-making and capable of being structured to meet social and ecological needs grows daily smaller. Even within liberal democratic states, the poorly socially accountable price/auction form of the market is increasingly permitted to invade the area available to democratic decision-making and to dominate and shrink the sphere of the political.

The market in this aggressive colonising form not only invades the public space in which oppositional citizen networks have flourished, but also wherever possible reduces collective welfare and forms of life to private, marketable goods, in the process frequently jeopardising many of the social and ecological functions they carry out. These tendencies are increasingly supplemented by political measures which further dismantle the corrective mechanisms expressed in regulation which have helped preserve a few collective and ecological areas of life from the ravages of liberal egoism.[15] Under neo-liberal forms of management, for example, private interests are emphasised to the point of irresponsibility, and many of the forms of collective life essential to the flourishing of nature lead an increasingly precarious and marginalised existence, subject to arbitrary elimination or pauperisation.[16]

The growth of radical inequality and the attack on collective forms of life undermine not only ecological responsiveness but also the main basis for the claim that liberal democracy represents freedom. This has rested largely on the concept of democracy as the making of laws 'for oneself' in a common polity, of freedom as autonomy and assent, self-government or self-determination involving the free recreation by all of social institutions.[17] However, liberal democracy increasingly assumes the form of groups of privileged citizens making laws punitive of marginalised groups – the homeless, women, illegal immigrants, future people, the criminalised, welfare recipients, animals – constructed as Others whose fate they can be sure they will never be required to share and who are excluded from full citizenship or political subjecthood. One does not need to assume an undifferentiated 'general will' in the fashion of Rousseau to observe that such oppressions and oppositions also undermine those forms of equality, intersubstitutability, and collectivity which make it plausible to describe what is done in the name of liberal democracy as 'self-government' or 'self-determination'.

As inequality increases and as key areas of economic management, depoliticised through excision from the sphere of popular political agency, are reconceived as part of the sphere of instrumental management by the purveyors of economic 'expertise' and 'prediction', the relationship of liberal society to necessity and freedom grows more and more distorted: the economy and technology are represented as engines of necessity, while nature, conceived as without limits, is represented as a sphere of freedom as unconstrained manipulation, of human conquest and prospect for human emancipation.[18] By protecting the major destructive social institutions from democratic re-evaluation and re-creation and displacing human hopes for betterment onto the control of the sphere of nature, the very structure of liberal democracy fosters a technocratic orientation and a disregard for natural communities and natural limits.

On the critical explanatory model, then, ecological failure would lead us to conclude that it is not democracy that has failed ecology, but rather liberal democracy that has failed both democracy and ecology. Although present forms of democracy have indeed failed ecology, this is not because they are democratic, but because they are liberal. That these same liberal forms have also failed democracy itself is attested by the realistic 'democratic' world we see around us, which is democratic mainly in rhetoric. For the many oppressed people who experience it, this 'democratic' world is not an imperfect through recognisable copy of a democratic ideal which our polity is striving to reach but, more often than not, a betrayal of democratic principles.

The Philosophical Roots of the Democratic Failure of Liberalism

A number of threads from feminist and critical theory can be drawn together to help theorise the interconnected democratic and ecological failures of liberalism and explain the weakness of its concept of ecological rationality. These suggest that we should view liberal democracy as a form of arrested development which provides a narrow understanding of democracy, limits and restricts this democracy excessively even in what it has designated as the sphere available to it, the political sphere, and fails to extend democratic principles to ecologically crucial areas of life including the economy and the sphere of paid work, as well as to 'private' areas such as the sphere of the household and personal life. These limitations and conflicts in liberalism reflect the tensions in the development of liberal democracy as the historical vehicle of a privileged, property-owning 'middle' class – simultaneously both an insurgent class needing to employ a discourse of universality and equality against monarchy and various kinds of despotism from above, and also a class of dominance aiming to maintain its own privilege against others such as women, 'savages', and animals, and to resist the extension of this universalising democratic discourse to excluded groups below it [*Pateman, 1988; 1989*]. Any project to liberate democracy must involve disentangling the inclusionary and exclusionary movements of liberalism [*Macpherson, 1973; 1977*]. Thus liberalism involves not only incompleteness, but also a set of inconsistent or exclusionary movements, the institutionalised denial of its own principles to areas and groups of Others with reduced political subjecthood and exempted from principles presented as universal. These areas and kinds of subjects exempted from the reach of democracy include both nature itself and the areas where the major relationships to and impacts on nature are found.

At the source of many of these exemptions and exclusions is a masculinist model of the citizen as independent (the 'man of property'), where the concept of independence incorporates various disavowed dependencies. Some of these denials are normalised in liberalism through the legitimation of forms of appropriation which deny the social Other by denying the dependence of property formation on collective forms of social life and infrastructure. These forms of appropriation also help constitute as less than full citizens specific groups of excluded Others whose contributory labour is denied and represented as background, as inessential and beneath recognition.

For all these primary Others, there is a common pattern or 'logic' of oppression or exploitation which arises from their assimilation to the status of 'nature'.[19] The primary Others who are exploited (that is, assumed but denied) in this master conception of property include, first of all, women, whose labour as 'nature' in the household is assumed but denied by the man of property as household head in his appropriation to himself of the wider social and economic rewards it makes possible [*Waring, 1988; Okin, 1989*]. Second, they include labouring, non-propertied citizens, and all those social Others whose contributions to production, and to the society and the infrastructure which makes this production and property possible, are assumed but denied in liberal forms of appropriation. Thirdly, these Others include the colonised, whose prior lands and prior and continuing labour are assumed but denied and appropriated in the formation and accumulation of the colonisers' property, often by assigning them the status of 'nature' [*Shiva, 1994*]. Fourthly, they include animals, nature and the earth itself, whose own prior agency and intentional organisation is denied and overridden in the foundation of property.[20] The man of property assumes the contribution of nature in the form of a continuing support base for production, accumulation and renewal, but also denies it, not infrequently in even stronger terms than he denies these human Others, failing to recognise and allow, in his economic and cultural systems, for nature's reproduction and continuation.[21] This denial establishes the basic ecological rationality characteristic of liberalism.[22]

These features of liberal property are reflected in the rational egoist form of the market, which assigns 'market values' to the contributions of excluded others such as women in accordance with this logic of denial [*Waring, 1988*]. The rational egoist variety of the market is founded on an anthropocentric denial of nature's intrinsic value and significance which is revealed in Locke's original argument for the legitimacy of property based on the 'mixing' of human labour as the source of value with a passive and valueless nature which contributes no 'value' or moral constraint on its own account. The anthropocentric representation of nature as nullity provides the basic model by which the exclusion of human others is framed and excused, in terms of their representation as nature in the framework of reason/nature dualism which I discuss in the final section [*Plumwood, 1993*].

Green liberalism and consumerism have hardly begun to address the problem of formulating a non-anthropocentric version of the market. Although some theoretical progress has been made in representing the instrumental value of certain forms of nature to the extent of allowing for their renewal in instrumental terms and of recognising nature's non-interchangeability and certain kinds of limits [*Pierce et al., 1989*], even these limited changes are usually deemed too radical for practical adoption in the context of actually existing liberal democracy, and it is unclear that anything less commodifying can be implemented within the boundaries of the liberal framework.[23] Envisaging a truly non-anthropocentric and ecological economy implies going much further still: envisaging nature as active agent and partner in the production of value [*Benton, 1989*], and challenging nullifying liberal conceptions of property, the market, and production.

The conception of self based on this denial and established as paradigmatic in the institutions and rationality of the liberal public sphere is that of the self-maximising and self-contained individual who is radically separate from others and from nature, rather than a satisficing[24] and relationally-expressed one. In this framework, egoism emerges as the normal and rational mode, altruism (like the Other) a problem to be explained or reduced to some version of egoism/self. These assumptions place the basic liberal forms of identity and rationality in conflict with the recognition of those relationships of kinship, care, dependency and mutuality which an ecological awareness requires us to recognise with future generations and with nature. [*Plumwood, 1993; Mathews, 1991a, 1991b*]. This element of the liberal tradition leads to the conception of the political encounter of democracy as occurring in a fundamentally instrumental community – that is, a community based on coincidence of interests, thought of as a means to ends conceived as only coincidentally shared. Similarly, liberal democracy sees as the essential political feature of individuals not the capacity for empathy and care for others but the capacity for rationality, usually interpreted as rational egoism in the pursuit of interests [*Jaggar, 1983*]. Dualistic models of freedom and reason converge to interpret freedom as distance from necessity and the body, and the dominance of the material conditions of life by reason as the essence of the higher self. This interpretation not only discounts other aspects of life and self, but gives major emphasis to a dominant Western conception of rationality which has been historically opposed to nature both within and without the human individual [*Plumwood, 1993*].

Reason/nature dualism has both provided the backdrop for the informal cultural climate of liberalism, and shaped its vision of formal political structure. Thus liberalism divides life into separate spheres which are organised hierarchically in accordance with reason/nature dualism. Those spheres identified with reason are the 'managers' which coordinate and rationally order the separate, split-off areas of 'interest' in which material desire and consumption, bodily need and care, material production and labour are organised as lower spheres representative of the body and nature. To the extent that direction is centralised into separate 'political' organs external to the sphere of material life, rather than spread widely throughout the social body, there is a parallel with the way in which the Cartesian reason-mind isolates and concentrates in an external organ the intentionality of the mind-stripped, mechanically-conceived body [*Plumwood, 1993*]. Reason supposedly forms the basis of qualifications for entry to the impersonal political sphere, directing and weighing impartially these lower spheres, according to the dictates of instrumental rationality. The supposedly rational public or 'political' sphere is divorced from the lower body of material and social life by the exclusionary characteristics attributed to reason – the exclusion of emotion, care, materiality and particularity – and conceived as a sphere of universality, freedom and choice divorced from considerations of material necessity. By means of these oppositions, the liberal dualisms of political and economic citizenship are established, and class and other forms of exclusion are articulated along axes of distance from nature as necessity, of recognition (or failure of recognition) of agency in labour, and in terms of 'rational' development, control and management of both the self and of subordinated Others.

Under the common liberal interpretation of individuals as self-contained, the liberal conception of freedom as absence of interference lends itself to an interpretation as separation from Others, especially non-human ecological Others, who are doubly excluded as outside even the human polity. Freedom comes to be interpreted in elitist and masculinist terms as lack of relationship and denial of responsibility, and self-determination as the rational mastery of external life conditions, through maximising transcendence of necessity and through control over the Other, over the 'lower' aspects of self as internal Other, and over nature. It is no coincidence that such freedom, defined as the denial of relationship associated with masculinism, selectively rewards those privileged, white, usually male subjects who succeed in the public sphere by avoiding or passing down to subordinated Others household and personal relationships and responsibilities [Okin, 1989]. In the *fin-de-siècle* neo-liberal orgy of the Nasty Nineties, security is interpreted not as a collective good resting in social trust, social 'capital' and the mutual provision of satisficing, basic life standards for all, but in the individualist terms of punitive law enforcement as social warfare waged against the criminalised Other, and in terms of each individual struggling to maximise self-shares in order to make provision for herself as best she can in an isolated battle against a hostile world. Thus the rationalist and individualist bases of liberalism [Addelson, 1994] lead it to define many of its key concepts – self, freedom, reason, security, and agency – in masculinist terms, in terms of opposition to those elements identified as Other, and in struggle with what is identified as nature.

Many other ecologically problematic features flow from these ways of conceiving the individual and his forms of rationality, including the marginalisation of collective forms of life, and the limitation of democracy and the political to interest group politics. As Carole Pateman notes, the liberal individual is conceived not just as ontologically self-contained but also as naturally contained within private life; '[liberal] citizenship is a "political lion's skin" which covers, temporarily, an individual whose natural habitat is private life' [1988: 104]. Liberal democratic citizenship becomes a bloodless, semi-fictional affair in which 'the liberal-democratic citizen does not vote as a political actor, but in defence of private interest', and public life is conceived in impoverished terms as a place for accomodating these private interests [Pateman, 1988; Walzer, 1992]. The resulting conception of democracy in terms of a central state mediating a multiplicity of competing (private) interest groups takes egoism, inequality and domination for granted, provides poorly for collective goods, militates against interests being balanced in a way which takes account of the weak, and legitimates the development and interest of a powerful security state as the central manager [Arblaster, 1987].

The liberal state's representative system reflects and enhances these problems, providing candidates lacking real critical strategies for the intractable social problems of liberal inequality with an alternative ground for competition in raising fear and distrust of the excluded Other. The resulting understanding of representation does not facilitate the processes of social communication or represent the outcome of collective decision-making, but rather permits representatives to adopt roles hostile to collective social forms and favourable to private interests selected in terms of power. Under the individualist interpretation of democracy, the concept that initially appeared to promise freedom as unlimited collective interrogation and free recreation by all of social arrangements degenerates into a formal show of managed electoral competition which all but the most repressive regimes can manage to stage in some form. Even where these are fair, their claims to ensure popular control are vitiated by their incompleteness, for only if the franchise were the major form of political power would voting begin to ensure widespread participation in communication and decision-making and therefore responsiveness to the degradation of collective ecological goods. As democracy is increasingly identified with its shallowest aspects, liberal commentators celebrate its spread in the modern world [*Marks and Diamond, 1992*].

Ecology and the Liberal Public/Private Division

Feminist political philosophy has shown that the liberal public/private division is one of the major means by which these masculinist limitations of vision are reproduced and sustained. It is also central to the means by which democratic activity and principle are kept confined to a narrow area of public 'political' life easily controlled by elites which benefit from environmental destruction. As a claim to exclude others from participation in the relevant sphere of decision-making, the liberal account of privacy has been used both to restrict the scope of the political, to effect the exclusion of women and other groups (servants, domestic animals) counted as part of the household, and also used to relegate most economic affairs to the realm of the private, to exclude them from democratic control and prevent their realisation as political, as subject to social discussion and determination [*Okin, 1991; Pateman, 1989*]. For feminists, households are primary political sites, and are only relatively unaccountable: the idea of the family as a sacred unitary space apart from the political and from others' knowledge and responsibility is now widely rejected in the treatment for example, of domestic abuse. Although few feminists argue for the elimination of household intimacy or in favour of incorporating it into the other dualistic pole of the public sphere,[25] feminists critical of both capitalism and patriarchy have stressed the way in which the concept of household privacy has been misused to put beyond challenge both the subordination of women and the private determination of an economic sphere which affects a much wider society [*Pateman, 1989; Bacchi, 1994; Fraser, 1987*].

The liberal private sphere thus includes both the sphere of particular relationships and ties, the realm of desire, care and value and, quite differently, the sphere counted as 'your own business', economic activity excluded, on the pretence that it affects no one else, from public knowledge and control, and therefore unaccountable and open to purely selfish determination. The liberal concept of privacy thus disjoins two quite different notions, with the intention and effect of transferring the hitherto uncontested status and small-scale decision-making basis of domestic privacy to the privatised economy. The dualistic structure designating the private-family and the private-economic as outside democratic control also exempts from democratic responsibility the two areas, consumption and production, where modern society impinges massively on nature.

Decisions about production and technology structure the frameworks within which private consumer choices are made. Any adequate ecological analysis of liberal democracy must move beyond the acceptance of these frameworks, expressed in green consumerism, to contest the exemption of the major areas of production and technology from democratic responsibility, and therefore to contest the way liberalism has shaped and used the public/private distinction. Feminist thought has provided many useful leads here on showing how liberalism denies and misrepresents the collective creation which shapes our lives [*Addelson, 1994*] and on the deconstruction of the liberal dualism of public and private spheres. The concept of privacy acquires great importance in liberal democracy as the seat of individual identity and freedom, and this tends to obscure the way in which it works, under the influence of the master subject, to perpetuate oppressive as well as emancipatory aims.

If, as Carole Pateman and others have noted, liberal theory locates the real individual in the private sphere, as the area of consumption and pursuit of desire, the 'public' world of citizenship, politics and collective forms of life will appear to lack importance except as instrumental to the private. As Young notes, the standards of professional and 'public' workplace behaviour also locate the 'real' individual in the private, along with her body, bodily needs and emotional satisfaction and expression [*1990*]. This private conception of the individual is ever more strongly asserted in contemporary life: thus in contemporary anti-taxation argument, it is only that part of your time you spend working for private appropriation that counts as truly 'working for yourself', implying that the 'public' aspects of self are external and 'other' to who you really are.

State and bureaucratic structures of regulation, often very extensively developed under liberal democracy as a substitute for as well as a concession to democratic management, tend to confirm this conception of collective life as alien, reinforcing the need to stress privacy as protection for the individual from sources of bureaucratic and state control and intrusion. All these factors combine to create the illusion that liberal privacy is invariably the saviour of freedom, and hence that ecological and other collective forms of responsibility must inevitably be on a collision course with freedom. What is overlooked when the collective aspects of self are thus marginalised is that liberal privacy, as well as having some liberating aspects, is also a major plank in the construction of many varieties of unfreedom – as subordination, discipline and vulnerability in both private and public worlds.

Feminist theorists such as Pateman and Okin have shown how liberalism's arrangement of public and private spheres effects the subordination of women, and these insights are also applicable to nature. The spheres of the family and the economy delineated by liberal concepts of privacy are articulated through gender, through the identities of the male producer and the female carer or consumer [*Fraser, 1987*], and inherit the problematic of masculine/feminine and of reason/nature dualism. Liberalism treats the public and the private as a dualism of sharply separated and opposed spheres, reflecting the dualism inscribed in male and female 'natures'. The extension of the democratic imaginary to the household is blocked by the assumption that the family, like woman's nature, is a unitary sphere of necessity sharply separate and radically other, a sphere of values and of relationships which are either naturally harmonious or naturally subordinate, but in neither case constructed in political terms.

Liberalism strives to construct and represent the public/domestic relationship in terms of a radical exclusion [*Plumwood, 1993*] which hyper-separates public politics and private care and intimacy, public freedom and private necessity, and hides the conflictual and political character of the household. 'Rational' public life adopts the instrumental, impartial, objectivist stance of reason and economic expertise in contrast to the domestic, conceived as the sphere of intimacy, care, need, emotion, value, empathy and natural community. This division also hinders the development of any public morality able to express care and responsibility for nature, other than that expressible in terms of 'interest group politics'. Within such superficial conceptions of the political and the democratic, what can be done to give social expression to concern for nature is very limited, being largely confined to green consumerism, participation in the instrumentally-oriented interest group politics of environmental lobby groups, and the politics of protest and embarrassment. This exclusion of the possibility of a public ethic has formed an important part of the critical case for replacing liberal conceptions of the polity by either a communitarian [*Sandel, 1982*], civic republican [*Skinner, 1992*], or a radical democratic conception [*Pateman, 1988; Mouffe, 1992b*].

One effect of the way in which the liberal public/private division has been shaped is that the liberal polity is 'systematically denuded of a set of public moral values' [*Pateman, 1988: 113*], which deficit includes any commitment to the health and viability of ecological systems, as well as to fairness to future generations. This creates an ethical vacuum in just that area where a commitment to an ecological ethic and an ecological economy would need to be founded. In the absence of the possibility in liberalism of a public ethic of care and responsibility for nature or the future, green consumerism tries to get by with a private ethic of care and responsibility for nature. But such a private ethic is patently inadequate for the main task of taking responsibility for the ecological impacts of larger social formations such as the structures of production, that is, for a democratic, ethical and ecological economy. The inability to conceive any public forms of moral life means that liberalism can at best yield a narrowly instrumental form of public policy in relation to nature, and is hard pressed to stabilise even enlightened instrumental forms in the tug of war between interest groups.

Liberal privacy does permit relationships based on recognition to occur in the private sphere, between particular individuals and nature. But although deeper possibilities can be realised by individuals on a private basis, the inability of liberalism to endorse any collective morality means that these possibilities are always in conflict with the instrumental rationality of the liberal public sphere, and can receive no genuine or unproblematic public, political or institutional expression. Thus liberalism cannot provide a stable conception of social good or democratic virtue in relation to nature or a framework for social practice based on respect for nature. At best it can exercise repressive tolerance towards such a practice, as the private practice of a few individual 'extremists'.

Radical Democracy and the Conditions for Ecological Citizenship

The demarcation of the household and the economy as private removes from political contest and democratic responsibility the major areas of material need satisfaction, production and consumption, and ecological impact. This is certainly not irrelevant to the persistence of ecological damage and inequality in liberal societies [*Green, 1985*]. It means that liberalism can recognise the other as an equal centre of agency in limited ways in a very limited sphere of political representation (political citizenship), but fails to extend this to provide wider recognition of the Other in the material sphere as an equal centre of need and responsibility in production, household and ecological life (economic and ecological citizenship). As Marx implies, the liberal tendency to recognise political but not economic and ecological citizenship rests on a form of mind/body dualism, a dualism then of the same kind that underlies Western inferiorisation and neglect of nature.[26] Marx however did not provide the basis for an adequate solution to this dualism, assuming that the political could be reduced to economic 'administration' and absorbed into the material and economic sphere. This reduction is not unconnected with the corresponding failure of Marxist societies to develop an adequate conception of democracy or political citizenship [Walzer, 1992]. A renewed effort to construct liberatory concepts of the political and of citizenship in the economic and ecological spheres is needed to resolve this dualism, which also plays an important role in maintaining the underdevelopment of democratic economic structures at the international level.[27]

The norms of democratic universality are often thought of as involving a recognition of the Other as a being of like agency and freedom, a different individual who is alike in meeting the conditions for political inclusion (reason or, what is different, agency and need). They also imply a setting of the boundaries of the political, the area in which power relations between political subjects are recognised as occurring and the area beyond which no such recognition is required or possible, the area of instrumental relationships. Liberalism strives to confine and minimise the area in which the political character of relationships is recognised and to limit recognition of appropriate subjects. This impoverished conception of the political is implicated in the conceptual blindness of formal liberal democracy to social relationships of domination [Young, 1990; Phillips, 1991; Mouffe, 1992b] and the restriction of equality to equal rights in a narrowly conceived legal and political sphere [Green, 1985]. A radical democratic and ecological objective would tend in the opposite direction, to maximise the recognition of political relationships and subjects and to recognise the plurality and pervasiveness of power relationships [Okin, 1991; Phillips, 1991; Walzer, 1992], as appearing for example in the sphere of gender relationships, in the household, in economic areas, in formations of knowledge, culture and identity, and in relationships with nature and animals [Plumwood, 1993]. Systematic and institutionalised failures and distortions of this recognition in the case of nature and animals can, I suggest, be thought of, in much the same way as in the human case, as political as well as ethical failings. Concepts of democratic communication also enable the extension to nature of some notions of political community (Dryzek, this collection), especially if we adopt the intentional stance in relation to nature [*Plumwood, 1993*].

But we also need to start from the other end to envisage the conditions for a concept of citizenship that could extend such recognition to integrate nature and concern for nature more fully into conceptions of political community, and especially into areas from which they are presently excluded in liberal polities. A fuller and less masculinist conception of citizenship can open space for renewing and extending the political and democratic impulse in key areas of exclusion, in the household and in economic and production organisation, including technology selection.[28] A number of theorists have argued that a better integration of democracy with everyday life can provide some of the necessary conditions for a public political morality.

Okin [*1989*] argues persuasively that democratising the household is essential to bring about a wider sense of social justice. Participatory theorists argue that the diffusion of democratic experience in both the household and the workplace develops democratic values and participatory competences [*Gould, 1988; Mill, 1969; Pateman, 1970; 1989*], diffusing practices of responsibility and care through areas from which liberalism strips them. Since an exclusive focus on workplace democracy can reflect a masculinist [*Phillips, 1991*] as well as a narrowly productivist orientation, it is important to stress a larger focus which supports a practice of democratic virtue across a wide area of life, including such female-identified areas as education and welfare. Economic citizenship must be conceived in wider terms which insert workplace democracy into larger networks providing community, regional and transnational accountability for economic policy and investment decisions [*Young, 1990*]. Without such insertions, there is nothing to prevent the exclusion of those not engaged in production from the decisions which shape the contours of their world, or a particular workplace from building its success in one community on ruining some other place [*Orr, 1994*].

Economic citizenship thus linked to widely diffused democratic values and practices has a crucial role in establishing not only political responsibility for other humans but also ecological responsibility for nature. A number of theorists have provided a basis for a conception which can extend such responsibility to nature: for example, Gould [*1988*] argues for economic citizenship from the idea that democracy involves a form of recognition of the other's equal agency. If recognising others in as many diverse ways and spheres of activity as possible can be thought of as a criterion of the political maturity of a society, it would follow that democratic recognition principles should extend to economic and household (private) life as well as to the recognition of others in nature.[29] The recognition account carries radical democratic implications subversive of a division of labour and working life which, under present forms of liberal capitalism, denies most workers agency and keeps for a minority of privileged professionals the recognition as self-determining agents implied in the ability to determine the meaning of their task and structure their own time and effort [*Ehrenreich, 1990; Young, 1990; Gould, 1988; Green, 1985; Pateman, 1970; Kropotkin, 1970*]. To find ways to renew and express the political and democratic impulse in this area, we need to mobilise a variety of democratic strategies and forms of organisation, not only direct democracy but novel democratic and representational forms, including demarchy (Burnheim, this collection). Democratic theorists suggest that where democratic structures and experiences are widespread and integrated into all the structures of everyday life, not split off as separate managerial organs for political elites, 'the democratic personality' [*Gould, 1988*] which emerges is one capable of infusing care and political responsibility into the tasks of daily life.[30] Such a practice can provide a basis for ecological citizenship as the recognition of others in nature, acknowledgement of the ethical and political character of relationships with animals and nature, and for ecologically responsible production and development behaviour as well as consumption and household behaviour.

If the core of such a shared political morality can be envisaged as respect for democratic values and participatory virtues in all spheres of life [*Mouffe, 1992b*], this provides a way to articulate a radical democratic conception of citizenship in which the individual is conceived as at home in public as well as private moral space. There is an important convergence here between such a radical democratic conception of citizenship as involving the diffusion of democratic practices and values throughout economic and political life, and an ecological citizenship capable of developing and giving expression to collective ecological concerns. The radical democratic reconception of citizenship involves a paradigm shift which effects a series of systematic displacements in the liberal framework which in turn bring it much closer to an ecological formulation of citizenship. Oppositional conceptions of reason can be displaced as the main conceptual basis for political entitlement and citizenship, to make room for a richer and less dualistically defined set of features.[31]

The self-contained conception of self characteristic of liberalism and its rationality of self-maximisation and instrumentalism can be replaced by a relational conception of self and its rationality of mutuality, which several theorists have argued corresponds to an ecological conception of self [*Plumwood, 1991; 1993*]. The identity of the individual in such a democratic order can be reconceived as expressed in the public as well as in private space, not, as in liberalism, as only exceptionally expressed in public, political action [*Pateman, 1989*]. The public aspect of identity as citizenship is expressed in political responsibility in the democratic forums of everyday life, and in the 'public-spiritedness' which aims to further the collective and cooperative forms of life marginalised in liberalism, whose health is necessary to the community and essential to the flourishing of nature, particularly biospheric nature.

This shift in identity opens a space for the development of moral values appropriate to the public sphere, replacing the empty and instrumental character of liberal morality by a substantive conception of public morality as 'principles of political right on which members of a self-managing democracy can consciously draw to order their political practice' [*Pateman, 1989*]. A commitment to such concepts of democratic virtue can provide a non-instrumental conception of political community which is inclusive of future generations and the non-human world. If the democratic community is envisaged as an unbounded community (Dryzek, Thompson, Mathews, this collection), these virtues would have to include such ecological values as taking responsibility for the ecological impacts of one's life, work and community, and not robbing future others for present generation benefits. Should we try to ensure this further by structuring into the forums of democratic communication political speakers for the interests of nature, representatives for nature and the future (Eckersley, this collection)? That idea is not limited to liberal representative politics, although it originates in the liberal framework. But the liberal framework is the very place where such a manoeuvre is least likely to be effective, where it would amount, given the rest of the liberal structure I have outlined, to sowing the wind, if only because such representatives would be unable in the liberal structure to address properly the major areas in which most impacts on nature originate. Economic citizenship is an essential condition for the usefulness of such a representational device, for only if we are equipped with democratic forums which address these major areas of impact in the making of decisions about production and economic life could such structures of representation for nature begin to be effective.

Radical democratic virtues can be based on the values inherent in participating in a political community as well as on the reintegration into the public of some of the care liberalism confines to the private, yielding a conception of responsibility for the Other that is not just human-centred in application. Communicative and democratic virtues include attentiveness and openness to the Other, tolerance, empathy, respect for the Other's difference, preparedness to share the means of life, to negotiate and accomodate needs with the other, generosity to and respect for the Other and recognition of their freedom and agency, and responsibility for one's life impacts on the other. All of these concepts can be applied directly to nature and animals to recognise them as part of the political and moral community,[32] yielding a concept of ecological morality and citizenship which resists the liberal reduction of ecology to the interests of the private pressure group. Of course, many of us will still seek private solace and joy in intimacy with nature, developing special relationships of love and care with particular others in nature, which can now be more in harmony with public ethics. But public ecological ethics need not and should not be reduced to such a private and intimate morality of love and friendship with nature. In this alternative democratic paradigm we are not obliged, as we are in the liberal paradigm, to rely on the hope that such personal values will somehow become universal, in order to build practices of democratic and ecological citizenship which respect the needs of nature.[33]

Reason/Nature Dualism and Democratic Culture

These concepts of democratic citizenship have much to offer in constructing ecological alternatives to liberalism, but in employing the discourse of public morality and stronger citizenship, we need also to be aware of various difficulties and dangers. These include a danger of positions such as civic republicanism using the concept of public morality to support a state-centred agenda which performs the converse reduction of the individual to the citizen and refuses the conditions of economic citizenship and diffused participation which are critical to ensuring that this discourse does not become another rhetorical cloak for elite control [Plumwood, 1994b]. Another area of difficulty is in the concept of moral pluralism, a prominent and widely admired landmark of modernity whose loss would mark our movement into unrecognisable political territory. Mouffe argues, convincingly in my view, that where a substantive conception of public morality is based on shared commitments inherent in democratic political practices, commitment to the procedural and communicative processes and values which make democratic practice and political community possible, public endorsement of these structural values is compatible with a strong commitment to moral pluralism in the non-structural field; in fact a commitment to pluralism and to the practices of multiculturalism can be considered one of the major democratic virtues [Mouffe, 1992b].

It seems clear that a commitment to ecological health should also figure among such structural commitments, first because the health of nature is not just another set of interests but the condition for any sustainable democratic practice, and second because nature and animals should be included in the political community in which such commitments operate. Mouffe is sceptical of such an extension, but I think that she has failed to see the possibilities for a political relationship to nature and animals based in the intentional stance and on communicative virtues, and for extending structural concepts of community membership and democratic virtue to nature. If this doubt indicates an area of debate, it also indicates a failure to recognise ecological responsiveness and citizenship as a key test of democracy.

Another major potential area of failure is in the area of responsiveness, ecojustice, and democratic culture. Richer conceptions of democracy help open the way for better information flows from those at the bottom who bear most of the costs of environmental damage, and hence better correctiveness and better accountability across a crucial range of areas. But simply widening areas of participation and providing a richer set of formal participatory structures by no means ensures that people, particularly the least advantaged people, will be able to participate. Feminists in particular have made the point that such structures can disadvantage women [*Phillips, 1991*]. Although this is in part a consequence of the liberal public/private division of labour which leaves women with the double day, it is also a consequence of lingering masculinism in conceptions of democracy. But there is also considerable work which shows that not only in liberal, but in non-liberal frameworks, those with most need to be considered are those least likely to participate in democratic structures [*Pateman, 1989*], and which suggests that a wider provision of structures of democracy may simply reproduce what Pateman calls 'miniature liberalism' in more areas. So multiplying formal participative structures will not on its own solve the urgent ecological problems of responsiveness and ecojustice, will not ensure that information and action on the degradation of nature flow freely through channels unclogged by elitism and inequality.

In our quest for ecological citizenship, we should not make the mistake of those political theorists who assume that formal political structures are all that we have to be concerned about, and who overlook the importance of democratic culture [*Pateman, 1989; Green, 1985*]. Deconstructing elite formations of culture in everyday life is essential if 'political activity is to become a part of everyday life, not something extra to it' [*Pateman, 171*]. And here it can be said that if reconceiving democracy is essential to fixing up our relationship with nature, reconceiving our relationship with nature is equally essential to fixing up democracy. This is because in Western culture, (which is now global technological culture), elite domination has particularly been elaborated through culture via the dialectic of reason/nature dualism, whose variations permeate everyday life and culture and are expressed especially in the structures of knowledge, labour and identity. Over 25 centuries of elite control of cultural resources have created a complex web of dualisms, in which 'lower' groups are represented as some version of nature or of body in contrast to the higher groups' appropriation for themselves of concepts of mind and rationality. Although the roots of these dualistic structures are old, they are constantly renewed to justify and create new forms of social hierarchy which defeat the possibilities for democracy, participation and political equality. Extending democracy into the area of political culture involves reconstructing this hierarchical reason/nature story, which, through its roots in the older Western project of rational mastery, has partially overshadowed and subverted the project of democracy.

To understand this subversion we need to understand how conceptions of reason and nature have been constructed as tools of hierarchy, and how an instrumental version of reason has evolved which supports a culture of rational meritocracy in which those considered 'more rational' acquire the right to dominate those constructed as less rational. We are conventionally offered a singular, unquestionable model of disengaged reason which has somehow escaped political influence in its formation. Yet for twenty-five centuries or more the essence of humanity has been identified with mind and reason, which has in turn been identified with elite groups, and the contrasting concepts of body, emotion and nature identified with those they dominate, with men over women, European over 'barbarian', civilisation over primitivism, and human over animal. It is not just a mistaken belief system we have to deal with here, one that we can set straight by claiming women, for example, to be equally rational; for, as feminist philosophers have argued, the dualistic exclusions which still form the framework for life in Western culture have deeply affected the dominant construction of both the body and reason, and thus of both who and what is seen as reasonable.

In both modern and classical forms of democracy, hierarchical concepts of mind and reason have been some of the major tools employed to contain universalist and egalitarian potentials and prevent the extension of democratic privileges to excluded groups. The retention in liberal democracy of a dualistic conception of reason which is traditionally opposed to the excluded lower realm designated as nature and body, means the corresponding retention of influential anti-democratic and anti-nature elements at the heart of liberal culture. Thus a strong theme of rational meritocracy has existed as a crucial subtext in liberal thought, excluding a variety of others represented as in opposition to reason – women, children, manual workers, those of non-European descent, non-whites, the mentally ill, those less educated – from the category of full political entitlement and participation. Mill wrote of his rational democracy: 'The best government must be the government of the wisest, and these must always be a few.'[34] Groups cast as outside or of lesser reason have often sought to contest exclusion from political entitlement on the basis of their possession of reason and hyper-differentiation from other lower orders thought to lack it, especially those from reason's major contrast class of 'brute nature'

[*Wollstonecraft, 1982*]. Thus, a strong motivation for seeing other 'lower groups' as inferior along the lines of reason/nature dualism is written into the foundation of the liberal turn, and is reinforced with each extension of democratic privilege to a new category of human society.

The liberal-rationalist subtext of rational meritocracy remains active within liberal democracy in justifying hierarchy and social inequality outside the formal political sphere, and constantly defeats efforts to obtain a more just and democratic society. Reason/nature dualism (and its special case, mind/body dualism) plays a significant role in the pervasive structuring of labour in terms of the division between socially esteemed 'mind-people', managers and professionals who design and direct their own labour and that of others, and their contrast class, the devalued and instrumentalised 'body people' who carry out these designs. These deep dualistic structures are part of the cultural complex of rational meritocracy that permeates basic cultural areas like knowledge and the culture of labour [*Green, 1985; Marglin and Marglin, 1990*]. They are reflected not just in ideology but, of course, in actual social ordering as divisions of prestige and reward, of knowledge and labour between higher and lower categories, between managers and 'hired hands', between men as doing the labour of freedom and achievement, and women that of necessity and care. Extending formal participative structures may mean little unless we can rework the dualisms that permeate the politics of work and leisure, knowledge and science, freedom and necessity, public and private, to subvert these oppositions of the higher order to the inferior orders, the head people to the body people, the 'civilised' to the 'primitive', the controlling, expert knower to the objectified known, the highly valued masculine life of freedom to the devalued feminine life of necessity, the rational, speaking human agent to the silenced, 'mindless' non-human object. Democracy, social equality and ecological citizenship must remain formal and superficial concepts and practices in a culture structured by the dualistic divisions and dualised identities which pervade the organisation of work and everyday life in existing liberal democracies. We must work to reconcile the anciently divided spheres of nature and culture, both in theoretical and political structures and in the culture and practice of everyday life, if we are to accomplish the increasingly urgent and convergent tasks of creating a society in which both human freedom and nature can flourish.

NOTES

1. Capture of much of the professionalised environment movement in the halls of power through the interest group framework is widely remarked [*Seager, 1993; Dowie, 1995*].

Another mark of the co-option of the eco-establishment through professionalism is the unwillingness of professionals to confront the intractability of the dominant political framework and the poverty of the strategy of promoting green consumerism and liberal reform. The professionalised movement is increasingly incapable of providing critical political direction and honest evaluation, or of generating effective strategies which face the reality that many failures have their roots in these political structures and are not just temporary and contingent setbacks. To the extent that movement professionals give top priority to guaranteeing their own advancement and projecting a 'successful' corporate image, they cannot entertain or admit failure or adopt a stance critical of structural barriers to change.

2. See Johansen [1993].

3. To the extent that environmental oligarchy is assumed to depend on 'objective science' to substitute for democracy as a reliable information source, its proponents depend on ignoring the substantial body of work on the social construction of science and on its production for the needs of the powerful. Much feminist work too has shown how power distorts conceptual frameworks and knowledges. Recent work on the way such distortions in science are generated by forms of power and oppression includes Harding [1991].

4. Privileged groups who have a stake in the problematic structures of accumulation will often be motivated to support mitigating forms of change which leave them intact, and it is this agenda especially which has influenced the forms of environmental politics they have been able to control [Dowie, 1995]. Although (relatively) non-privileged groups such as workers may have their choices constrained in ways which lead to their obstructing change, they are likely to play a much less significant role in constructing the overall choice context, and to have less stake in protecting it. Many of these forms of redistribution downward are also directed to future people, who, in terms of consideration for their interests and welfare, have to be considered highly disadvantaged.

5. Although they can already use their superior access to resources to mitigate the personal ill effects of diffused forms of environmental degradation, and will be able to do so to an increasing degree as technologies which enable selective insulation develop.

6. The effects of power are amplified by the perceptual politics of ecological bads, whose highly particularised forms are often those which are most noticeable, and appear most clearly as contingent and avoidable. These are the forms most likely to arouse effective political action for positive change, but also the forms most liable to redistribution to the poor in a society of inequality. The highly diffused forms of environmental degradation, such as nuclear radiation, acid rain and general biospheric degradation, tend to be harder to perceive, and are subject to notorious problems of political responsibility and effective action.

7. This was the argument recently employed by the President of the World Bank to justify Third World waste dumping.

8. See Pateman 'The Civic Culture: A Philosophic Critique', in Pateman [1989].

9. Surveys persistently show high levels of public support for environmental action. See Luke [1993].

10. This is one way to get something useful from the 'veil of ignorance' framework elaborated by Rawls, which otherwise can function as a justification for liberalism by preserving liberal egoism while introducing philosophical instruments to abort its normal effects. It is not the failure of 'the veil of ignorance' which we should hold responsible however, in the context of inequality, but political and cultural structures which favour the privileged.

11. As Castoriadis [1991] notes, environment portfolios solve the problem of what to do with junior ministers.

12. On nature as the condition for speech, see Kirk [1995].

13. See recent works by Alterman [1992], Bagdikian [1992], Baker [1994], Kofsky [1994], Mazzocco [1994], Parry [1992], as well as many others.

14. For an account of some of these in the form of corporate influence and lobbying in the environmental case, see Dowie [1995]. Other liberal mechanisms which reduce the accuracy of representative systems themselves, (for example 'power trading' identified by Burnheim, this collection) can also be implicated in loss of ecological responsiveness.

15. It is important to stress that the problem does not just lie in capitalist control of the economy,

but also in systems of knowledge, in political and administrative systems, and the complex interaction between these factors. The existence of interactive structural features of liberal capitalism which render it unable to respond to the complexity of problems of an environmental nature has been persuasively argued recently by John Dryzek [*1990; 1992*]. Dryzek argues that capitalism generates through its own growth and profit logic environmental problems which it cannot solve itself but must displace into the spheres of administration and representative democracy. But the political sphere of liberal democracy is also imprisoned by the requirements of economic growth, while administrative systems are prevented from dealing adequately with the complex, boundary-crossing problems of the environment by their hierarchical structure, instrumental rationality, and commitment to the economic system. The logics of all systems combine to block an effective, non-piecemeal response to the kinds of problems the large-scale degradation of nature represents. Many seasoned environmental activists have trodden the well-travelled avenues of bureaucratic frustration and democratic failure this structure generates.

16. This extends to the environment movement itself: the successes of environmentalism in the past twenty years have depended heavily on collective forces within liberal democracy which are now in decline [*Keane, 1984; Held, 1993*], such as effective regulatory institutions and funding support for citizen associational networks for nature.

17. The other major argument for this identification of liberal democracy with freedom, that from free contract, is also undermined by gross inequality, since unequal or forced contracts which take place in contexts which have structured out other choices (often by past violence) do not represent freedom and have no moral force. Who could be said freely to strike so disadvantageous a social bargain as that which attends gross inequality?

18. This distorted relationship to necessity also appears in other areas. Thus corporate generosity is directed, through 'advantage' systems and other perks for star consumers, to those who need it least, but withheld from the homeless and destitute.

19. On this common logic, see Plumwood [*1993*]. These features correspond to an anthropocentric structuring of the market, as well as an androcentric and eurocentric one.

20. For detailed discussion of Locke's argument and its assumption of the nullity of nature, see Plumwood [*1993*].

21. The sphere of domination does not of course stop with the exclusion of these four groups of primary Others, which are simply those which have had a crucial initial constituting role in defining the master subject. For a more complete contemporary account of kinds of oppression, see Young [*1990*].

22. Feminist thought particularly has contributed to understanding the peculiarities of this form of denial, with its assumption of the contribution of the other and simultaneous refusal to recognise this. On the form of this denial, see Marilyn Frye [*1983*].

23. For some critique of the neoclassical model, see Jacobs [*1994*].

24. Where satisficing replaces maximising by the concept of 'enough', as in Buddhist economics.

25. There are three major exceptions. First, some forms of Marxist feminism, which aim to absorb the private in a new fraternal public sphere. Second, the radical feminism of Shulamith Firestone. The third exception is the nineteenth-century 'material feminist' movement which aimed to socialise the household via the market, through the replacement of women's unpaid labour by specialist or professional services [*Hayden, 1984*]. When feminists speak of democratising the household [*Okin, 1989; Pateman, 1989; Phillips 1991; Young, 1990*], they do not of course mean that it should become open to the 'tyranny of the majority', state regulation or regulation by general voting in a single, universal public sphere: they mean that household relationships themselves should take on the characteristics of democratic relationships, and that the household should take a form which is consistent with the freedom of all its members. Mill's principle for selecting decision-makers in terms of who is affected may be used here.

26. See K. Marx [*1967:225–6*]. Note that this dualism connects closely with the liberal conception of the essential feature of citizenship as the capacity for rationality, which is what the political sphere is taken to represent. Marx does not of course explore the connections between this fundamental dualism and the inferiorisation of nature, since he is himself

committed to this inferiorisation. See Plumwood [*1981*].

27. On the importance of democratising international relations, see Held [*1991; 1993*].
28. On the role of democracy in technology selection, see Winner [*1986*].
29. This is also the conclusion which follows from the application of Mill's principle that those most affected by decisionmaking are those who should be most involved in it. This is one of a number of points at which Mill's principles conflict with capitalism and point towards economic citizenship. See Macpherson [*1973*].
30. The recognition of nature can follow some of the same logic as other political forms which acknowledge the other as a fellow subject and agent, another who is, like the self, a centre of choice, freedom and needs, but a different one [*Benjamin, 1990; Laclau and Mouffe, 1985*], a logic which requires the recognition of both community with and difference from the other. In addition to recognition of the other as a fellow agent, democratic norms also require respect for the other as of value for their own sake [*Gould, 1988: 77*]. This criterion of the political corresponds to the familiar idea that the political sphere is that in which power is contested or exercised over another. Distortions of the recognition process are indicators of the familiar dynamics of power – exploitation, domination and oppression – involving treating the other as means, denying or attempting to subsume their agentic capacities, and failing to acknowledge either their agentic commonality and interdependence or their agentic boundaries, difference and independence from self [*Benjamin, 1990*].
31. For example by the concepts clustered around agency, which include purposiveness, need, intentionality, and self-directedness. If this is the key cluster of concepts for political community, a reconception of nature as active, intentional agent [*Merchant, 1980; Haraway, 1990; Mathews, 1990; Plumwood, 1993*] helps us to extend elements of political community to nature.
32. The thesis that the main elements of the recognition account apply directly to nature is argued in detail in Plumwood [*1993*].
33. Even if they were, somehow, to become universal, it is not clear that they could become effective in the liberal framework, because of the nature of liberal and institutional rationality.
34. J.S. Mill, quoted in Arblaster [*1987: 49*]. For a tracing of the themes of dualism and rational meritocracy, see Marglin [*1990*] and Plumwood [*1993*]. Many feminist and postmodernist writers have explored the theme of the dualistic construction of identity.

REFERENCES

Addelson, Kathryn Pyne (1994), *Moral Passages: Towards a Collectivist Moral Theory*, New York: Routledge.
Alterman, Eric (1992), *Sound and Fury*, New York: Harper Collins.
Arblaster, Anthony (1987), *Democracy*, Milton Keynes: Open University Press.
Bacchi, Carol (1994), 'From Anti-Discrimination to Managing Diversity: How Did We Get Here from There?' *Political Science*, RSSS, Australian National University.
Bagdikian, Ben (1992), *Monopoly*, Boston, MA: Beacon.
Baker, C. Edwin (1994), *Advertising and a Democratic Press*, Princeton, NJ: Princeton University Press.
Benjamin, Jessica (1990), *The Bonds of Love*, London: Virago.
Benton, Ted (1989), 'Marxism and Natural Limits: An Ecological Critique and Reconstruction', *New Left Review*, pp.51–86.
Beck, Ulrich (1995), *Ecological Enlightenment*, Altantic Highlands, NJ: Humanities Press.
Burnheim, John (1985), *Is Democracy Possible?*, Oxford: Polity Press.
Castoriadis, Cornelius (1991), *Philosophy, Politics, Autonomy*, Oxford: Oxford University Press.
Chomsky, Noam (1991), *Deterring Democracy*, London: Vintage.
Dowie, Mark (1995), *Losing Ground*, Cambridge, MA: MIT Press.
Dryzek, J. (1990), *Discursive Democracy*, Cambridge: Cambridge University Press.
Dryzek, J. (1992), 'Ecology and Discursive Democracy: Beyond Liberal Capitalism and the Administrative State', *Capitalism, Nature, Socialism*, Vol.3, No.2, pp.18–42.
Fraser, Nancy (1989), '"What's Critical About Critical Theory"', in Seyla Benhabib and Drusilla

Cornell (eds.), *Feminism as Critique,* Oxford: Polity.
Frye, Marilyn (1983), *The Politics of Reality,* New York: Crossing Press.
Gould, Carol (1988), *Rethinking Democracy,* Cambridge: Cambridge University Press.
Green, Philip (1985), *Retrieving Democracy: in Search of Civic Equality,* London: Methuen.
Harding, Sandra (1991), *Whose Science? Whose Knowledge?,* Milton Keynes: Open University
    Press.
Haraway, Donna (1990), *Simians, Cyborgs and Women,* London: Free Association Books.
Hartsock, Nancy (1985), *Money, Sex and Power,* Boston, MA: Northeastern University Press.
Hayden, Dolores (1984), *Redesigning the American Dream,* London: W.W. Norton.
Held, David (1991), *Political Theory Today,* Cambridge: Polity Press.
Held, David (1993), *Prospects for Democracy,* Cambridge: Polity Press.
hooks, bell (1995), *Outlaw Culture,* London: Routledge.
Jacobs, Michael (1994), 'The Limits of Neoclassicism: Towards an Institutional Environmental
    Economics', in M. Redclift and T. Benton (eds.), *Social Theory and the Global Environment,*
    London: Routledge.
Jaggar, Alison (1983), *Feminist Politics and Human Nature,* Totowa, NJ: Rowman & Allanheld.
Jennings, Cheri Lucas and H. Bruce Jennings (1993), 'Green Fields/Brown Skin: Posting as a
    Sign of Recognition', in Jane Bennett and William Chaloupka (eds.), *In the Nature of Things,*
    London: University of Minnesota Press, pp.173–96.
Johansen, Robert (1994), 'Military Policies and the State System as Impediments to Democracy',
    in Held [1993: 213–34].
Keane, John (1984), *Public Life and Late Capitalism,* Cambridge: Cambridge University Press.
Keane, John (1988), *Democracy and Civil Society,* London: Verso.
Kelsey, J. (1993), 'Globalisation, Trade and the Nation-State: Reflections from Aotearoa/New
    Zealand', *Law and Society Conference,* Sydney, Dec. 1993.
Kirk, Gwyn (1995), 'Ecofeminism and Environmental Justice: Bridges Across Gender, Race, and
    Class', *Ecofeminist Perspectives Colloquium,* Dayton, OH.
Kofsky, Frank (1994), *Harry Truman and the War Scare of 1948: A Successful Campaign to
    Deceive the Nation,* New York: St. Martin's.
Kropotkin, Peter (1970), *Kropotkin's Revolutionary Pamphlets,* (ed. Roger N. Baldwin), New
    York: Dover.
Laclau, Ernesto and Chantal Mouffe, (1985), *Hegemony and Socialist Strategy,* London: Verso.
Lindsay, A. D. (1943),. *The Modern Democratic State,* Oxford: Oxford University Press.
Luke, Timothy (1993), 'Green Consumerism: Ecology and the Ruse of Recycling', in Jane
    Bennett and William Chaloupka (eds.), *In the Nature of Things,* London: University of
    Minnesota Press, pp.154–72.
MacKinnon, Catharine (1989), *Towards a Feminist Theory of the State,* Cambridge MA: Harvard
    University Press.
Macpherson, C.B. (1973), *Democratic Theory: Essays in Retrieval,* Oxford: Oxford University
    Press.
Macpherson, C.B. (1977), *The Life and Times of Liberal Democracy,* Oxford: Oxford University
    Press.
Marglin, Frederique Apffel and Stephen A. Marglin, (1990), *Dominating Knowledge:
    Development, Culture and Resistance,* Oxford: Clarendon Press.
Marks, G. and L. Diamond (1992), *Reexamining Democracy,* London: Sage.
Martin, Brian *et al.* (1986), *Intellectual Suppression,* Sydney: Angus & Robertson.
Marx, K. (1967), in L. Easton and K. Guddat *Writings of the Young Marx on Philosophy and
    Society,* New York: Anchor Books.
Mathews, Freya (1991a), *The Ecological Self,* London: Routledge.
Mathews, Freya (1991b), 'Democracy and the Ecological Crisis', *Legal Service Bulletin,* Vol.16,
    No.4 pp.156–9.
Mazzocco, Dennis (1994), *Networks of Power,* Boston, MA: Southend Press.
Mendus, Susan (1992), 'Losing the Faith: Feminism and Democracy', in John Dunn (ed.)
    Democracy: the Unfinished Journey, Oxford: Oxford University Press, pp.207–20.
Merchant, Carolyn (1980), *The Death of Nature,* London: Wildwood House.
Mill, John Stuart (1969), *The Collected Works of John Stuart Mill,* J.M. Robson (ed.) Toronto:

University of Toronto Press.

Mouffe, Chantal (1992a), 'Democratic Citizenship and Political Community', in Chantal Mouffe, *Dimensions of Radical Democracy*, London: Verso, pp.225–39.

Mouffe, Chantal (1992b), *The Return of the Political*, London: Verso.

Okin, Susan Moller (1989), *Justice, Gender and the Family*, New York: Basic Books.

Okin, Susan Moller (1991), 'Gender, the Public and the Private', in Held [*1991*].

Orr, David (1994), *Earth in Mind*, Washington, DC: Island Press.

Parry, Robert (1992), *Fooling America*, New York: William Morrow.

Pateman, Carol (1970), *Participation and Democratic Theory* Cambridge: Polity Press.

Pateman, Carol (1988), *The Sexual Contract*, Cambridge: Polity Press.

Pateman, Carol (1989), *The Disorder of Women*, Cambridge: Polity Press.

Phillips, Anne (1991), *Engendering Democracy*, Cambridge: Polity Press.

Plumwood, Val (1991), 'Nature, Self and Gender', *Hypatia*, Vol.6, No.1, April, pp.4–32.

Plumwood, Val (1993), *Feminism and the Mastery of Nature*, London: Routledge.

Plumwood, Val (1994a), 'Science, Silence and Survival: the Politics of Scientific Rationality', in R. King (ed.), *Intellectual Dissent: Papers from Society for Social Responsibility in Science Conference*, Latrobe University Department of Education.

Plumwood, Val (1994b), 'Republican Ambiguities', *Arena* (13), Oct., pp.25–8.

Plumwood, Val (forthcoming), 'Androcentrism and Anthropocentrism: Parallels and Politics', in K. Warren (ed.), *Ecofeminist Perspectives*, Bloomington, IN: Indiana University Press.

Plumwood, Val (1981), 'On Karl Marx as an Environmental Hero' *Environmental Ethics*, Fall , pp.237–44.

Pierce, David *et al.* (1989), *Blueprint for a Green Economy*, London: Earthscan.

Sandel, Michael (1982), *Liberalism and the Limits of Justice*, Cambridge University Press.

Schor, Juliet (1991), *The Overworked American*, New York: Harper Collins.

Seager, Joni (1993), *Earth Follies*, New York: Routledge.

Shiva, Vandana (1988), *Staying Alive*, London: Zed Books.

Shiva, Vandana (1994), *Close to Home*, London: Earthscan.

Skinner, Quentin (1992), 'On Justice, the Common Good and the Priority of Liberty', in Mouffe [*1992a*].

Waring, Marilyn (1988), *Counting for Nothing*, Sydney: Allen & Unwin.

Walzer, Michael (1992), 'The Civil Society Argument', in Mouffe [*1992a: 89–107*].

Winner, Langdon (1986), *The Whale and the Reactor: The Search for Limits in an Age of High Technology*, Chicago, IL: University of Chicago Press.

Wollstonecraft, Mary (1982), *A Vindication of the Rights of Women*, London: Dent.

Young, Iris (1989), 'Polity and Group Difference', *Ethics*, 99, pp.250–74.

Young, Iris (1990), *Justice and the Politics of Difference*, Princeton, NJ: Princeton University Press.

Liberal Democracy and the Rights of Nature: The Struggle for Inclusion

ROBYN ECKERSLEY

Is there a necessary, in-principle connection between ecocentric values and democracy or is the relationship merely contingent? Is it possible to incorporate the interests of the non-human community into the ground rules of democracy? Through an immanent ecological critique of the regulative ideals and institutions of liberal democracy, it is suggested that ecocentric values and democracy can be connected to some extent – at least in the same way that liberalism and democracy are connected – through an extension of the principle of autonomy and the rights discourse to include ecological interests. However, the move from autonomy, to rights, to an ecologically grounded democracy encounters a number of hazards, not all of which can be successfully negotiated owing to the individualistic premises of the rights discourse. While the rights discourse may be extended to include human environmental rights and animal rights in relation to captive and domesticated species, it becomes considerably strained and unworkable (ontologically, politically and legally) in relation to the remaining constituents of the biotic community.

After more than two decades of public environmental concern there is now a growing disquiet among many environmentalists that the regulative ideals and institutions of liberal democracy may be inadequate to the task of addressing the ecological crisis.[1] While most environmentalists would concede that liberal democratic states have proved their *relative* superiority to single party communist states on the issue of environmental protection (as in many other areas), very few would regard this comparison as a vindication of liberal democracy (or of capitalism). To be sure, liberal democratic institutions have provided scope for the political mobilisation of environmental concern, ranging from mass protests to the formation of green parties. Moreover, it has been argued that environmental activism on

Robyn Eckersley teaches in the Politics Department, and is Program Director for Environment and Development at the Institute of Ethics and Public Policy at Monash University, Australia. The author is very grateful to Freya Mathews for valuable feedback on an earlier draft of this contribution.

the part of citizens and non-governmental organisations has, in turn, helped
to enhance liberal democratic institutions and processes [*Paehlke, 1988*].

Yet the response of Western parliaments to heightened environmental
concern has been largely reactive rather than anticipatory. The spectacular
growth in environmental legislation and the proliferation of new
environmental agencies in the last three decades has done little to arrest the
growth in the rate, scale and seriousness of ecological problems, many of
which are irreversible (for example, species extinction and global
warming). Indeed, the 'public interest' in environmental protection fares
particularly badly in the corporatist political bargaining processes that
characterise 'actually existing liberal democracies'. Environmental
protection largely depends on public interest advocacy that is able to 'give
a voice' to long-term, generalisable interests (for example, future
generations) as well as the interests of non-human species. The members of
this extended environmental constituency obviously cannot vote or
otherwise influence political decisions made by any given political
community, yet their welfare can be directly affected by decisions made by
that community.

Liberal democracies generally operate on the basis of very short time
horizons (corresponding, at most, to election periods). Existing liberal
democratic bargaining processes also deal very poorly with the uncertainties
and complexities of ecological problems. Indeed, there seems to be an
intrinsic tendency for decision-makers to postpone action on a 'wait and
see' basis rather than take anticipatory and preventative action [*Jänicke,
1990: Ch. 4*]. Liberal democracies also presuppose political competition
between selfish human actors in the struggle for 'who gets what, when and
how'. Such a 'politics of getting' [*Rodman, 1980: 65*] puts groups and
organisations that are well resourced (in terms of money and information),
well organised and strategically located (for example, having easy access to
politicians and bureaucrats) at a distinct advantage to poorly resourced,
poorly organised and dispersed groups, such as community environmental
groups (see also Dryzek [*1992: 22–3*]). When these limitations in the
political bargaining process are set against the broader structural constraints
facing the modern state, particularly its fiscal dependency on ongoing
private capital accumulation, it is not difficult to see why the longer term
public interest in environmental protection (including the interests of future
generations and non-human species) is systematically traded off against the
more immediate demands of capital and labour.

Many environmental activists have responded to these problems by
disparaging and rejecting conventional liberal democratic channels of
political participation and, in some cases, the rule of law. The growth of
mass environmental protests, non-violent civil disobedience and direct

action, which began in the 1960s and reached its peak in the 1980s, is symptomatic of a deep and widespread frustration and dissatisfaction with the reactive and piecemeal environmental measures emanating from the liberal democratic parliamentary process. In some cases, this frustration has prompted the practice of 'ecotage' or monkeywrenching [*Foreman, 1991*]. Radical environmental groups such as the US *Earth First!* organisation have gained considerable notoriety for their refusal to make political concessions within the liberal democratic framework – a refusal that is encapsulated in their slogan 'no compromise in defence of mother earth' (for a general discussion, see List [*1993*]).

Many of the contributors to the early wave of ecopolitical theorising have been similarly disgruntled with liberal democracy. However, many of these theorists [*Ophuls, 1973; 1977; Hardin, 1972; Heilbroner, 1974*] looked to ecoauthoritarian solutions rather than to mass protests, civil disobedience or ecotage. Reacting to the 'limits-to-growth' literature of the early 1970s, these 'doomsday' ecopolitical theorists warned that we faced a choice between 'Leviathan or Oblivion' [*Ophuls, 1973*], that the urgency of the ecological crisis demanded tight, centralised government environmental regulation, energy and resource rationing, population control and a suspension of normal channels of political participation where these were seen to interfere with a swift and decisive governmental reponse to the crisis [*Hielbroner, 1974*].

However, by the time a distinctly green political theory began to develop self-consciously in the late 1970s, the emphasis had shifted to finding 'stronger' forms of democracy than liberal democracy. The decision-making rules and frameworks that have been typically defended in green movement and party circles since that time have usually followed a string of variations on a participatory and deliberative democracy theme (for example, consensus, grassroots democracy, direct democracy, local and/or 'face-to-face' democracy). For example, recent theoretical work on 'green democracy' has drawn on Habermasian-inspired notions of 'communicative rationality' [*Dryzek, 1987; 1992*] or on classical Athenian democratic ideals [*O'Neill, 1993*]. These green theorists rightly point out that environmental protection largely depends on public interest advocacy that is able to represent long term generalisable interests rather than short term selfish individual interests. As Dryzek [*1987: 204*] explains, the protection of life-support systems 'is *the* generalisable interest *par excellence*, standing as it does in logical antecedence to competing normative principles such as utility maximisation or rights protection'. More deliberative, pedagogical forms of free and impartial public debate are therefore defended as more conducive to securing long-range environmental protection than what Lindblom [*1965*] has called the 'partisan mutual adjustment' that is expected and encouraged in existing liberal democracies. For Dryzek, communicative rationality is likely to be facilitated by locally scaled decision making structures that are more flexible and more attuned to feedback signals from the local environment.

Whereas the early ecoauthoritarians (and the more recent 'ecosaboteurs' or, after Foreman [1991] 'eco-warriors') have shown a preparedness to sacrifice some measure of democracy at the altar of ecological principles, most greens theorists and activists (including those who have practised non-violent civil disobedience) have defended democracy as a desirable form of decision-making but have sought a style and form of democratic communication that is *more conducive* than liberal democracy to achieving environmental protection. What is common to all of these responses, however, is that a distinction is made between the desired outcome (environmental protection) and a range of possible social choice mechanisms (the forms of action and decision-making – non-violent civil disobedience, ecotage, authoritarian government, consensus etc.) that might conceivably produce the desired outcome.

Such a characterisation of the problem facing greens supports the contention that there is no necessary connection between the principles and procedures of green politics [*Goodin, 1992; Saward, 1993*]. According to Goodin, a distinction must be made between a green theory of *value* (which is consequentialist rather than a deontological theory that is concerned to protect 'natural values') and a green theory of *agency* (which must be understood as a separate and subsidiary component of a green theory of value). A green theory of agency would not insist, in advance, on any particular social choice mechanism (including the forms of agency typically recommended by greens). Rather, a green theory of agency would examine the available means and choose those that are found to be most conducive to achieving the desired outcome. According to Goodin's assessment, many of the familiar green forms of agency (such as rotation in office, decentralisation and locally scaled decisions) have served as obstacles to securing green outcomes. If greens are not to remain 'an amusing parliamentary sideshow', he argues, they must form parties of the standard kind, fight elections in the standard way, compromise and enter into coalitions [*1992: 171*).

In a similar vein, Saward has pointed out that although 'grassroots democracy' is generally included in the shopping list of green political principles, the putative link between ecology and democracy is 'an artificial unity'; democracy is supported on instrumental grounds, not on grounds of green principle. Indeed, Saward [*1993: 69*] argues that there is a 'natural compatibility between liberalism and democracy which does not obtain between ecologism and democracy'. We must understand democracy as 'a

politics without certainty'; greens must stop claiming that there are
ecological imperatives that override democracy and accept that 'persuasion
from a flexible position based on uncertainty can be their only legitimate
political strategy' [*1993: 77*].

Does this apparent distinction between political principles and
procedures hold for liberalism as well? That is, is democracy merely
instrumental to liberalism or is it also a liberal end in itself? Is there, as
Saward suggests, a 'natural compatibility' between liberal values and
democracy which does not (yet?) exist between green values and
democracy? If this is the case, then can green values be reformulated in
ways that might be more compatible with particular forms of democracy –
at the level of principle? Historically, liberalism has provided both an
impetus and platform for democracy while also serving as a major
constraint [*Beetham, 1992: 41*]. Would green political theory, in developing
a broader and stronger platform for democracy, also provide a new set of
constraints?

In this contribution, I want to challenge the claim that the connection
between green values (defined in ecocentric terms) and democracy is
necessarily as tenuous as that suggested in the foregoing discussion and
suggest that green values and democratic procedures can be linked at the
level of principle (rather than instrumentally). This challenge will be
mounted in the course of showing how one of the regulative ideals and
institutions of liberal democracy – namely, rights – might be enlisted and
developed in an ecocentric direction.

The general argument will run along the following lines: if it is accepted
that the rights discourse has provided a means of *connecting* liberalism with
democracy – *morally, politically and legally* – then could a reformulated
rights discourse, grounded in a *prima facie* respect for the autonomy of *all*
life-forms, also serve as a linchpin between ecocentric values and
democracy? Such an argument could be pursued on behalf of humans and,
more provocatively, on behalf of non-humans as well . This study will focus
on the more provocative case.[2]

Attention will be directed to the adaptability of the form and
composition of arguments that link liberalism and democracy via a rights
discourse, as well as the possible scope and content of non-human rights.
Additionally, the rights discourse will be analysed as a means of political
persuasion by the green movement, as a form of rhetoric that is accessible
to the *political animal*. As Aristotle observed, 'rhetoric is not the art of
political persuasion; but the art of being able to discern in each case *the
available means* of persuasion' (my emphasis) [*Rees, 1980: 492*]. What,
then, are the possibilities and what are the pitfalls of the rights discourse for
greens as a means of extending recognition and protection to the non-human

members of the biosphere?

A Treble Duty

The rights discourse has served a treble duty for liberalism – moral, political and legal. That is, it has provided a *moral foundation* for limited government by the consent of the people; it has provided a successful rhetorical device for the *political recognition* of a new, rising class (the bourgeoisie) and a *political challenge* to the existing class (the aristocracy); and it has provided a *legal institution* by which certain forms of conduct, or more precisely, certain social and economic relationships between people, have been sanctioned or penalised by the state.

John Locke, for example, in his *Two Treatises of Government* of 1690, argued that humans possessed 'natural' and 'inalienable' rights to life, liberty and property. Although these rights were held to belong to all human beings 'by nature', independently of positive law (this is the *moral* dimension of the argument), representative government gave them *political* and *legal* recognition. The construction of political and legal rights through the social contract thus facilitated the enjoyment, and protected against the infringement, of 'natural' or 'basic' rights. For Locke, rights provided both a justification for representative government and a limitation on government.

Of course, the moral, political and legal dimensions of rights are rarely separated out in practice and they are sometimes conflated in theory. It is well known that Benthan rejected natural rights as 'nonsense on stilts'. Rights, he argued, were created by convention and by positive law, not by God or nature – an argument that is now widely accepted. However, Bentham's criticism applied only to Locke's *moral* argument (indeed, Bentham's argument provided an explicit recognition of the political and legal applications of the rights discourse). Nowadays, the rhetoric of rights has expanded well beyond its classical liberal formulation. Rights now form part of ordinary language and a central part of the discourse of *Realpolitik*, providing a 'court of appeal' in which the justice of actions or proposed actions may be judged. In this everyday sense, the appeal to rights is less concerned with the distinction in ethical theory between 'the right' and 'the good'. (Indeed, one occasionally finds the political rhetoric of rights being employed by utilitarians!) As political rhetoric, rights are usually invoked not as something that is God-given or 'natural' but merely as statements concerning the standard of conduct that we should expect from citizens, communities or the state.

Can the rights discourse also serve this treble duty for greens – moral, political and legal? If rights fail to pass muster in one of these arenas, can they none the less be enlisted in one or other of the remaining arenas? More generally, can the language of rights be used by greens as a means of translating complex moral ideas about intrinsic value into ordinary political language and legislation?

The remaining discussion will seek to present the rights approach in its best light in order to determine what green mileage might conceivably be gained. I will then seek to 'round up' the various critiques of the rights discourse – critiques that will inevitably open out into a more general ecological critique of the individual premises of the rights discourse and of liberal democracy. Finally, I offer some general reflections on the circumstance in which the rights discourse (in its moral, political and legal applications) might, despite its limitations, serve as a stepping stone towards, or a complement to, an ecocentric democracy.

The Democratic Connection: The Good versus the Right

According to C.B. Macpherson 'the justifying theory of Western [that is, liberal] democracies rests on two maximising claims – a claim to maximise individual utilities and a claim to maximise individual powers [or individuality]' [*Macpherson, 1973: 3*]. The former claim may be traced to Bentham while the latter claim finds its most articulate expression in the writings of J.S. Mill. Both claims are liberal claims because they maintain that liberal democratic society enables the maximisation of individual human self-realisation. However, they are based on different maximising claims and different models of the individual. In short, utilitarians seek to maximise utilities while deontological theorists seek to maximise autonomy (or, in the case of J.S. Mill, individuality).[3]

Utilitarians believe that collective choices should be made by aggregating individual human preferences (preference utilitarianism) or maximising the sum of individual pleasures and pains of human (and non-human) sentient creatures (hedonistic utilitarianism). Either way, aggregation is seen to be the most equitable way of reconciling conflicting individual preferences or desires, thereby providing the greatest happiness for the greatest number (each individual's set of preferences or pleasures and pains count as one). However, the standard criticism of utilitarianism is that aggregation of individual preferences or pleasures (utilities) may result in the subjugation and abuse of certain minorities for the benefit of the majority.

In contrast, the deontological tradition insists that there are certain 'basic' rights of individuals (however defined) which must not be bargained away by simple majorities. They provide a framework which constrains what may be decided in the name of the general welfare. Such basic rights (whether substantive and/or procedural) are derived not from law or convention but from a set of moral principles that ultimately rest on respect for the inherent dignity and value of each and every individual. The idea that each and every individual possesses inherent dignity and value is basic to the democratic impulse.

As a justificatory basis for liberal democracy, the rights-based strand of liberalism offers a more secure form of recognition, inclusion and protection for minorities against 'the tyranny of the majority' than its main liberal rival, utilitarianism. This particular expression of the liberal regulative ideal of autonomy could, if developed and extended to non-human life-forms, provide a 'protective service' that cannot be provided by utilitarianism. In this sense, environmentalists have much in common with deontologists in arguing that there are certain rights or interests which should not be traded off in liberal democracies. As Laurence Tribe puts it: 'It is Kant, not Bentham, whose thought suggests the first steps toward making us "different persons from the manipulators and subjugators we are in danger of becoming"' [*Tribe, 1974: 551–2*].[4]

Although Bentham was prepared to include the pleasures and pains of all sentient creatures (whether human or non-human) in his utilitarian calculus – an inclusion that has provided the theoretical touchpoint for Peter Singer's defence of 'animal liberation' [*Singer, 1975: 1993*] – this inclusion still does not prevent a majoritarian sacrifice of human or non-human minorities. Indeed, the 'tyranny of the majority' can still occur irrespective of whether non-human interests are incorporated into the utilitarian calculus either directly, through an estimate of the likely pleasure or pain to be experienced by non-human sentient beings, or indirectly, through the inclusion of *human* preferences for the 'existence value' of non-human species [*Pearce, Markandya and Barbier, 1989: 61–3*].

The broad deontological/utilitarian distinction within liberal thought finds an approximate parallel within environmental thought in the division between Conservationists and Preservationists, or what Brian Norton has called Aggregators and Moralists [*Norton, 1991: 6–10*]. The Aggregators, sometimes referred to as 'wise-use environmentalists', apply scientific resource management techniques to the natural environment to obtain the 'maximum sustainable yield' or the greatest utility for the greatest number (usually humans, but, as we have seen, this has now been extended to include other life-forms, whether vicariously or directly). In contrast, the Moralists usually rely on moral and aesthetic arguments to demonstrate that the non-human world is valuable not only for its use value but also for its own sake (or for its 'intrinsic' value). Humans, individually and collectively, are seen as having a moral responsibility to live their lives in ways that allow non-human life-forms to pursue their own evolutionary destiny, untrammelled by various forms of human domination (this argument is further developed below).

Rights as a Critical Tool

Both the deontological and utilitarian traditions of liberal theory have been the subject of intense scrutiny and criticism from environmental philosophers (in the case of rights, these criticisms will be rehearsed below). However, the rights tradition has received relatively little attention from political theorists in the context of debates about democracy, rights and the 'representation', recognition and protection of non-humans. By re-opening the 'rights of nature' debates in a broader political and legal (rather than simply moral) context, we may discover some new critical tools which might help to guide the form and focus of green campaigns.

Political struggles for further 'democratisation' and liberation have often involved struggles for political recognition and *inclusion* through the extension of rights. In such struggles for recognition, the rights discourse has been used as a means of strengthening democracy, often by way of an 'immanent critique' of liberal democratic ideals. Roderick Nash, a well-known American champion of the 'rights of nature', suggests there are strong parallels between the campaigns of the American anti-slavery movement and the campaigns by radical environmentalists to extend legal and moral recognition to non-human species. As Nash puts it, 'Nature in their [the environmentalists'] eyes is just the latest minority deserving a place in the sun of the American liberal tradition' [*Nash, 1990: 212*]. Clearly, Nash sees the liberal rights tradition as having the capacity to take on the latest, and possibly the final, phase of our widening moral horizons.

However, the rights discourse has also been subjected to a sustained critique, most notably from socialists. For example, the liberal rights discourse has served to challenge existing power relations while also serving to construct and sustain new power relations [*Stammer, 1993*]. It is precisely because the liberal rights discourse serves to connect liberalism with democracy that it has this double edge: it has been used as an ideological smokescreen to blur the differences between the theory and practice of rights and it has been used as a powerful critical tool to expose these differences. In particular, the liberal rights discourse has been used by socialists to wage an 'immanent critique' of liberalism, exposing stark discrepancies between the formal existence of rights and the substantive enjoyment of rights. Such critiques have provided compelling arguments for more deep-seated social and political changes to ensure that 'heavenly rights theory' meets 'earthly rights practice'. The upshot of campaigns such as these has been that the growth of the welfare state since the Second World

War has been accompanied by a gradual extension of the rights discourse to include a range of economic, social and cultural rights alongside the traditional Lockean 'natural' rights to 'life, liberty and property'. This growth in 'welfare rights' has been justified, in part, as necessary for the proper exercise of the more traditional rights. Moreover, welfare rights are also increasingly recognised as morally valid claims in their own right. The development of a discourse on rights for non-humans (complementing a discourse on human environmental rights) would therefore furnish a further rationale for more substantial social and economic transformations towards ecological sustainability.

Green Democracy and Rights

The emerging debates about green democracy are surprisingly silent on the questions of rights. However, it is noteworthy that the model of liberal democracy that is rejected by defenders of deliberative democracy [e.g., *Miller, 1992; O'Neil, 1993; Dryzek, 1987; 1992*] is utilitarian (based on individual preference aggregation) rather than deontological (which seeks to uphold individual autonomy).[5] These theorists have argued that when it comes to reaching agreed judgements about generalisable interests (such as environmental protection), individual preference amalgamation is inferior to deliberative democracy. Preference amalgamation merely *registers* the preferences of individuals (who may choose selfishly or magnanimously); deliberative democracy requires a preparedness on the part of individuals, acting as citizens, to have their preferences *transformed* through reasoned debate about generalisable interests. Thus deliberative democracy seeks to educate through dialogue rather than simply reflect the sum of individual desires. It demands access to all relevant information; and it requires citizens to be generous and 'public spirited'. Both Dryzek and Miller point out that deliberative democracy is more likely to be achieved in small-scale communities or among trusted friends than in mass electorates (attended by competitive 'party machines').

There is certainly much to be gained from developing more deliberative forms of democracy in state institutions and civil society – both as a supplement to, or in some cases an alternative to, liberal democracy. In this respect, I endorse Dryzek's argument that a discursive 'communicatively rationalised' form of social choice [*Dryzek 1987: 239*] is undoubtedly more likely than liberal democratic bargaining practices to lead to better environmental protection.

However, given the characteristics and conditions of deliberative democracy, it is uncertain how far it can be generalised for society (and international society) as a whole. As Held [*1992: 19*] points out, 'the classical participatory model cannot easily be adapted to stretch across space and time'. Given existing social inequities and resource, knowledge and power disparities among different social classes and groups, to what extent will the abstract norms of free and impartial public discussion continue to reflect the experiences and interests of dominant groups? What new institutions can give effect to these 'stronger' principles of democracy? Finally, and most importantly for present purposes, to what extent can green democracy secure the protection, or at least ensure the systematic consideration, of non-human interests that might be at odds with generalisable human interests?

Despite the attractiveness of the case for deliberative democracy, it does not attempt to restructure the ground rules of decision-making to provide any explicit protection or recognition of non-human interests. That is, it is generally assumed that debates and decisions about generalisable *human* interests will effectively incorporate non-human interests. Yet these interests are not identical. Only those aspects of the non-human world that have a bearing on general human welfare need be considered. Non-human species that have no apparent use to humans could quite reasonably be considered dispensable and their habitats destroyed on behalf of generalisable human interests (the possibilities of potential human benefit in the future could be dealt with via preservation *ex situ* in gene banks).

What is lacking in accounts of deliberative democracy is some kind of guardianship or trusteeship, some institutional form whereby citizens are able to fulfil a human fiduciary responsibility or duty towards non-human beneficiaries who cannot represent themselves in the public arena. Non-human rights may provide one possible means whereby this trustee relationship might be instantiated, while also providing a language for arguing for the recognition and respect of the autonomy of non-human beings as subjects 'in their own right'. As we have seen, adopting the rights discourse also opens the way for a possible 'immanent ecological critique' of liberal democracy (in the same way that the left has enlisted the rights discourse to perform an 'immanent social critique' of liberal democracy).

Green Values and the Principle of Autonomy

Recall the opening argument that there is no necessary connection between the principles and procedures of green politics. This argument holds if a green theory of value is formulated as a consequentialist theory of natural (understood as non-human) values [*Goodin, 1992*]. However, if green values were to be grounded in a critique of domination (of humans and other species) and a general defence of autonomy (the freedom of human and non-human beings to unfold in their own ways and live according to their 'species life'), then processes and outcomes might conceivably be linked – at least in the way that liberalism and democracy have been linked. The connection between ecology and democracy would no longer be tenuous. That is, authoritarianism would have to be ruled out at the level of green principle (rather than on purely instrumental grounds) in the same way that it is ruled out according to liberal principle: it fundamentally infringes the rights of humans to choose their own destiny.

In developing this liberal form of argument in an ecocentric direction, an obvious complication arises in so far as non-humans cannot 'choose their own destiny' in a political sense. However, if the general moral premise of respect for the autonomy of *all* beings is accepted (this case is argued further below), then humans (as the only moral *agents*) must collectively acknowledge that human choices need to be constrained by a recognition and consideration of the interests of non-human beings – just as they must be constrained by a recognition and consideration of the interests of other humans to make the principle of autonomy workable. Liberal theorists have provided the justification for a range of constitutional restrictions on what the legislature may enact, based on the prior recognition of certain fundamental human rights; they have also defended general principles which qualify the ways in which both the state and individuals may exercise their powers or rights (such as J.S. Mill's 'harm principle'). These restrictions and qualifications are justified on the ground that they maintain democratic processes and structures and thereby maximise individual autonomy for everyone.

Ecocentric theorists would similarly extend this form of argument to include non-human life. The extension of rights to non-humans would necessarily involve a corresponding adjustment, restriction or redefinition of human rights. The challenge for green theory would be to develop principles that would enable the reconciliation of human and non-human autonomy. If all beings have a *prima facie* right 'to live and blossom', then we need to know in what circumstances this prima-facie right might be overridden by humans (as the only moral agents) in cases of conflict. The deep ecology principle of 'vital needs' provides a useful starting point for determining the general circumstances whereby human interference with nonhuman life may be justified. According to this principle, humans have 'no right' to reduce the richness and diversity of life-forms except to satisfy vital human needs [*Naess, 1989*]. There is, of course, plenty of room to argue over what constitutes a 'vital need' – a debate that would obviously need to take account of cultural variability. However, the principle places the onus on humans to justify any interference – a shift that is quite revolutionary. Moreover, it suggests, at the very least, that where humans (both individually and collectively) have a range of different possible courses of actions or technologies from which to choose, they ought to choose the course of action or technology that provides the least interference with the richness and diversity of life.

On the basis of the foregoing general argument, a case could be made that certain fundamental rights of non-human species (such as the right to exist) should be incorporated and entrenched alongside fundamental human rights in a constitutional bill of rights to ensure that they are not 'bargained away' by a simple majority in Parliament. Indeed, this would seem to be the only way in which non-human interests might be incorporated into the ground rules of democratic decision-making. The upshot would be that any legislation, or any administrative or other decision, that authorised action that posed a threat to the survival of endangered species could be challenged as constitutionally invalid.

The Moral Premise: Enlarging a Familiar Principle

The foregoing discussion is based upon the moral premise of respect for the intrinsic value of all life-forms – which is expressed in terms of a *prima facie* right or freedom of all life-forms to unfold in their own ways. This moral starting-point is by no means universally accepted (or understood) in moral and political debate.[6]

However, the narrower moral premise of respect for the intrinsic value of all humans *is* widely accepted. Among the cluster of ideas that make up the liberal democratic tradition is the idea of the *universal and equal worth of each individual*, an idea that underpins the principle of one person one vote. This idea – a secularisation of the Christian idea that each individual human being is of equal spiritual worth before God – has been a powerful driving force in the long struggle for universal suffrage to the point where it is now enshrined in the Universal Declaration of Human Rights of 1948. It is noteworthy that this particular declaration refers to *human* rights, not *citizen* rights. That is, human rights are declared to belong to every individual human in the world, irrespective of his or her membership of any particular political community. In this sense, they function as basic international moral and political standards, which may be translated into civic and legal obligations (through International Covenants and the domestic law of states).[7]

Arguing by analogy and anomaly, defenders of non-human rights have sought to demonstrate that *there is no good reason* for not extending this notion of respect for intrinsic worth to other animals, to other sentient beings or to all life. As Tribe explains, by starting with the familiar, 'the very process of recognising rights in those higher vertebrates with whom we can already empathize could well pave the way for still further extensions as we move upward along the spiral of moral evolution' [*Tribe, 1974: 1345*].

Tom Regan has provided one of the more influential moral defences of the rights-based approach in relation to animals [*Regan, 1983; 1985*].[8] According to Regan, all beings (human or non-human) who are the 'experiencing subjects of a life' (all conscious beings who have an individual welfare that matters to them, which Regan takes to be all mature mammals) possess 'inherent value' [*Regan, 1985: 22*]. Moreover, Regan argues that all beings who possess inherent value possess it equally, whether or not they are human. Thus all mammals have a *prima facie* equal right to respect (though not necessarily equal treatment). The theory of animal rights is presented as part of, rather than antagonistic to, the theory of human rights. As Regan explains, the animal rights movement is 'cut from the same moral cloth' [*Regan, 1985: 24*].

Now the traditional objection to the case for rights for non-humans has been that right holders must be competent moral, rational or linguistic agents, capable of fulfilling reciprocal obligations. Since non-humans cannot engage in moral reasoning, cannot reason, cannot talk and cannot discharge moral obligations, they therefore cannot be right holders. How, then, can a theory of animal rights be 'cut from the same moral cloth' as the theory of human rights?

Regan and other defenders of animal rights have typically responded to this criticism by way of human analogy. In meeting these traditional objections, animal rights theorists usually point out that it is not necessary for humans to be competent moral, rational or linguistic *agents* in order to be worthy moral and/or legal *subjects*. After all, many humans (for example, infants, intellectually handicapped, the comatose, the senile) do not possess the full repertoire of human attributes that are normally seen to distinguish humans from other animals, yet they are recognised as possessing certain basic rights, which create direct moral obligations on the part of morally competent humans. According to this argument, it is therefore arbitrary and unjust to exclude non-human species from moral consideration when it is clear that they can be harmed from human actions in ways that are not substantially different in kind from human 'moral patients'. The disqualification of nonhuman animals from moral and legal consideration *simply because they are not human* is therefore exposed as an unwarranted human prejudice, as human chauvinism.

Yet while resort to human analogies helps to break down resistance to the idea of extending rights beyond the human fold, it does so only in relation to a limited category of non-humans which bear significant resemblances to humans (in Regan's case, this amounts to mature non-human mammals). Many environmental philosophers concerned with the erosion of biodiversity have criticised Regan's case for being unduly restrictive [*Callicott, 1980*]. Why take the *human* case as paradigmatic of moral considerability? Must non-humans be significantly analogous to humans in order to be recognised as having any moral worth? Are not fish, birds, reptiles, and insects morally worthy? And what about plants and natural entities such as ecosystems?

Perhaps the most adventurous attempt to push the rights discourse into uncharted territory has been Christopher Stone's influential essay 'Should Trees Have Standing?' [*1974*]. Here Stone's argument proceeds not by way of human *analogy* but rather by way of legal *anomaly* [*Rodman, 1977*].[9] According to Stone, extending legal rights to natural entities is not 'unthinkable' when it is remembered that legal rights are conferred on 'non-speaking' persons such as infants and foetuses, on legal fictions such as corporations, municipalities and trusts, and on entities such as churches and nation states [*Stone, 1974: 34*]. Given that there is no common thread or principle running through this anomalous class of right holders, Stone argues that there is no good reason *against* extending legal rights to natural entities.

Stone has argued that the time has come when we ought to consider subordinating some human claims to those of the environment, especially in relation to wilderness and so-called 'useless species' [*Stone, 1974: 43*]. Stone suggests that his idea can be made operational through the appointment of a legal guardian who could ensure that the interests of a natural entity is protected through the administration of a trust fund and the instigation of legal actions on its behalf in order to make good any injury inflicted on it. Stone also discusses a range of procedural safeguards that would ensure that the 'interests of the environment' are taken into account by government agencies and private corporations. The legal guardian could enjoin the agency or corporation if the procedures were not followed. Courts could build up a body of environmental rights as disputes were litigated. Stone also suggests that more fundamental environmental rights (along the lines of the right to freedom of speech) might be introduced by setting up a constitutional list of 'preferred objects' that are defended by the courts [*Stone, 1974: 39*]. Stone even flirts with the idea of 'an electoral apportionment that made some systematic effort to allow for the representative 'rights' of nonhuman life' [*Stone, 1974: 40*].

Whereas Regan has provided a moral case for animal rights (without addressing legal rights), Stone addresses the question of independent legal standing as a mechanism for protecting non-human entities without explicitly mounting a moral argument as to why non-human entities should be protected. However, his unstated ethic is clearly an environmental ethic that is concerned to protect 'natural entities' as well as self-conscious, individual subjects of a life; in this sense it is implicitly Leopoldian. Stone's case therefore represents an even more daring extension of the liberal rights discourse than Regan's because it breaks with liberalism's concern for the well-being of identifiable *individuals*.

Unlike Regan, Stone does not develop a moral case for 'basic rights'; he simply shows how we may use the law as a means of protecting natural entities (by showing how the protective ambit of the law already extends to 'non-persons') and as a vehicle for shifting public opinion. His proposed legal reforms (including the development of a body of law that determines the meaning and ambit of environmental rights) are defended as a means of facilitating a general change in consciousness. His essay appealed to at least one American Supreme Court judge (Justice Douglas) in the famous Mineral King decision, which involved a proposed development in the Mineral King mountain range.[10]

It is important to disentangle the different moral bases of Regan's and Stone's defence of non-human rights. Although both Regan and Stone enlist the liberal rights discourse as a means of protecting nonhumans, they actually represent two of the main rival positions in the non-anthropocentric ethical literature – positions that are encapsulated in the familiar animal rights/environmental ethics controversy (for an overview of this controversy, see Hargrove [*1992*]).

Whereas Regan's theory of animal rights is broadly consistent with the philosophical premises of the liberal rights discourse, it is none the less vulnerable to a range of social and ecological criticisms. Whereas Stone's unargued Leopoldian premise escapes at least the ecological criticisms, his enlistment of the rights discourse for non-human entities introduces a degree of conceptual strain that many ecocentric theorists are likely to find unacceptable. Can these rival philosophical positions be reconciled? Does it mean we must abandon the rights discourse entirely or merely recontextualise it? Each of these problems will be addressed in turn.

The Socialist Critique

Until Ted Benton's *Natural Relations: Ecology, Animal Rights and Social Justice* appeared in 1993, the influential case for animal rights had been subjected to an extensive ecological critique [e.g., *Rodman, 1977*] but it had largely escaped the extensive socialist critique of individual 'bourgeois' liberal rights.[11] According to Benton, the tendency of animal rights theorists to draw on liberal, individualistic human-centred moral discourses has prevented a constructive dialogue between social welfare advocates and animal welfare advocates.

Although Benton's critique is primarily directed against Regan's case for animal rights, it may also be extended to the more general case for 'the rights of nature'. Three main socialist criticisms of the animal rights discourse may be distilled from Benton's wide-ranging discussion (which builds on, and extends, the socialist critique of liberal human rights): the problems of causality, epistemology and realisability.

The causality problem refers to the fact that the liberal rights discourse acknowledges only those harms that can be attributed to identifiable moral agents. However, there are many other sources of harm to humans and other species that are systemic, deriving from impersonal structures and dynamics. Ecological problems are also notoriously diffuse, which makes it difficult to find the requisite causal connections in order to attribute responsibility to particular moral agents.

The epistemological problem refers to the fact that non-human beings, unlike humans, cannot define and press their own claims. Human guardians must therefore 'second guess' what amounts to harm or injury to their non-human beneficiaries – a problem that creates a difficult set of epistemological challenges and also provides considerable scope for misguided (albeit well meaning) paternalism on the part of humans.

According to the realisability critique, the liberal rights discourse does not call into question the form of society in which human and non-human autonomy may be maximised. That is, in the absence of profound changes in our general socio-economic relations, human and non-human rights are likely to remain largely unfulfilled under capitalism. This criticism challenges not only the realisability of liberal rights under capitalism but also the very concept of individual well-being posited by liberals.

Benton's primary objection to the liberal rights discourse is that it ignores both the social and ecological 'embeddedness' and 'embodiment' of individuals. According to Benton, rights must be seen as '"boundary posts" erected between the territories of estranged individuals. A socialist conception of rights must answer the conceptual critique of liberal rights and widen their horizons by addressing the conditions of life that will enable their fulfilment' [Benton, 1993: 203]. This critique applies equally to the case for human and non-human rights. Benton argues that we must recontextualise the liberal starting point by moving from an atomistic individualism to a relational understanding of individuation which incorporates yet goes beyond the socialist focus on social interdependence to include biophysical embodiment and ecological interdependence – both of which are seen as indissolubly bound up with the individual's identity and experience of self.

Yet none of the foregoing arguments need be fatal to the case for rights – whether on behalf of human or non-humans. Just because right holders (or their guardians) may not be able to trace all sources of harm to assignable agents does not, of itself, mean that rights should therefore be abandoned entirely. Rather, the existence of systemic harms (which perpetuate the disparity between the formal existence of rights and their substantive enjoyment) provides a powerful set of arguments for more general social and political change that will ensure that rights are substantively enjoyed.

As to the epistemological challenges, there is no doubt that human paternalism is unavoidable in the case of non-humans. Our understanding of animal behaviour, animal welfare and the general functioning of life-support systems is highly incomplete. Indeed, recent developments in modern science (for example, physics, chaos theory) suggest that human understanding may never be complete in the sense that we may, in principle, never be able to predict the behaviour of non-linear dynamical systems (that is, most natural systems). However, again, this argument should not defeat the case for rights. Rather, it merely points to the need for guiding rules (such as the precautionary principle) to deal with the problem of uncertainty. We must work with the best available information, recognising that it may need to be revised from time to time. Moreover, the potential for the disenfranchisement of lay people by 'professionals' and 'experts' (such as bureaucrats and scientists) can be avoided by ensuring that amateur naturalists, schools, community environmental organisations and the wider public are involved in the monitoring and enforcement of non-human rights.

As to the realisability criticism, it is not clear whether rights would be rendered superfluous in a new post-capitalist socio-economic setting. In the meantime, it would be foolish to abandon the valuable, albeit imperfect, kinds of protection that legal rights are able to offer. As we have seen, the rights discourse can also serve as a vehicle for public education and as an 'immanent lever' for socio-economic transformation.

The foregoing defence points to the educational, transformational and protective advantages of the rights discourse – arguments that are employed by Stone in his defence of legal rights for non-human entities. However, these arguments still leave one crucial question unanswered: *how far* can the rights discourse be extended in relation to the non-human world (mammals, all animals, fish, plants and so on)?

The Ecological Critique

Although there are important differences in the premises and scope of the socialist and ecological critiques of the liberal rights discourse, they are structurally similar. That is, both insist that the well-being of individuals is indissolubly linked with the well-being of the broader social and ecological communities of which they are part. In this respect, an ecological perspective has a greater affinity with a socialist ontology than a liberal ontology. Individuals do not exist a priori and then enter into social and ecological relations; they are *constituted* by these relations.

However, the ecological critique operates from a broader premise and therefore has a wider scope than the socialist critique. As we have seen, many ecocentric theorists see no good reason for taking the individual human case as paradigmatic in determining what is morally considerable (a premise which has been extended by Regan to include all mammals). They point out that the relational ontology of an ecological perspective undermines claims that there is an absolute and consistent dividing line between us and the rest of nature on which to ground claims for restricting moral considerability to humans or other animals who are analogous to humans.[12] It is the broader network of ecological interrelationships (that include yet go beyond the human community) that should be the over-arching field or region of human care and moral responsibility.

This analysis would appear to provide a fundamental challenge to enlistment of the rights discourse, which is ordinarily tied to individual interests. After all, individual interests do not always coincide with the 'interests' of ecological communities. Animal rights theory does not encounter this problem because it remains individualistic, its primary focus of concern being animal suffering. Yet this 'humane' animal welfare position has attracted considerable criticism from defenders of a more holistic ecological ethic, such as Leopold's land ethic [*Leopold, 1949*]. To take the most obvious example, it is not in the *individual* interests of prey to be eaten by their predators, but it is in the 'interests' of the larger biotic community that certain individuals meet this fate.

Indeed, the problem of species diversity exposes the most serious flaw in the 'humane' moral starting point adopted by defenders of human and animal rights. In focusing on individual animal welfare, animal rights theorists are unable to discriminate between domesticated or abundant species, on the one hand, and 'native', rare or endangered species, on the other hand. They therefore cannot provide any sensible ecological criteria for the protection of endangered populations, gene pools or species considered as a whole. In contrast, a more holistic ecological ethic, such as Leopold's land ethic, explicitly adopts an ecologically informed perspective in focusing on the need to maintain the integrity and stability of the biotic community. Such an ethic locates humans within the ecological food chain, and therefore sanctions the killing of non-human species (at sustainable rates) to serve human needs along with the culling of feral species in order to protect indigenous species. Regan, however, explicitly rejects ecological holism (such as Leopold's land ethic) as 'environmental fascism' because it condones the sacrifice of individual animals for the benefit of the whole [*Regan, 1983: 362*].

Have we finally reached the limits of a theory that is 'cut from the same moral cloth' as the theory of human rights? Can a 'humane ethic' do 'ecological justice'? And can an ecological ethic do human justice? The different dimensions of the rights discourse will be examined in turn.

The Moral Dimension Revisited

So far, we have defended a very general moral principle that all life-forms have a *prima facie* right to unfold, or 'to live and blossom'. We have provided a general principle for determining the circumstances in which humans (as the only moral agents) may legitimately interfere with the 'right' of other life-forms to unfold in their own ways. That principle is the principle of vital needs (that is, humans have 'no right' to reduce the richness and diversity of life-forms except to satisfy vital human needs). However, we have not yet clarified the criteria for determining what is a life-form. Moreover, if an ecocentric perspective rejects atomistic individualism and proceeds instead from a relational ontology, and if ecological systems are as important as individual organisms, then on what basis can we mediate or discriminate between entities and individual organisms for the purposes of the ascription of rights?

Leopold's land ethic not only suffers from vagueness, it also suffers from 'excessive holism' in not providing any explicit recognition of the value of individual organisms. Let us turn instead, then, to the more comprehensive environmental ethic known as 'autopoietic intrinsic value theory', which I have defended elsewhere as providing one possible theoretical basis for determining what beings and entities have intrinsic value [*Eckersley, 1992: 60–61*]. Following Fox [*1990: 165–76*], autopoietic ethics attribute intrinsic value to all entities, *including individuals,* that display the property of autopoiesis, which means 'self-production' (this is essentially a definition of life-forms). Autopoietic entities are characterised by the fact that they are 'primarily and continuously concerned with the regeneration of their own organisational activity and structure'; in this sense they may be taken as 'ends-in-themselves' [*Fox, 1990: 171–2*]. This is essentially the same as Freya Mathews' criterion for the identification of 'self-realising' beings and systems [*1991: 98*]; such beings and entities 'embody their purposes in themselves' [1991: 101]. Included in this category would be all individual biological organisms (for example, human and non-human animals, birds, fish, reptiles, plants, and micro-organisms) as well as identifiable ecological entities such as ecosystems and, indeed, the biosphere considered as a whole.

The primary advantage of autopoietic intrinsic value theory over Leopold's land ethic is that it overcomes the individual/community (or atomistic/holistic) tension in the animal rights versus environmental ethics debate by recognising the moral considerability of *both* individuals and ecological entities. It also provides a dynamic and relational rather than static and atomistic understanding of individual and community development. Finally, it suggests some broad principles for ecologically sustainable development that would reconcile the tension between ecosystem integrity, animal welfare and human welfare, which we might dub 'Callicott's triangle' (see Callicott [*1980; 1988*]). That is, the rights of individual organisms would need to be framed in the context of the requirements of larger autopoietic entities, such as ecosystems, in ways that maximise the opportunities for both individuals and ecosystems (on which individual organisms are dependent) to flourish. In broad terms, such an ethical framework would seek a system of governance that is able to maintain biodiversity (the abundance and variety of nonhuman species); protect ecosystem integrity (for example, the waste assimilation and recycling services of ecosystems); and ensure that renewable resources (such as forests and soils) are utilised at a sustainable rate. We thus return to the basic normative requirement that the range of choices open to humans must be circumscribed and conditioned by broader requirements of ecological sustainability on the grounds that these requirements provide the conditions that maximise the autonomy of all life-forms.

The Political and Legal Dimensions

But even if we were to accept this ecologically plausible (and admittedly very general) ecocentric ethical framework as providing the regulative ideals for what Christoff [forthcoming] has called 'ecologically guided democracy', are legal rights an appropriate political and legal vehicle for achieving it? Does Stone's attempt to assign rights to *collective entities* rather than individual members of particular species overcome this impasse?

According to Norton [*1992: 77*], it is one of the minimal conditions of rights ascription that the right holder be an identifiable individual [*Sagoff, 1993: 91–2*]. This would suggest that Stone has made an illegitimate move in ascribing rights to entities. An individual organism may have rights, but a species, considered as a whole, cannot [*Sagoff, 1993: 91*]. But if the claims of right holders may be made not only against identifiable *individuals* but also against identifiable legal *entities* such as corporations or the state, then why cannot right holders also be identifiable entities? This might, for example, take the form of a *class* of rights holders. We are all familiar with class actions on behalf of individuals belonging to an identifiable human group (for example, rate-payers, women, environ-mentalists, indigenous peoples, and so on). Moreover, in political discourse, we often hear of 'the right of self-determination' of political communities. So why can human environmental guardians not bring actions on behalf of an identifiable *class* of non-human beings, such as threatened populations or species?

However, the challenge of fashioning an ecocentric rights discourse increases exponentially as we move from a consideration of individual organisms, and classes of organisms, to systemic entities such as ecosystems. Although we have offered ecologically informed criteria for determining what beings or entities are 'ends-in-themselves' along with some general principles restraining human intervention in ecosystems, we encounter problems of boundary definition when it comes to delineating and ordering the rights of 'autopoietic entities'. That is, while it may be a relatively simple matter to identify individual organisms, populations and species, it is no easy matter to determine the boundaries of ecosystems or other collective entities *with the degree of precision that would be required for the purposes of rights ascription.* Indeed, identifying what is an entity for the purposes of assigning such rights is likely to be a very difficult, and ultimately, arbitrary exercise. Whatever autopoietic entity or ecosystem we choose (for example, a lake) it is likely to form part of a larger collectivity (for example, a larger watershed). Even in the unlikely event that we were to solve the boundary problem and develop a more precise and intricate hierarchy of individual and collective rights for the purposes of conflict adjudication, how might these rights be practically upheld or administered? How could we avoid excessive litigation or bureaucratic paralysis? As Norton [*1992: 81*] points out, 'As one expands the class of rights holders to larger and larger portions of nature, one necessarily increases the number of conflicts'.

In short, we have reached the limits of the rights discourse. Indeed, many ecocentric theorists have called into question the ascription of rights not only to natural entities, but also to non-humans in general. According to John Livingston [*1981: 62–3*], extending liberal egalitarian ideals to nonhumans merely 'anthropomorphises the non-human world in order to include it in a human ethical code'. John Rodman also suggests that it is subtly degrading to animals to include them within the human ethical code by analogy with 'defective humans' (that is, humans who are not competent moral agents). According to Rodman, the 'liberation of nature' requires not the extension of human-like rights to non-humans but the liberation of the non-human world from 'the status of human resource, human product, human caricature' [*Rodman, 1977: 101*]. Extending rights to non-humans entities is too strained and ungainly and (for Rodman) subtly degrading.

However, this ecocentric critique does not necessarily require the abandonment of the quest to adapt the institutions of liberal democracy to ensure more systematic environmental protection. Nor does it demand the total abandonment of the rights discourse. Rather, it requires a further elaboration of the circumstance in which rights ascription might be appropriate in a world of nested communities with soft and overlapping social and ecological boundaries. As we shall see, the ecologically inspired moral framework defended here both incorporates the rights discourse in human and human analogous cases while also transcending it.[13]

The Rights and Wrongs of Rights

We humans are connected to nature in many significant ways, but we also stand in a very special relationship to nature. Which of these connections and which of these discontinuties make a difference? In any discussion of connections and communities, '*Where we draw boundaries depends on the particular relationships we are interested in defining*' [*diZerega, 1992: 11*].

Drawing on the work of Midgley [*1983*], Callicott [*1988*], Wenz [*1988*], Benton [*1993*] and diZerega [*1992; 1993*], one might approach this problem by constructing a broad three-tiered framework of nested moral communities: the human community, the 'mixed community' (of humans and dependent animals brought within human social relations) and the 'biotic community'. We humans are part of all of these communities, yet we have different sets of responsibilities in each, *which derive from the different relationships that constitute each community*. For example, whereas 'predation' is injurious to a human political community, it is part of the fabric of ecological communities [*diZerega, 1992: 19*]. There is a significantly greater set of social (and in many cases, psychological) interdependencies between humans and captive and domestic animals than there is between humans and so-called 'wild' animals. Clarifying these relationships and associated moral responsibilities will help to determine which responsibilities might be appropriately discharged through legal rights and which might be appropriately discharged by other means.

In the human community, the extension of full *citizenship rights* to slaves, blacks and women was appropriate because they are all people who are capable of participating in political life. Following Benton, we can argue that the human entitlement to basic environmental conditions must also be postulated as a basic right existing *alongside* (rather than prior to or consequent upon) citizenship rights. Such basic rights not only enable individuals to realise their potential; they also enable political participation. That is, if we are to accord citizenship rights to all humans, then we must ensure that all humans have access to the social and environmental conditions that enable those rights to be exercised. As Benton [*1993: 182*] has explained, environmental rights would satisfy not only biophysical needs but also 'identity needs' – particularly in the case of indigenous peoples. A human environmental rights discourse would be able to take full advantage of the general protective, educational and transformational benefits of a rights discourse discussed earlier in this chapter. In particular, if human environmental rights were developed alongside a comprehensive set of social and environmental indicators intended to detect disparities in the enjoyment of such rights, disadvantaged social classes (and nations) would have a potent political argument for substantive socio-economic changes and wealth redistribution.

Unlike humans, non-human animals do not form part of the polity because they are incapable of political participation. Accordingly, it is inappropriate to apply notions of citizenship rights to non-humans. However, we may recognise a basic moral right. These rights take their character in the context of a different kind of community that is constituted by a different set of relationships.

In 'mixed communities' (of humans and other animals), the human moral obligation to ensure animal welfare arises because animals are beings whose ability to meet their own needs autonomously has been undermined by human practices [Benton, 1993: 212]. By creating a situation of dependency on the part of captive and domesticated animals, humans have a positive moral duty to such animals [Wenz, 1988: 151–2; 191]. Accordingly, such animals should possess a corresponding right to proper human care that is appropriate to the animals' particular bodily and social requirements.[14] Such rights could also take a political and legal form and would need to be enforced by human guardians (or maybe a specialised Animal Welfare Defender's Office) either as class actions or actions on behalf of particular animals.

Wild animals *primarily* belong not to the human community of citizens, nor to the 'mixed community' but rather to their own specific ecological communities, which are part of the biotic community. Unlike domestic and captive animals, *individual* wild animals are not *directly* dependent on humans for their well-being and sustenance. Accordingly, humans do not have the same direct moral obligation towards individual wild animals as they do towards captive and domesticated animals, and individual wild animals would not have the same kind of rights in relation to humans. Wenz [1988: 151–2; 191] has expressed these differences by arguing that whereas domesticated animals have positive rights in relation to humans, wild animals have merely 'negative rights' (that is, freedom from harm) in relation to humans. Communities of wild animals can be directly or indirectly harmed by human activities (such as land clearing, pollution or the introduction of exotic animals). Humans, as morally responsible members of the biotic community therefore have a generalised moral obligation to ensure that animal communities are not jeopardised by human activity. This human obligation to prevent harm to wild animal communities might be enforced by class actions. Such actions would need to be enforced by an independent institutional guardian to ensure that the interests of wild species are not jeopardised by human decisions.

One way of upholding this right to 'freedom from harm' might be to establish a well resourced, independent Environment Defender's Office as a statutory authority empowered to scrutinise the implementation of environmental legislation and instigate actions against governments, corporations and individuals in cases where biodiversity interests are infringed. The Environment Defender's Office could also act as a political advocate in public debates, supplementing the intitiatives of 'ecological citizens' [Christoff, 1996] and the campaign work of community environmental organisations.

The broadening of legal standing rules for individuals and community environment groups would also serve to complement the activities of the Environment Defender's Office. Ecological citizens could be empowered to bring actions not only to enforce their own environmental rights[15] but also to bring actions as guardians on behalf of non-human species. Legal aid would need to be extended to concerned individuals and community organisations to enable them to exercise their rights and responsibilties as 'good ecological citizens'.

However, when we turn to the remaining constituents of the biotic community, we find that the rights discourse becomes considerably strained and unworkable, morally, politically and legally. The attempt to ascribe rights not only creates unfathomable problems of boundary definition; it also demands a degree of precision that cannot be delivered on the basis of our limited understanding of essentially open-ended and highly contingent biological and ecological processes. Accordingly, the human obligation to ensure ecological sustainability, which the human community owes to itself and to the broader biotic community, would be best discharged through the systematic application of the precautionary principle and more general sustainability planning. Such planning would be facilitated by developing more deliberative forms of democracy, improving citizen access to environmental information, and encouraging the direct involvement of the community in environmental problem solving and monitoring.

Conclusion

This contribution has sought to extend the current debates about green democracy in two ways. First, it has suggested how green values might be connected to democratic theory in principle (rather than merely instrumentally) by way of an extension of the liberal rights discourse and the liberal principle of autonomy. Second, it has suggested some possible ways in which the interests of non-human beings might be incorporated into the ground rules of democracy. In both cases, liberal regulative ideals and institutions (autonomy and rights) as well as liberal forms of argument have been enlisted in an attempt to conduct an 'immanent ecological critique' of liberal democracy.

The exercise has been insightful in a number of respects. The move from 'autonomy' to 'rights' to an 'ecologically grounded democracy' encountered a number of hazards, not all of which can been successfully negotiated owing to the individualistic premises of the rights discourse. However, there is considerable scope for greens to argue for rights in human and human analogous cases, both on behalf of individuals or as class actions on behalf of particular non-human populations and species. Here rights can serve the 'treble duty', moral, political and legal. However, the rights discourse becomes considerably strained (in all its dimensions) when we come to consider ecological entities. Although the general principle of autonomy can stretch to accommodate this new class of constituents, the rights discourse cannot. None the less, we have sketched an ethical basis for setting ecological parameters on the exercise of both human rights and animal rights. This contribution has sought to highlight some of the possibilities and limitations in enlisting the regulative ideals and institutions of liberal democracy in pursuing green campaigns. There is no doubt that the likely proponents of ecocentric democracy – the local, national and international environment movement, green parties, and some members of knowledge-based communities such as scientists and bureaucrats – will face stiff opposition. However, the extension and development of familiar regulative ideals and institutions may possibly pave the way for more far-reaching reforms.

NOTES

1. As Miller [*1992: 54*] points out, the relationship between the *institutions* of liberal democracy and the *regulative ideals* of liberal democracy is by no means straightforward. For example, the same set of institutions may be justified according to different regulative ideals and the same regulative ideals may be implemented by different institutions. These regulative ideals may be traced to different strands of liberal theory, such as utilitarianism, the classical social contract theories or the broader deontological or liberal rights tradition. However, many of these regulative ideals have also been critically reinterpreted by social democratic, socialist, feminist, and more recently, green theorists. None the less, despite the growth of the welfare state, the present 'Western' *system* of governance is still more usually described as *liberal* democratic rather than *social* democratic because it is intended, in theory at least, to prevent despotism and the abuse of power in order to secure the liberty of the subject. For the purposes of discussion, I will employ a slightly embellished version of

Beetham's [1992] useful characterisation of liberal democracy as a benchmark. This characterisation is set forth in the Appendix.

2. Although the focus will be on non-humans, the case for environmental rights for humans will be briefly discussed.

3. Mill reacted against what he saw to be the crude utilitarian view of the individual as a mere consumer or bundle of appetites. According to Macpherson [1973: 5] this reaction revived older elements of the humanist tradition which saw humans as rational, purposive beings. Mill argued that a liberal democratic government should be concerned with enabling individuals to develop their own special human attributes, their own forms of excellence – in short, their individuality.

4. Kant, of course, maintained that only humans were ends-in- themselves [Pybus and Broadie, 1978]. Ecocentric theorists, as we shall see, argue that there is no good reason for such a restrictive moral premise.

5. Although Miller's discussion of deliberative democracy does not specifically address green democracy, his discussion of generalisable interests has a clear application to environmental problems.

6. For a discussion of some of these misunderstandings, see Eckersley [1992: Ch.3].

7. The International Covenants, both passed by the United Nations in 1966, are the International Covenant on Civil and Political Rights and the International Covenant on Economic, Social and Cultural Rights, both of which place international legal obligations on those countries that ratify the covenants.

8. Singer's defence of animal liberation has been equally influential, although Singer employs the language of rights merely as a rhetorical device. His theory is grounded in the utilitarian tradition rather than the deontological tradition. Nonetheless, other animal rights theorists have used Singer's criterion of sentience as the basis for ascribing moral, and in some cases legal, rights.

9. Stone's discussion primarily addresses the political and legal dimensions of protecting nonhuman natural entities; he does not argue the moral case for rights [cf. Stone, 1987]. None the less, his discussion proceeds on the basis of an implied environmental ethic (discussed further below). More recently, Stone has explicitly rejected the idea that legal recognition must necessarily be in the form of legal rights, or that legal rights must necessarily be connected to moral rights. Recognising something as a 'legal person' is merely a convenient fiction which enables the law to provide protection [Stone, 1987: 43].

10. For a discussion of this case, see Stone [1974: Part II].

11. For an extended critical review essay of Benton's contribution, see Eckersley [1994].

12. For a fuller discussion of this relational ontology, see Birch and Cobb [1981]; Mathews [1991]; and Eckersley [1992: Ch.3].

13. Considered on its own, Regan's case for animal rights would certainly provide a strong basis for the protection of domestic and captive animals from human cruelty and maltreatment. Indeed, these kinds of harm (stemming from such practices as vivisection and factory farming) have been the major preoccupation of animal rights theorists. Animal rights theory can also deal with the problem of habitat destruction of domestic or 'wild' mammalian species when it can be shown that such animals are likely to be harmed from a failure on the part of humans to take steps to protect habitat. Those who apply broader moral criteria for animal rights, such as sentience or self-consciousness, would be able to cast the net much wider in terms of the range of habitats that might be protected. Even here, however, a point might be reached where the relationship between animal suffering and habitat destruction becomes contingent [Norton, 1992: 83] For example, animals could be relocated to new, 'designer' habitats or 'free range' zoos – a move that would offend most ecocentric environmentalists.

14. Although Benton concedes that positive rights may serve a useful protective function for domesticated animals brought within human social relations, he nonetheless concludes, contrary to my argument, that they should be treated merely as 'moral patients', without corresponding rights [Benton, 1993: 212].

15. For example, the Michigan Environmental Protection Act confers on citizens a substantive right to sue to prevent significant environmental harm and even challenge the adequacy of

environmental standards applied by government agencies [*Sax and Dimento, 1974*].

REFERENCES

Beetham, D. (1992), 'Liberal Democracy and the Limits of Democratisation', *Political Studies*, 40 (Special Issue), pp.40–53.
Benton, T. (1993), *Natural Relations: Ecology, Animal Rights and Social Justice*, London: Verso.
Birch, C. and J. Cobb, Jr. (1981), *The Liberation of Life*, Cambridge: Cambridge University Press.
Callicott, J. Baird (1980), 'Animal Liberation: A Triangular Affair', *Environmental Ethics* 2, pp.311–338.
Callicott, J. Baird (1988), 'Animal Liberation and Environmental Ethics: Back Together Again', *Between the Species* 5, pp.163–69 (also reprinted in Hargrove).
Christoff, P. (1996), 'Ecological Citizens and Ecologically Guided Democracy', in B. Doherty, and M. de Gues, (eds.), *Democracy and Green Politics*, London: Routledge.
diZerega, G. (1992), 'Individuality, Community and the Foundation for Ethics: The Contemporary Relevance of Native American Insights', unpublished MS.
diZerega, G. (1993), 'Deep Ecology Meets the Market: Empathy and the Relational Self', paper presented to the Libertarian Party Convention, Salt Lake City, Utah, Sept.
Dryzek, J. (1987), *Rational Ecology: Environment and Political Economy*, Oxford: Blackwell.
Dryzek, J. (1992), 'Ecology and Discursive Democracy: Beyond Liberal Capitalism and the Administrative State', *Capitalism, Nature, Socialism*, Vol.3, No.2, pp.18–42.
Eckersley, R. (1992), *Environmentalism and Political Theory: Toward an Ecocentric Approach*, London: UCL Press.
Eckersley, R. (1994), 'Natural Justice: From Abstract Rights to Contextualised Needs', review essay of Ted Benton, *Natural Relations: Ecology, Animal Rights and Social Justice*, *Environmental Values*, Vol.3, No.2, pp.161–72.
Foreman, D. (1991), *Confessions of an Eco-Warrior*, Boston: Harmony Books.
Fox, W. (1990), *Toward a Transpersonal Ecology: Developing New Foundations for Environmentalism*, Boston, MA: Shambhala.
Goodin, R. (1992), *Green Political Theory*, Cambridge: Polity Press.
Hardin, G. (1972), *Exploring New Ethics for Survival: The Voyage of the Spaceship Beagle*, New York: Viking.
Hargrove, E. (ed.) (1992), *The Animal Rights/Environmental Ethics Debate: The Environmental Perspective*, Albany, NY: State University of New York Press.
Heilbroner, R. (1974), *An Inquiry into the Human Prospect*, New York: Norton.
Held, D. (1992), 'Democracy: From City-state to a Cosmopolitan Order?' *Political Studies*, Vol.40 (Special Issue), pp.10–39.
Jänicke, M. (1990), *State Failure: The Impotence of Politics in Industrial Society* (translated by Alan Braley), Cambridge: Polity Press.
Leopold, A. (1949), *A Sand County Almanac*, Oxford: Oxford University Press.
Lindblom, C. (1965), *The Intelligence of Democracy: Decision Making Through Mutual Adjustment*, New York: Free Press
List, P. (1993), *Radical Environmentalism: Philosophy and Tactics*, Belmont, CA: Wadsworth Publishing Co.
Livingston, J. (1981), *The Fallacy of Wildlife Conservation*, Toronto: McClelland & Stewart.
Macpherson, C.B. (1973), *Democratic Theory: Essays in Retrieval*, Oxford: Clarendon Press.
Mathews, F. (1991), *The Ecological Self*, London: Routledge.
Midgley, M. (1983), *Animals and Why They Matter*, Athens: University of Georgia Press.
Miller, D. (1992), 'Deliberative Democracy and Social Choice', *Political Studies*, Vol.40 (Special Issue), pp.54–67.
Naess, A. (1989), *Ecology, Community and Lifestyle* (translated by David Rothenberg), Cambridge: Cambridge University Press.
Nash, R. (1990), *The Rights of Nature*, Leichhardt, NSW: Primavera Press.
Norton, B. (1991), *Toward Unity Among Environmentalists*, New York: Oxford University Press.

Norton, B. (1992), 'Environmental Ethics and Nonhuman Rights', in E. Hargrove (ed.), *The Animal Rights/Environmental Ethics Debate: The Environmental Perspective*, Albany, NY: State University of New York Press, pp. 71-94.

O'Neill, J. (1993), *Ecology, Policy and Politics*, London: Routledge.

Ophuls, W. (1973), 'Leviathan or Oblivion?', in H. Daly (ed.), *Toward a Steady State Economy*, San Francisco, CA: Freeman, pp.215-30.

Ophuls, W. (1977), *Ecology and the Politics of Scarcity: A Prologue to the Political Theory of the Steady State*, San Francisco, CA: Freeman.

Paehlke, R. (1988), 'Democracy, Bureaucracy, and Environmentalism', *Environmental Ethics*, Vol.10, No.4, pp.291-308.

Pearce, D., Markandya, A. and E. Barbier (1989), *Blueprint for a Green Economy*, London: Earthscan.

Pybus, E. and Broadie, A. (1978), 'Kant and the Maltreatment of Animals', *Philosophy* 53, pp.560-61.

Rees, W.L. (1980), *Dictionary of Philosophy and Religion: Eastern and Western Thought*, Atlantic Highlands, NJ: Humanities Press.

Regan, T. (1983), *The Case for Animal Rights*, Berkeley, CA: University of California Press.

Regan, T. (1985), 'The Case for Animal Rights', in P. Singer (ed), *In Defence of Animals*, Oxford: Blackwell, pp.13-26.

Rodman, J. (1977), 'The Liberation of Nature?', *Inquiry* 20, pp.83-145.

Rodman, J. (1980), 'Paradigm Change in Political Science: An Ecological Perspective', *American Behavioral Scientist*, 24, pp.49-78.

Sagoff, M. (1993), 'Animal Liberation, Environmental Ethics: Bad Marriage, Quick Divorce' in M. Zimmerman *et al.* (eds.), *Environmental Philosophy: From Animal Rights to Radical Ecology*, Englewood Cliffs, NJ: Prentice Hall.

Saward, M. (1993), 'Green Democracy?' in Andrew Dobson and Paul Lucardie (eds.) *The Politics of Nature: Explorations in Green Political Thought*, London: Routledge.

Sax J. and J.F. Dimento, (1974), 'Environmental Citizens Suits: Three Years' Experience Under the Michigan Environmental Protection Act', *Ecology Law Quarterly*, Vol.4, No.1.

Singer, P. (1975), *Animal Liberation*, New York: Avon Books.

Singer, P. (1993), *Practical Ethics – Second Edition*, Cambridge: Cambridge University Press.

Stammer, N. (1993), 'Human Rights and Power', *Political Studies*, 41, pp.70-82.

Stone, C. (1974), *Should Trees Have Standing?: Toward Legal Rights for Natural Objects*, Los Altos, CA: William Kaufmann.

Stone, C. (1987), *Earth and Other Ethics: The Case for Moral Pluralism*, New York: Harper & Row.

Tribe, L. (1974), 'From Environmental Foundations to Constitutional Structures: Learning from Nature's Future', *Yale Law Journal*, 84, p.545.

Wenz, P. (1988), *Environmental Justice*, Albany, NY: State University of New York Press.

APPENDIX A

Beetham's characterisation of liberal democracy singles out those components of liberalism that are seen to be indispensable to liberal democracy at the level of the nation state. According to Beetham [*1992: 41-42*], the indispensable components of liberal democracy are:

(1) The protection of individual rights to freedom of expression, movement, and association along with other rights which are necessary to secure popular control over elected representatives (such as the right to vote).

(2) The institutional separation of powers between the legislative, executive and judicial branches of government and the maintenance of due process and the 'rule of law'.

(3) A popularly elected representative assembly (or federation of assemblies) having power to make laws with respect to a defined territory.

(4) The idea of a limited state and some degree of separation between the 'public' and the 'private' spheres of life.

(5) The 'epistemological premise' that there is no superior knowledge or ultimate truth concerning the public good. It is up to citizens, and their elected representatives, to decide for themselves the meaning of the public good. The institutions of liberal democracy should be procedurally neutral and should be able to accommodate a diversity of opinion.

'Monkeywrenching' and the Processes of Democracy

ROBERT YOUNG

The practice by radical environmentalists of 'monkeywrenching' – deliberately interfering with industrial and commercial activities that are judged to be destructive of the natural environment – has been claimed by critics to be a form of ecological terrorism. Despite there being some features in common between monkeywrenching and terrorism it is misleading to see the one as a form of the other. Rather, monkeywrenching is far more accurately represented as a form of civil disobedience. That being so, it is important to consider whether, in the Western societies where it is practised, it is consistent even with the prevailing rather weak understanding of democracy. I argue that it is and, indeed, that its selective use may serve to strengthen the democratic process in polities where acts of civil disobedience are seen not as thuggery against the rule of law but as directing our attention to the need for reform of particular laws and related social practices.

It is a commonplace that the scale and complexity of modern societies make for difficulties in the realisation of the classical understanding of democracy as participation on an equal footing with other citizens in collective decision-making. The invention of institutions of representation is best seen as a direct response to the problems posed by mass society for the classical form of democracy. Parliamentary and congressional forms of democracy are the most familiar institutional expressions for us of the idea of democracy, but they are in important ways much weaker forms of democracy than the classical conception. While these forms have enabled the solving of some of the problems inherent in involving citizens of complex societies in the decision-making process, they are incapable of facilitating equality in collective decision-making. There are several reasons why this is so.

First, the device of representation puts a gulf between those who are

Robert Young teaches in the School of Philosophy, La Trobe University, Australia. Thanks are due to members of the Democracy and Environment Group and to an anonymous referee for helpful comments on an earlier version of this contribution.

supposedly the ultimate holders of power (the community as a whole) and those who exercise it on the community's behalf. This gulf has widened further, as political representation has become a professional career (so that the very livelihood of representatives turns on their being re-elected), and as insistence on individual representatives being subject to party discipline has been elevated above independence of thought and action. Second, various interest groups within societies have concluded that to protect their sectional interests they must make use of the extra-parliamentary power they possess to ensure that parliamentary representatives do not take decisions that unduly threaten those interests. This is particularly the case for the media and large corporations, the trade union movement and professional bodies, but also, in some societies at least, for religious and other special interest groups. Lobbying by these groups gives them a much greater say in the decision-making process than is the case for individuals or less influential groups. Third, while we know that democratic structures, even in the weaker, representative mode, are more stable and work more effectively where there is relative economic independence, a history of peaceful evolution of social institutions, tolerance of differing views and a significant degree of consensus about values and social goals, it is also clear that the emergence in recent times of plural and diverse conceptions of life has made the achievement of consensus far harder.

This last point is of special concern in the present context. Though there has been a growing popular appreciation of the importance of protecting the natural environment, there certainly is no consensus about affording it the sort of protection that many environmental activists would wish. One consequence of this has been to pose the problem for such activists of whether it is best to work for their values through the parliamentary mechanisms, to work for them in extra-parliamentary ways, or to endeavour to promote their cause through some combination of these.

The history of seeking to achieve environmental protection exclusively through the first means is not encouraging. Single-issue representatives have commonly been marginalised by those whose constituency is more broadly based. Whenever other issues than the single one of the environment and its protection are perceived to be more pressing, as when economic concerns dominate in times of economic downturn or high inflation, representatives elected on behalf of a single-issue are easily rendered ineffective. Since the single issue representative is likely to believe if not in the paramount importance of the interest being represented, at least in its great significance, this is apt to be an especially galling outcome.

Even when environmentalists choose to exert whatever influence they can through extra-parliamentary rather than parliamentary means, there are going to be times when they will be unable to obtain a good hearing. Faced with an unresponsive community or unresponsive institutions of representation, and given their conviction about the high stakes being played for, some activists have found it necessary to raise the stakes. The result has been that in recent years a number of environmentalists have resorted to radical forms of political action and have, in turn, been accused of engaging in ecological terrorism ('ecoterrorism'). The accusation stems from the ways in which they have responded to what they consider to be violence being done to the natural environment. Their responses have included actions aimed at stopping or seriously hindering timber cutting, oil and gas exploration, mining, various sorts of construction work, the use of off-road vehicles, trapping, whaling, off-shore fishing and so forth.

In this contribution I will first consider whether these actions are accurately to be characterised as 'terrorism', for in that case they would properly be thought of as involving a rejection of democratic processes. I will argue that, in fact, they are not acts of terrorism and should rather be thought of as acts of civil disobedience. I will go on to argue that not only can such acts, under appropriately specified circumstances, be morally justified, but that they are consistent with democratic principles. Indeed, I shall argue, they can be seen as strengthening the very processes of democracy.

'Monkeywrenching' as Civil Disobedience, not Terrorism

To make a proper classification and assessment of the kinds of action that have provoked the accusation of ecoterrorism, it will be necessary to have before us a more complete account of the offending actions and an analysis of the nature of terrorism.

Radical environmentalists have pulled up forest survey stakes, 'spiked' trees[1] due to be logged, destroyed machines such as bulldozers, rendered dirt roads in wilderness areas impassable to vehicles, destroyed trap lines, sabotaged power lines and burned property, all with a view to blocking environmentally destructive projects or making them so expensive as to be economically unattractive.[2] According to their radical environmentalist practitioners, these acts are best characterised as 'monkeywrenching'. They throw a large spanner into the works of those engaged in activities that are severely detrimental to the natural environment. They are thus a means of resisting the destruction of natural diversity and wilderness areas. Exponents of these means are adamant that their targets are only ever inanimate things and that great care is taken to ensure that no living things come to any harm (since to violate this requirement would be incompatible with the adoption of a biocentric perspective). They profess no revolutionary goals, only a concern to defend the environment. In response to the charge that monkeywrenching, especially tree spiking, poses serious risks of injury to people (such as timber workers) and is accordingly properly to be spoken of as ecoterrorism, radical environmentalists claim that no act of monkeywrenching by them has been documented to have caused injury.[3]

Of course, we cannot just accept the say-so of these environmentalists that they are not (ecological) terrorists. To help us make our own assessment we will need before us an account of what makes something an instance of terrorism.

Notoriously, 'terrorism' is a term that suffers from indeterminacy because of its use for partisan purposes. Thus what the 'baddies' do is called terrorism while what the 'goodies' do is never so described. None the less, in my view it is possible to set aside this difficulty, for if we focus on what are indisputably terrorist actions a clear enough idea for our purposes will emerge as to what terrorism is.[4] First, and fairly obviously, terrorist actions are expressions of a particular political view and so can properly be described as political actions. Second, terrorist actions are violent political actions. Generally the violence is physical and is directed towards persons (or quasi-persons such as the state) or their property, but it may also be psychological. This links with a third point to be made, namely that it is commonly, if not always, the intention of those who carry out terrorist actions to generate or maintain a state of terror. Fourth, since terrorist actions are not the preserve of revolutionary groups alone but may be engaged in by states as well, the conclusion to be drawn is that terrorism is not something typically carried out by isolated individuals but is a form of organised political action. Fifth, though some contend that terrorism is violent political activity carried out by organised groups which is targeted only at the innocent or those with non-combatant status (or their property) [*Coady, 1985: 54f*], it is surely more reflective of the facts to see terrorism as not being restricted in this way. Violence aimed at army personnel or their barracks, or at police engaged in the guarding of political figures or state property can certainly constitute terrorism. It is quite implausible to regard such individuals as having non-combatant status in order to save the theoretical claim. Similarly, where a state systematically employs violence against members of groups who oppose it, it would be foolish to claim that the state's actions could not possibly be terroristic because its opponents are neither innocents nor combatants. Finally, while it is often said that terrorism involves the indiscriminate use of violence, this is, in fact, misleading. Often terrorist targets are non-specific as, for example, when a terrorist group is chiefly concerned to establish an atmosphere of terror. But to conclude from this, as those who make the charge do, that terrorist actions are characteristically acts of uncontrolled violence, would be to make a serious mistake. Quite apart from the consideration that, in the sort of circumstances mentioned, warnings will typically have been given, terrorism for the most part is aimed at specific targets and so, in the relevant sense, can be said to be very discriminating.

These points are, I believe, sufficient to characterise the nature of terrorism. However, there are cases of terrorism (especially of the revolutionary variety) that have features of a contingent kind and these should be noted in passing. These features are also more often than not present in cases of monkeywrenching and so may influence the answers that people give to the question of whether acts of monkeywrenching are acts of (ecological) terrorism. What I have in mind are features such as the cloak of secrecy under which most acts of terrorism are carried out, and the lack of conventional political power of those (other than states) who carry out terrorist acts. Terrorist activities typically require co-operation with other conspirators and the keeping of confidences prior to the deed being done. The sharing of a particular ideology is generally sufficient for providing and maintaining the attendant cloak of secrecy – without the concealment this provides, operatives would find it much harder to avoid detection let alone to terrorise. Monkeywrenchers, too, act in secret though they are more likely to engage in their clandestine acts of sabotage as lone individuals. In each case it would seem that it is the relative political weakness, occasioned by being isolated from conventional political power, that drives the respective practitioners to don the cloak of secrecy.

Though these latter two features are, I have suggested, only contingently connected with terrorism it is not without plausibility to think that their presence in instances of monkeywrenching has influenced some people's opinion that monkeywrenching is nothing but terrorism. In both cases we have acts of political violence carried out through subterfuge by people who have been unable to achieve their political goals through conventional political means. In such circumstances opponents of those radical environmentalists who engage in monkeywrenching have found it easy to point an accusing finger at them and to claim that they are terrorists by any other name. The first question for us to answer is: are they right to point such an accusing finger?

My contention is that they are not. To begin with, acts of tree spiking, of destroying mechanical equipment, of plugging up factory outlets such as smokestacks and drains, and so forth, cannot with any plausibility be regarded as directed at the generation or maintenance of a state of terror (which I have claimed is commonly, if not always, a feature of terrorist actions). Consider the action of spiking trees in old-growth forests, the action which has led to most of the uproar over alleged ecoterrorism. Tree spiking is supposed to have nuisance value or to be an impediment to ordinary commerce. It is accompanied by warnings and is done in the knowledge that milling companies nowadays routinely use metal detectors to locate spikes. Moreover, as long as milling companies properly maintain their band saws no injury to workers is likely to happen. So, despite the indeterminacy involved in the use of the term 'terrorism', it would be misleading in the extreme to think of tree spiking as terrorism, rather than as, at worst, vandalism or sabotage. We are a long way along the spectrum of violent political acts from, say, the violent attacks on people and, to a lesser extent, their property, of the IRA or the UDA in Northern Ireland and England. If this is so for tree spiking it is even more obviously so for the other forms of monkeywrenching which I have mentioned.

But it may be replied that this is too hasty. After all, have not many radical environmentalists been more than happy to adopt the language of warfare in their defences of monkeywrenching? Witness, for example, the way they tend to think of themselves as 'eco-warriors'. If there really is a 'war' going on concerning the environment, would it not be quite reasonable to think of some of the more extreme, guerrilla-style actions as terroristic? After all, do not the IRA and the UDA think of themselves as conducting a guerrilla war, too?

The fact that some eco-warriors see themselves as engaged in a last resort guerrilla-style defence of the natural environment does not, however, show them to be terrorists. Not all acts of political violence done as a matter of last resort are acts of terrorism. If they were, then the violent destruction of a sacred object by religious believers who prefer the destruction of such an object to its capture by infidels would (implausibly) be a terrorist act.

But there is a deeper point to be made. It was noted above that monkeywrenchers are committed by their beliefs to the preservation of life forms (and, even for the most misanthropic among them that presumably includes human life). It may seem, then, that, just like terrorists, monkeywrenchers are standing up for their political beliefs and prepared to use violence, albeit more selectively, in the process. So, notwithstanding the fact that they confine themselves to attacking inanimate things, are not the critics right to suggest that, for all relevant purposes, monkeywrenching is morally indistinguishable from terrorism? The answer still seems to me to be 'no'. The reason is as follows. Even if monkeywrenching, like at least some acts of terrorism, is understood as a means of defence (whether of the 'ecological self' or on behalf of an ecosphere that is ultimately a defenceless innocent), it does not follow that there is no distinction between the two kinds of political activity. Not every act of self-defence or, as some would say, 'counter-force' [*Goodin, 1992: 133ff*], is properly to be regarded as an act of terrorism. So even if we take the rhetoric of the eco-warriors at face value, their acts of guerrilla warfare do not automatically count as acts of terrorism.

That still leaves us, of course, with the question of how we should classify the behaviour of monkeywrenchers. I suggest that the sabotage carried out by monkeywrenchers is most accurately thought of as being continuous with civil disobedience. I do not doubt that there may be some radical environmentalists and even some animal liberationists who practise monkeywrenching who would put their hands up if asked whether they were terrorists.[5] Radicals of this ilk may think it impossible to protect the natural environment or captive animals without a revolutionary attack being directed against what they consider is a destructive social and political system. But they are by no means representative, or even typical, of the radical environmentalist movement. Not only do most of those who consider themselves to be part of the movement repudiate such revolutionary goals, but some practitioners of monkeywrenching have in recent times questioned the tactical value of those forms of monkey-wrenching that create even quite remote hazards for others, particularly tree spiking [*Manes, 1990: 177ff; Scarce, 1990: 266; Foreman, 1991: 158ff, 167ff*]. (It should be said, though, that many mainstream environmentalists have claimed that their very moderation has come to be seen in a favourable light by those offended by the activities of more radical environmentalists, and so to have resulted in their obtaining a better hearing than they otherwise would. No doubt they would nevertheless prefer to see such activities cease even given the resultant loss in advantage to their own position.) It is true that part of the reason for the rethinking has been the concern of monkeywrenchers over the violence of the responses to the threat of tree spiking made by those working for forest service and commercial organisations [*Foreman, 1991: 125ff*]. But the main cause for the questioning of monkeywrenching would appear to be a wish not to engage in activities with the potential to harm others, for fear that that would move environmental protest along the spectrum of political activism in the direction of out-and-out terrorism. Were that to happen it would become extremely difficult to defend such activism as being demanded by the need to defend biocentric rights while also acknowledging the importance of other civil rights.

Suppose I am right that most radical environmentalists see themselves as in the business of trying to get the wider public to acknowledge the need for an expansion in the boundaries of the ethical (and legal) community. Does that help make sense of their more extreme activities, such as monkeywrenching? I think the answer is that it does. The best parallels to the kinds of civil disobedience in which present day environmental activists are engaged are acts like those committed in defiance of the Fugitive Slave Laws in the nineteenth century in the United States, those carried out by resistance movements during the Second World War and those that were directed against the apartheid laws in South Africa during their heyday.

As with these earlier cases, monkeywrenching is clandestine in order that its practitioners can escape being detected and captured by the legal authorities. It is true that many of its practitioners have emphasised the *civility* of civil disobedience, so that those, for example, who engaged in civil disobedience during the civil rights protests of the suffragettes, and the protests against racism in the United States and Australia in the 1960s, commonly offered only passive resistance, preferring to be arrested and subsequently punished. It is also true that clandestine acts against morally objectionable practices are most easily justified when they are resorted to in a context of vicious (state) repression. None the less, as the examples I gave above make clear, it is not a necessary condition for an act's being one of civil disobedience that its perpetrator be willing to be punished [*Schochet, 1972*]. Nor is the use of violence precluded in acts of civil disobedience (despite the claim of those who insist on the need for civility in such acts).

Some of those who, in the recent past, have practised civil disobedience have so abhorred violence that they have been meticulous in insisting on civil disobedience being non-violent protest. Within the green movement the examples of Gandhi and Martin Luther King have often been pointed to as models of passive or non-violent resistance. Indeed the West German Green Party included in its policy platform a statement about its commitment to non-violent forms of resistance. However, many of the party's members took the principle of direct non-violent action to exclude all violence against sentient creatures, but not to rule out damage to property [*Langguth, 1986: 78ff*]. Such a view is not uncommon in green groups where opposition to violence (at least against property) has been for tactical rather than principled reasons so as to ensure that attention is not drawn away from the focus of protest.

In short, it is a mistake to think that civil disobedience is *essentially* a non-violent form of protest. Sometimes the use of violence serves to highlight an injustice in a way that no other form of protest can match. Sometimes the violence may be an inescapable means to the resistance of an injustice or a rights violation (especially where tyranny reigns). And sometimes, as has been pointed out by protesters who have resorted to violence, including some radical environmentalists, it is not until there is violent protest that any meaningful response to wrongs is likely to be made in many a society.[6]

It is considerations like these which lend support to the claim that acts of civil disobedience (including clandestine ones) can actually enhance democratic processes. Where protesters are at a disadvantage as regards participating on an equal footing with other citizens in collective decision-making (because they lack adequate and equal opportunities not merely to express their views but to have them listened to, or because they would be subject to sanctions whose very application contributes to the stymieing of open debate), or where public discussion is hindered because the dominant sources of information are unreliable or inadequate, protest can be a stimulus to greater democracy. Indeed, in the quite recent past, protest in several countries against involvement in the war in Indo-China led to greater citizen participation in decision-making about that involvement and, ultimately, to changes in policy. Not all of the protests were carried out openly and not all were non-violent. Some protesters were willing to be punished because they saw that as a way of achieving publicity for their cause, others thought it tactically more effective to wage their campaign of sabotage from the underground.

So neither the secrecy that surrounds some acts of monkeywrenching, nor the fact that they involve violence, shows that it is incorrect to think of such protest as a form of civil disobedience. The presence of these features, and especially that of the violence, does, however, point up the importance of providing a moral justification for such political acts. The next section of this study will be devoted to examining whether such a justification can be found. I will proceed by way of a consideration of various objections which have been levelled at monkeywrenching. My conclusion will be that there can be no blanket rejection of the practice.

Breaking the Law to Facilitate the Democratic Process

A recurring theme among critics of monkeywrenching is that breaking the law is wrong and, therefore, that acts of sabotage by radical environmentalists which involve breaking the law are wrong. Unfortunately, this claim is too sweeping to be plausible. There is a prima-facie obligation to obey the law within a reasonably democratically governed community. Indeed it is probably correct to go further and say that the onus is on those who break the law in such a community to justify their actions. But that onus can certainly be discharged should the law be broken to uphold a more important value. The breaking of laws against assisting fugitive slaves in the nineteenth century in the United States, the breaking of apartheid laws and the breaking of laws requiring contributions to immoral causes such as unjust wars are cases in point.

The critical issue, given this approach to justification, is whether the values upheld in protecting old growth forests from being logged, or in saving wilderness areas, or in protecting environmental diversity, outweigh the prima-facie obligation to obey laws protecting property such as machines, survey markers, roads and the like. That is a matter which is unlikely to be resolved in isolation from other objections, despite the confidence of radical environmentalists about the order of precedence. So, for the time being, judgment must be reserved on the availability of such a justification.

There are, of course, other ways in which to try to justify the civil disobedience which I have argued provides the best way of understanding the political activism engaged in by monkeywrenchers. In particular, there is a longstanding tradition of seeing civil disobedience as about raising the consciousness of a democratic polity, or, put slightly differently, as a way of changing the political discourse accepted within a particular democracy. Here the focus is less on the particular actions taken by protesters (and so their justification), and more on how effective protest is in getting the community to think anew about the issue in question. If monkeywrenching is seen in this light it is probably best considered as a way of dramatising the issues surrounding protection of the ecosphere. Indeed, many ecological protesters would contend that because of the typecasting of the issues, and the stage managing in the media of much of the debate, anything short of such dramatisation would fail to get the attention of the public. Until people's attention is grabbed there can, of course, be no conversation with them. From the point of view of the ecological protester, then, the resort to civil disobedience may be seen as a necessary means to educating the public and so of helping make the democratic structures effective. There remains the question, however, of the place of violence in such a conception. Here a protester might respond that a strategic resort to violence against replaceable property is defensible when those with something important to say are unable to command attention in the democratic forums and so have to take measures born out of desperation. If powerful forces such as the public media have shut out alternative voices it may be necessary for protesters to try to get the attention of the public in the most dramatic way open to them.

Whatever the merits that some protesters will find in the justification for ecological civil disobedience that I have just rehearsed, there will be others who will consider it a sell-out. I have in mind those who claim that monkeywrenching is not an attempt to persuade but an expression of moral outrage at what they see as a concerted attack on the ecosphere. Those who take such a view are usually pessimistic about democracy (especially in its liberal, parliamentary forms) being a helpful means to the protection of the ecosphere. While it is likely that those who adopt this sort of stance would align themselves with a position that I outlined earlier – that there are more important values to uphold than respect for the law – they might well consider such talk to be too concerned with ranking values in terms of consequences in the external world. They would instead see the matter as having to do with the maintenance of their own integrity, just as Martin

Luther did when he declared that, from where he stood, he could 'do no other' [*Luther, 1958: 109–13*].

Now that we have before us these sketches of the ways in which civil disobedience (including monkeywrenching) might be defended, we can better consider other objections that have been urged against monkey-wrenching.

According to some, the destruction of property is a wrong that could not be outweighed by the values monkeywrenchers aspire to defend. Even staunch environmentalists have condemned the tactic on this ground [*Manes, 1990: 181ff*].

Radical environmentalists are able to make an obvious response: surely it is a mistake of major significance to value more highly a bulldozer or some marker pegs (or whatever other piece of replaceable property is the target of the monkeywrenching), than an intact ecosystem which provides support for a community of plants, insects and animals? Of course, when property is damaged it is not just that damage that we need to consider. We also have to take into account the impact on the interests of the owners of the property (and related indirect effects on the interests of those whose employment may be affected). So a more accurate statement of the choice is that it is between the evil of ecological destruction or damage and the evil of violence against inanimate objects, the latter evil commonly issuing in either or both direct and indirect effects on human interests.

Some will see this as not a real choice because they consider it to be between incommensurable values. I am not persuaded that they are right to do so. It is true that many radical environmentalists think of wilderness areas and old growth forests for which they fight as like sacred objects, and hence that the destruction of such things is abhorrent. Their moral outrage at the suggestion of a trade-off makes them adamant that there can be no compromises because there can be no replication of nature's original once it is destroyed [*Elliot, 1982*]. We have already observed that for these environmentalists there can be no truck with those whom they see as having corrupt values.

Perhaps more typically, though, many radical environmentalists see the natural environment as merely an extension of the social community and so urge that it is as entitled to respect as the human component of that community. From this point of view, destruction and disturbance have to be justified by reference to how necessary they are to satisfy vital interests. The mere fact that humans have certain interests does not, of itself, make them *vital* interests so they have no automatic precedence.

This point of view is decidedly different from one which sees the environment as a sacred object. More importantly, it is possible for there to be a *rapprochement* between those with this more typical radical outlook and those who oppose monkeywrenching because of its effects on human interests. What I have in mind is to emphasise the points of contact (rather than of disagreement) between these differing outlooks with a view to making use of democratic processes to resolve the disagreements. In particular, there is good reason to think that agreement can be reached in democratic polities that many present day forest projects do not serve vital human interests and so can be foregone. In those instances, at least, a suitable scheme of compensation for leaseholders and owners should be capable of being devised so as to permit our leaving wilderness areas and old growth forests intact.

Naturally the community as a whole has to accept responsibility for providing satisfactory compensation for the losses in economic opportunity suffered by property owners and leaseholders such as timber companies, by workers who lose employment and by rural communities which lose their very *raison d'être*. But that can obviously be a democratic choice. Moreover, monkeywrenchers could rightly claim some of the credit for getting their society to clarify its values through such choice and thereby aiding the democratic process. That would surely be a satisfactory response to the objection we have been considering. Though such an outcome would be democratically satisfactory it is important to recognise how high a value is being placed on the likes of old growth forests by those who demand their protection. For the community to be brought to agree with the demand is for it to accept that the forests and their inhabitants are worth more than the impact on people's lives, homes and work *and* that compensation has to be paid. Only thus can the costs of the demand to leave the forests alone be spread fairly.

There are those who insist, however, that monkeywrenching cannot claim any credit for making democracy work better, because it is ineffective. What exactly is it that such critics require of monkey-wrenching? Do they require that every project ever sabotaged has to have been stopped for the practice to be effective? To insist on such a standard would be unrealistically harsh (consider, for instance, the implications for judgements about the effectiveness of widely accepted parliamentary tactics if success on every occasion of their use were demanded). If we suppose a less rigorous standard, then radical environmentalists certainly have claimed many successes in halting environmentally damaging projects in connection with mineral exploration, industrial pollution, in anti-whaling activities, in preventing cattle ranching in ecologically fragile regions, as well as in the more celebrated forestry cases [*Foreman, 1991: 133ff*]. But, more importantly, monkeywrenchers claim that the significance of their impact is best gauged through the discouragement their activities have given to those thinking of undertaking environmentally sensitive projects.

They frequently speak of their activities as a stalling tactic to give the environmental movement time to raise public awareness about the ecologically destructive nature of much present day industry.[7]

Suppose this to be right and that some time has been bought through their monkeywrenching by those who espouse biocentric values. Might it not still be the case, as opponents of monkeywrenching claim, that in a democracy such tactics are unacceptable because the breaking of (democratically enacted) laws constitutes an attempt to coerce others into agreement? At the beginning of the present section I responded to the claim that monkeywrenching must be rejected as a political tactic because it requires the breaking of (democratically enacted) laws, by pointing out that it is sometimes morally required of us that we break particular laws in order to uphold more important values. This present objection differs from the earlier one in that it is now being alleged that we should find fault with monkeywrenching because of the way it affects the democratic processes themselves. It is alleged to be morally faulty as a tactic because it is aimed at coercing other participants in those democratic processes and so is inconsistent with the achievement of democratic outcomes.

Those who put forward this objection have a tendency to think of the operation of the rule of law as the hallmark of a democracy. Accordingly they do not accept that civil disobedience is defensible because they consider that a society that operates under the rule of law has made provision for lawful means of registering protest. Protesters are apt to respond that civil disobedience is resorted to only where the lawful means have been tried without success – that is, where all efforts have failed to persuade. Opponents will retort in turn that this lack of success is the very thing that shows it is the protesters who are out of step with the majority view (as reflected in the law).

This last point brings us to the nub of the issue. Is democracy to be understood as the expression of majority wishes and values through the rule of law? Certainly societies which function along these lines are considered to be democracies. But this is an extremely weak sense of the ideal as compared with the classical understanding outlined at the beginning of this study. Moreover, deciding who will govern, by reference to majority opinion, is, at best, a democratic decision procedure not democracy itself. We saw earlier that at the heart of the idea of democracy is that everyone is to have an equal share in power so that each may participate on an equal footing with every other in collective decision-making.[8] Existing parliamentary-style democracies do provide for some sharing of power but they certainly do not ensure that there is equality of power. Given that the societies with which we are familiar (and within which radical environmentalists are endeavouring to have their say), simply do not display the equal sharing in collective decision-making which is the true hallmark of democracy, the objector's case fails.[9]

If existing political structures fall short of what is required for fully-fledged democracy, the civil disobedient is in a strong position to reply to the objection we have been considering. The radical environmentalist who resorts to civil disobedience in order to have a more effective say in his or her society's collective decision-making about the fate of the environment, can once again argue, with some plausibility, that such actions further the democratic process. They do so by giving those with less power than, for instance, the media, large corporations and the trade union movement, an opportunity to have a say with a serious likelihood of being heard. They do so as well by alerting other citizens to issues of concern to the protesters and so contribute to a more enlightened electorate.

Against this, objectors are apt to say that civil disobedience, far from being an enhancer of democratic debate, interferes with the orderly continuation of the bargaining that underlies contemporary pluralist societies. Moreover, it is likely to be said that where the interference is in the form of violent protest, as with monkeywrenching, such protest is quite anti-democratic. It is anti-democratic because, to reiterate a part of the objection stated earlier, it is aimed at coercing opponents (in this case, the majority of the electorate).

These sentiments seem rather selective. To begin with, it is not obvious that any such interference with the processes for achieving collective agreement in pluralist societies is nearly as serious as that of powerful media proprietors who use their media outlets to campaign vigorously for particular interests, including some antithetical to the preservation of the natural environment. Second, it is certainly less disruptive to the democratic process than the actions of large corporations who make significant donations to political parties, threaten to withdraw from projects or to disinvest in a region in order to influence legislative outcomes. (Similar points could be made about the lobbying of the trade union movement.) Third, it is hard to see how such selective protesting as monkeywrenchers engage in, could be thought to match the capacity of the bureaucracy to thwart the public in its attempts to achieve democratically supported outcomes. So even if it were agreed that monkeywrenching had a coercive effect on the democratic process it would hardly be alone in that regard. But the truth seems rather to be that monkeywrenching is far less likely to be coercive than many other activities that are already thought of by objectors as being part of the democratic process. I conclude that a last resort use of strategic monkeywrenching does not amount to assaulting the democratic process. It is considerably less likely to damage that process than many other actions already being carried out by others who are opposed to a strong defence of the natural environment, including those who have employed violence against environmentalists in an attempt to intimidate them.

Even if the responses we have considered have successfully rebutted the objections raised against the more extreme forms of political action undertaken by radical environmentalists, the question remains whether they are morally commendable forms of environmental activism. As with those who engaged in civil disobedience in the past in order to defend civil rights, monkeywrenchers, to judge by their writings, are morally serious people. They risk a good deal because of their actions – damage to reputation, fines or imprisonment, and violent retaliation from those who oppose their activities. Given this token of their good faith and given that they ensure that their sabotaging actions do not degenerate into sheer vandalism or threaten the lives of sentient beings (for their actions would then be morally inconsistent with their overall goals), they are to be respected for dramatising ecological issues and bringing them before the public. They follow in the tradition of those who opposed participation by outsiders in conflicts like the war in Indo-China. Just as hindsight has enabled us to see the moral justifiability of many of the protests against that war, a clearer vision may enable us to see many acts of monkeywrenching as equally justifiable. Finally, while it is true that criticism, dissent and protest of the kind seen in monkeywrenching are only tolerated in democracies, especially those which show significant respect for individuals and their conscientiously held beliefs, such activities should be seen as contributing to the health and vigour of democratic processes. Repressive violence is likely, in the absence of the rule of law, to be the response by those in authority to protest. But in societies that value tolerance, acts of civil disobedience can be seen against the backdrop of the rule of law as directing our attention to weaknesses in, and failures of, particular laws. From the perspective of those concerned to protect the natural environment against threats to its integrity, not only do democratic structures represent their best hope for ensuring such protection, but their very efforts can be seen as strengthening those structures on which they needs must rely.

NOTES

1. Tree spiking is the practice of driving nails or spikes into trees to prevent or hinder milling and so logging. The spike does not harm the tree but can damage expensive saws if not removed (at great expense) prior to milling.
2. For accounts of such acts see, for example, Manes[*1990*, especially Part 2]; Scarce [*1990*]; Foreman [*1991: Chs. 11–15*].
3. Foreman [*1991: 149ff*] contends that the much publicised case of a timber worker who was injured in California in 1987 when the band saw he was helping operate shattered after

striking a tree spike embedded in a redwood log, has been shown to have resulted from the continued use of a saw that was overdue for replacement and, more to the point, that the chief suspect for having implanted the spike was a disgruntled neighbour of the milling company.

4. For more extensive discussions of the nature of terrorism see, for example, Young [1977] and Coady [1985].
5. See, for example, the views of the so-called 'Circle A' anarchists who broke away from the Earth First! movement in the United States, as reported in Scarce [1990: 88ff].
6. For perceptive discussion about the relation of violence to civil disobedience, see Cohen [1971: 22–30].
7. This idea is taken up by several contributors, including Foreman himself, in Foreman [1985] and in various articles in publications like Earth First!: The Radical Environmental Journal.
8. For a valuable discussion of the ideal of democracy see Dahl [1982].
9. See, for example, Norman [1987, especially Ch.8].

REFERENCES

Coady, C.A.J, (1985), 'The Morality of Terrorism', Philosophy, 60, pp.47–69.
Cohen, Carl (1971), Civil Disobedience: Conscience, Tactics and the Law, New York: Columbia University Press, pp.22–30.
Dahl, Robert (1982), Dilemmas of Pluralist Democracy, New Haven, CT: Yale University Press.
Elliot, Robert (1982), 'Faking Nature', Inquiry 25, pp.81–94.
Foreman, Dave (ed.) (1985), Ecodefense: A Field Guide to Monkeywrenching, Tucson, AZ: Ned Ludd Books.
Foreman, Dave (1991), Confessions of an Eco-Warrior, New York: Harmony Books.
Goodin, Robert (1992), Green Political Theory, Oxford: Polity Press.
Langguth, Gerd (1986), The Green Factor in German Politics: From Protest Movement to Political Party, Boulder, CO: Westview Press.
Luther, Martin (1958), 'Speech at the Diet of Worms', reprinted in Luther's Works, Philadelphia, PA: Fortress Books, Vol.32, pp.109–13.
Manes, Christopher (1990), Green Rage: Radical Environmentalism and the Unmaking of Civilization, Boston, MA: Little, Brown.
Norman, Richard (1987), Free and Equal: A Philosophical Examination of Political Values, Oxford: Oxford University Press.
Scarce, Rik (1990), Eco-Warriors: Understanding the Radical Environmental Movement, Chicago, IL: The Noble Press.
Schochet, Gordon J. (1972), 'The Morality of Resisting the Penalty', in Virginia Held, Kai Nielsen and Charles Parsons (eds.), Philosophy and Political Action, New York: Oxford University Press, pp.175–96.
Young, Robert (1977), 'Revolutionary Terrorism, Crime and Morality', Social Theory and Practice, 4, pp.287–302.

The Greening of Participatory Democracy: A Reconsideration of Theory

BRONWYN M. HAYWARD

Concern about the slow progress of liberal representative democracies on questions of sustainable development has encouraged research into alternative forms of democracy which might better inform environmental decision-making. Forms of deliberative, strong or 'participatory' democracy which emphasise greater public involvement in decision-making have particular appeal for many environmentalists. However, there has been surprisingly little critical evaluation of these theories in an environmental context. This contribution evaluates theories of participatory democracy in the context of environmental management in New Zealand where major restructuring has created new opportunities for experimentation. This opportunity to 'green' theories of democracy should force theorists to consider ecological rationality, community diversity, the needs of future generations, claims of intrinsic value, and the political sovereignty of indigenous peoples.

Environmental problems present a challenge for contemporary democracies. Democracies are forced to make difficult choices about how limited resources will be used. These choices are complicated by the often vastly differing attitudes people have about the environment, its problems and what actions (if any) should be taken to address these. Nevertheless, no matter how difficult, conscious choices eventually have to be made. Environmental degradation is unrelenting. Indicators suggest that, rather than go away, many environmental problems will only get worse. The scale and nature of environmental problems demands a collective response.[1]

But can our democracies respond adequately to environmental problems? Many environmental policy analysts are doubtful. Some have

Bronwyn Hayward teaches public policy in the Department of Parks, Recreation and Tourism at Lincoln University, Canterbury, New Zealand.
The author would like to acknowledge the valuable comments of the *Environmental Politics* reviewer and discussion with Robert Bartlett, Ton Buhrs, John Dryzek and Iris Marion Young. Earlier versions of this contribution were also presented in a Political Economy panel at the International Political Science XVI World Congress held in Berlin, August 1994 and the Ecopolitics VIII Conference, Lincoln University, August 1994. The author would like to thank the participants in those conference panels for their helpful comments.

expressed particular concern about the limited progress liberal democracies have made on environmental problems [*Fischer, 1993; Eckersley, 1992; Dryzek, 1992*]. While recognising some significant achievements, critics argue that the majority of liberal democratic initiatives fail to respond adequately to complex environmental problems. They complain that liberal democracies are committed to competitive elections, individual liberty and private property [*Milbrath,1984: 27–28; Porritt, 1984: 122–5*]. This commitment encourages short-sighted environmental policies, and generally favours the interests of developers and capital accumulation at the expense of environmental protection [*Dryzek, 1987: 67–87*]. Moreover, critics argue, liberal democracies use methods for making policy choices that are ecologically irrational [*Bartlett, 1986; Dryzek, 1987*]. Drawing on the heritage of the Enlightenment, liberal democracies tend to adopt instrumental analytic reasoning to inform policy development, disaggregating problems and applying mechanisms of a free market and polyarchy to environmental management.[2] These practices are argued to displace rather than to resolve environmental problems [*Dryzek, 1987: 10–11*].

Frustrated with the environmental performance of liberal democracies, some environmentalists and policy analysts have looked for alternative ways of making environmental decisions. For example, some argue that we should reform existing liberal democratic institutions by requiring more rigorous environmental impact assessment procedures or mandatory environmental accounting (see Paehlke and Torgerson [*1990*]). Others have advocated a more ecofascist approach: critical environmental choices cannot be left to ill-informed citizens or their elected representatives; difficult decisions should be made by experts trained in ecological sciences or those who are able to exercise strict political control [*Heilbroner, 1974; Ophuls, 1977*]. Others still have argued that citizens should have more input into decision-making, advocating a more 'participatory' democracy as the means of tackling environmental problems [*Dryzek, 1990; 1992a; DeLeon, 1992; Hillier, 1993; Robynson, 1993*]. It is this last argument that is the focus of this contribution.

I shall discuss the various forms of participatory democracy and the contested nature of environmental policy before considering the case of New Zealand, where attempts to involve citizens directly in environmental management have raised wider questions for theorists of participatory democracy. When considering these questions I wish to compare the work of two theorists in particular: John Dryzek [*1987; 1990; 1993*] and Iris Young [*1994; 1995*]. Discussion will assess the extent to which Dryzek and Young's theories of participatory democracy help us to address questions which have emerged from environmental practice.

Participatory Democracy: Strong, Deliberative or Communicative?

I use 'participatory democracy' to refer here to democratic theories that advocate active citizen participation in the process of governance, for example through face to face discussion in multi-stakeholder forums, public meetings, referenda or interactive polling [*Pateman, 1970; Macpherson, 1977; Barber, 1984; Dryzek, 1990; Fishkin, 1991; Young, 1994*]. I am not focusing here on anarchist or Marxist forms of democracy which suggest institutions of government or class should give way to self regulation or the collective governing of public affairs.³ While these ideas have had an important influence on many environmental movements, the forms of democracy of interest to me are those often also called 'strong' democracy [*Barber, 1984; Fishkin, 1991*]. In participatory or strong democracies, active citizen participation is essential. Freedom to participate in common life is valued as an end in itself, as part of the 'good life'. Participation in collective affairs is also valued because through such activity, people define themselves as citizens, and become educated about collective problems and democratic principles (see Nelson [*1980*]). Through the experience of self determination it is hoped that people will be transformed to become 'other regarding citizens' with a strengthened commitment to applying the principles of democracy in public life [*Warren, 1992*].

Advocates of participatory democracy differ over the extent to which everyone is required to participate all the time, in all social institutions. Most envisage a direct form of participatory democracy with opportunities for citizen participation through decentralised forums which include local/regional government, political parties, workplace organisations, neighbourhood assemblies or voluntary organisations.⁴ These forums are often small in scale. Other writers relax the requirement for direct participation by all; they have advocated greater citizen participation in the context of representative government, for example by establishing multi-stakeholder citizen forums on a regional or international scale [*Fishkin, 1991; Young, 1990*].

Two significant variations of participatory democracy are 'discursive' democracy and 'communicative' democracy. John Dryzek [*1987; 1990; 1993*] is a notable advocate of discursive democracy and Iris Young [*1990; 1994; 1995*] coined the latter term. Both Dryzek and Young emphasise active citizen participation, and greater opportunities for public deliberation. Dryzek's theory of democracy focuses on the process of critical argument along the lines of an ideal speech situation in which people come together to talk under conditions of free and open discourse and where decisions are reached through the force of the better argument [*Dryzek, 1990: 36–7*]. In contrast, Young proposes a model of democracy which

attends to social difference and the way power enters speech itself [*Young,
1995*]. Young argues that ideal speech situations cannot achieve free debate
because even if such situations eliminate the influence of economic power,
social inequalities would still arise because ideal speech situations privilege
some styles of speaking over others.

Young uses the term 'communicative democracy' to describe a situation
in which a variety of methods of communication (beyond critical argument)
are used to both promote democratic deliberation and acknowledge
community heterogeneity. Young's aim is to privilege equally '... any forms
of communicative interaction where people aim to reach understanding
across their differences' [*Young, 1995*]. In this way, Young hopes to
eliminate the cultural bias inherent in critical argument and enable a wider
variety of viewpoints or 'situated life experiences' to inform community
deliberation [*Young, 1995*]. Young and Dryzek's theories, together with the
ideas of strong democracy, will be collectively referred to in this contribution as theories of 'participatory democracy' to highlight the way these
approaches share a common aim – to facilitate greater citizen participation
in collective decision-making.

The Contested Nature of Environmental Problems

The highly contested, intersubjective nature of environmental problems
presents a challenge for democracies. Contemporary environmental
problems are best described as 'wicked' policy problems, problems which,
as Frank Fischer argues, 'lend themselves to no unambiguous or conclusive
formulations and thus have no clear cut criteria to judge their resolution'
[*Fischer, 1993: 173*]. The contested character of environmental problems
stems in part from the complexity of the interrelationships between the
biotic and physical components of ecosystems [*Begon et al., 1986*]. These
relationships are open to alternative interpretations. But the contested nature
of environmental problems also stems from the myriad socio-economic
values that people attribute to ecosystems. These values include resource,
amenity, aesthetic, historical, sense-of-place, spiritual, and intrinsic values.
Socio-economic values give an environment an important meaning which is
beyond the sum of its biotic and physical components. For example,
resource values are the 'use values' people attribute to components of
ecosystems, reflecting the way minerals, soils, water, or forests and so on
are valued for production purposes. Amenity values are those physical
qualities or characteristics of an area which contribute to human
appreciation of its recreational potential. In practice, amenity values are
closely related to aesthetic values – people's appreciation of beauty or
coherence [*Handbook of Environmental Law, 1992*]. When we respond to a

place or an area, it may also be on the basis of stories, myths, events or experiences we associate with that area. Those associations can be referred to as 'sense of place' values.

In addition to the values identified above, the environment also has other significant values for many people. For example, for New Zealand's indigenous Maori community the spiritual value of the environment is crucial. For Maori, the ecosystem with its mountains, rivers and landforms is part of a complex spiritual sphere – from which Maori draw strength and in which Wairua or spirit can be invoked. Intrinsic values have also been attributed to the environment by Maori. Claims of intrinsic value refer to the way ecosystems possess value independent of their use for human purposes.[5] Maori speak of the Mauri or life force which is possessed by all the elements (human and non-human) of ecosystems. Mauri is a vital, intrinsic, spiritual quality which exists independently of humans and cannot be invoked. Others who speak of intrinsic environmental values refer to the 'non-relative' or inherent properties possessed by ecosystems such as their genetic or biophysical diversity, or to their 'objective' value [O'Neil, 1993]. Objective value is value independent of the attitudes or preferences of valuers, where this includes characteristics which determine the integrity, form, function or resilience of ecosystems [Handbook of Environmental Law, 1992].

The variety of socio-economic values identified above which are attributed to the environment illustrates why it is difficult to make collective choices about environmental problems. There are so many variables and values to be addressed. Given the crucial but contested nature of environmental problems, what is required is a political arrangement which can help us address environmental issues as normative policy questions. But what form should that political arrangement take? Many have argued that a participatory democracy is appropriate for reasons I shall briefly review.

Participatory Democracy: Its Appeal for Environmentalists

Given the complexity of environmental problems, it may seem surprising that some would want to complicate decision-making further by involving more participants. The ideas of participatory democracy have been heavily criticised on a number of grounds – the most common being the argument that in today's large communities, methods of decision-making based on citizen deliberation are too cumbersome or time consuming. Critics argue that active citizen involvement in decision-making simply will not work – it slows decision-making and is too demanding – people are just not that interested in politics, casting a vote is quite enough involvement for many, anything requiring more active participation is simply too much. There are other serious concerns that have been raised. Firstly, there is the difficulty of coordinating local action to combat transboundary environmental problems; secondly, there can be inadequate consideration of the context in which decentralisation might occur (for example, are natural resources distributed evenly amongst communities?); and lastly, the mechanistic assumption that an understanding of complex global environmental problems will build from direct experience in decision-making at a local level is open to criticism.

Moreover, critics point out that while Athens of the fifth century BC is frequently cited as the quintessential example of a participatory democracy, Athenian citizens were carefully vetted – slaves, immigrants, men under twenty and women were not accorded the privileges of citizenship [Beethham, 1993]. Disquiet about the ideals of this form of democracy have even arisen from within the participatory camp itself. Pateman [1988; 1989] has revisited the writings of Rousseau, often described as the 'exemplar' of participatory democracy. Pateman now argues that Rousseau's democracy was a masculine preserve in which the political right of self-government was exercised only by men – women, according to Rousseau, lacked the natural restraint, order and reason necessary for citizenship [Pateman, 1989].

Given such significant criticisms, why have the ideas of participatory democracy continued to have an appeal for many environmentalists? First, it is interesting to note that the appeal of participatory democracy cuts across ideological boundaries within the environmental movement. Support for active citizen participation in decision-making has been expressed both by environmentalists who adopt an anthropocentric perspective and by some who adopt an ecocentric perspective.[6] For most environmentalists much of the appeal of citizen participation is instrumental. Participatory democracy appears to provide a way of better informing environmental decisions. Environmentalists have frequently complained that liberal democracies tend to deny local communities the opportunity to take an active part in decision-making [Bührs and Bartlett, 1993]. They argue that environmental decisions are made too often by experts or elected elites. They would prefer a wider variety of voices contributed to decision-making and that decisions were arrived at through a process of collective reasoning rather than a 'competitive struggle for self-interested votes'.[7] Many environmentalists also argue that small, decentralised decision-making forums will enhance decision-making by enabling a more rapid response to the signals of degradation coming from the immediate environment [Dryzek, 1987: 217].

Participatory democracy also appeals to environmentalists for differing instrumental reasons. For example, Eckersley has argued that environmental activists who adopt an anthropocentric perspective tend to favour participation as a means to achieve distributive justice [*Eckersley, 1992: 9*]. She argues that anthropocentric environmentalists aim to facilitate the inclusion of groups formerly marginalised in decision-making about resource use. From this perspective, small-scale participatory forums such as neighbourhood councils are pursued primarily as a means of achieving self-determination in an environmental context.

The importance of self-determination for many environmentalists was highlighted at the Earth Summit. Green critics of the Summit complained angrily that '... issues central to the work of grassroots groups – in particular the right of local communities to determine their own future (had been) excluded from the agenda (of the Earth Summit) ... ' [*The Ecologist, 1993: vii*].

For environmentalists who adopt an ecocentric perspective, Eckersley suggests that participation appeals because of its transformative potential [*Eckersley, 1992: 10*]. Through the experience of active participation, it is hoped, citizens will become better educated about environmental problems and 'transformed' from 'self regarding' individuals to 'other regarding' citizens with an appreciation of their common (environmental) interests and compassion for non-human nature [*Dryzek, 1987; Eckersley, 1992; Hillier, 1993*].

Participatory democracy is also favoured by many environmentalists (particularly those of an anthropocentric persuasion) for intrinsic reasons – active citizen participation is valued as part of the 'good life'. For example, New Zealand's contemporary environmental movement grew out of the 1960s campaign to save a lake threatened by hydrodevelopment (Lake Manapouri) and a campaign against large-scale aluminium smelting at a site called Aramoana. These proposals became the subject of national controversy. The groups that were formed to oppose these schemes renewed enthusiasm for the human emancipatory potential of participatory democracy, in a manner similar to the North American and European New Left movements of the 1960s [*Wilson, 1982*]. This enthusiasm for participatory democracy was reflected in the subsequent structure of New Zealand's green political parties, including both the Values Party of the 1970s and today's Green Party.[8]

Citizen Participation in New Zealand's Environmental Management

Given environmental interest in forms of participatory democracy, it is surprising how little evaluation there has been of the theoretical questions that arise from the practice of participatory decision-making [*Deleon, 1994; Fischer, 1993; Laird, 1993*]. New Zealand provides one opportunity to explore such questions because New Zealand's environmental administration has been dramatically restructured, in part, to provide more opportunities for public participation in environmental management.

Between 1984 and 1991, all existing governmental institutions in New Zealand with responsibility for environmental issues were dismantled and replaced, and all environmental legislation was reviewed. This restructuring involved widespread public consultation. A national 'Environmental Forum' was held in 1984 at which a large variety of community groups and organisations were canvassed about environmental issues [*Bührs and Bartlett, 1993: 122*]. A working party was then appointed by government to tour the country, holding numerous public meetings about options for future environmental administration [*ibid.*]. Following this process, two notable agencies were created, one for conservation management (the Department of Conservation), and one to provide policy advice (the Ministry for the Environment). This restructuring of environmental administration was complemented by the complete restructuring of local government. To facilitate more effective control over environmental management, new tiers of 'regional' government were created and charged with the task of managing resources. The boundaries of these regional governments were established on an ecological basis – following watersheds as well as human communities of interest [*Memon, 1993*].

Once these new structures were mapped out, the government set about reviewing all environmental legislation. The review replaced over 50 environmental statutes and regulations with a single piece of legislation – the Resource Management Act (1991). The central principle of the Act was 'sustainable environmental management' and its aim was to integrate all aspects of resource use in a comprehensive management statute. This mammoth legislative project itself involved wide spread consultation through public meetings, several rounds of public submissions, toll free phone-ins, and public information campaigns [*Bührs and Bartlett, 1993: 123*]. Once passed, the Resource Management Act was heralded for introducing greater opportunity for citizen participation by providing the following: rigorous pre-hearing meetings – to be called by developers or local government early in the development process; a requirement for all levels of government to consult extensively with Maori as the indigenous community (*Tangata Whenua* – people of the land); requirements to consult affected publics more rigorously when preparing or modifying plans and policy documents; and new opportunities for environmental mediation in local government decision-making.[9]

Obviously this restructuring of the New Zealand government's environmental administration does not amount to the creation of a participatory democracy. Despite the rhetoric of government, most of the changes were modest, simply providing more opportunity for public consultation. However, although modest, these reforms are significant for theorists of participatory democracy for two reasons. First, the process of restructuring New Zealand's environmental administration has put questions of citizen participation back on the institutional agenda as a topic for debate. This is important because there has been very little opportunity for citizen input on policy issues in New Zealand over the last decade. Since 1984, successive governments of both the Left and Right have introduced far-reaching market-orientated reforms which have deregulated, corporatised (and subsequently privatised) a dazzling array of state-owned assets and services from post offices to coal mines, airlines to telecommunication and health services, with breath-taking speed – displaying a contempt for the process of public consultation, which earned it the description of an 'elected dictatorship' [*Mulgan, 1990*]. In fact, New Zealand's executive has had so few constitutional restraints on its decision-making power that a New Zealand political scientist and constitutional lawyer turned prime minister, Geoffrey Palmer, once described New Zealand as 'the fastest law in the West' [*Palmer, 1987*].

New Zealand's attempts to provide more opportunity for public consultation on environmental issues are also worth considering because, although these reforms were not intended to achieve the ideals of a participatory democracy, democratic theorists can learn from these experiences. New Zealand's experiments with public consultation raise wider questions for those interested in developing and/or applying theories of participatory democracy. In this study I wish to consider some of the questions that have emerged in practice. In discussion I will compare the ways that theories of democracy, as espoused by John Dryzek [*1987; 1990; 1993*] and Iris Young [*1990, 1994; 1995*] in particular, might help us address these questions.

Participatory Democracy – Some Questions from Environmental Practice

On the basis of New Zealand's experience, it can be argued that before any form of democracy can persuasively claim to deal with environmental problems, it must address some questions which have emerged in practice. These questions are as follows: is it ecologically rational; does it deal with the diversity of community attitudes and values about the environment; is it self limiting, in the light of claims to political sovereignty made by indigenous people; does it facilitate consideration of claims of future generations or intrinsic value; and finally, is it resilient enough to meet the challenges of contemporary economic practice? These questions are raised here in the environmental context of New Zealand, but they are not unique to this policy area or that country. They echo problems raised by democratic theorists grappling with assessments of democracy in other social and economic contexts [*Held, 1987; 1993*]. I shall now examine these questions in turn.

Is Participatory Democracy Ecologically Rational?

In New Zealand the *Resource Management Act* 1991 requires governments to manage, develop and protect ecosystems in a sustainable way (Resource Management Act, 1991: Section 5). However, given the complexity of ecosystems, many environmentalists argue that sustainable decision-making will need a whole new method of reasoning. Environmental problems require a method of reasoning that is 'ecologically rational'. Ecological rationality reflects ' ... the rationality of biogeochemical systems, their integrity, maintenance, reproduction and evolution' [*Bartlett, 1986: 234*]. A democracy can be described as exhibiting *functional* ecological rationality if it is structured to produce, increase or preserve the life-supporting capability of ecosystems consistently [*Bartlett, 1986: 234*].

John Dryzek has addressed the question of ecological rationality, and argues that discursive democracies are likely to exhibit functional ecological rationality. Dryzek readily acknowledges the possibility that citizens of a discursive democracy may choose outcomes which degrade the environment [*Dryzek, 1987: 204*]. However, he suggests that this would be unlikely to happen often. He argues that a discursive democracy is more likely to exhibit functional ecological rationality because it is structured according to theories of practical reason – in particular, the ideal speech situation as developed by Habermas. Choices are made on the basis of reasoned collective deliberation. Discussion is free and open, all participants have the ability to inform the discussion and the only authority is that of the better argument [*Dryzek, 1987: 201*]. Under an ideal speech situation, a course of action may be chosen because it has appeal when held up to shared values or norms during deliberation [*Dryzek, 1987: 201*]. Dryzek argues that options that preserve ecological integrity are placed in a strong position in this situation because the fact that human life depends on environmental integrity means that environmental integrity is an 'obvious generalizable interest' [*Dryzek, 1987: 204*].

The limitations of Dryzek's argument will be discussed shortly, but before that it should be noted that Dryzek goes on to suggest that if any form of democracy is to be judged ecologically rational it must be able to provide negative feedback (that is, to react against human-induced shortfalls in life support capability) and to coordinate responses and actions across different circumstances. It must also be robust (that is, be able to perform in different conditions), flexible (capable of adjusting to new situations) and resilient (able to correct severe disequilibrium) [*Dryzek, 1987: 11*]. Dryzek argues that discursive democracies encourage *co-operation* because people have freely consented to norms or principles for action [*Dryzek, 1987: 207*]. He also suggests that when public discussion takes place in small-scale, self-sufficient forums, ecological rationality is enhanced because the community is able to *respond quickly* and *flexibly* to local environmental indicators [*Dryzek, 1987: 20*]. Furthermore, Dryzek suggests that discursive democracy is *resilient* because policies are developed using critical argument – not simply on the basis of myth or tradition [*Dryzek, 1987*]. Dryzek also points out that actions can be *coordinated* across local government boundaries using techniques of 'limited bargaining' and practical reason across 'functional' areas – as demonstrated by the Berger Inquiry which travelled the Canadian North to debate the effects of an oil and gas pipeline [*Dryzek, 1987: 233; 1990: 127–9*].

Iris Young's model of communicative democracy does not help us address the question of ecological rationality directly. However some of Young's ideas raise questions about the extent to which a discursive democracy can achieve functional ecological rationality. At present discursive democracy faces a major limitation – the ideal speech situation is most likely to promote ecological rationality if each person has a chance to inform the community's understanding of environmental problems, but in practice the use of critical argument can silence some voices in environmental decision making. In New Zealand, for example, Maori communities use oratory (*whaikorero* or rhetorical speech making), singing (*waiata*) and public prayer (*karakia*) and ritualised greeting ceremonies (*powhiri*) as other important methods of establishing understanding during public deliberation. Research by Kathy Irwin indicates that when public discussion takes place using the method of critical argument alone, the voices of both Pakeha (European) men and Maori men are privileged at the expense of Maori women who traditionally participate in public deliberation through informal conversation, *waiata* and *karakia* [*Irwin, 1992*].

Young's model of communicative democracy helps us broaden our social understanding of environmental problems because it provides opportunities for citizens to communicate in a variety of ways. Young argues that we need to find ways of speaking across the differences of culture, social position and need [*Young, 1995*]. She suggests this could be achieved by attending to the conditions under which discussion takes place. As noted earlier, Young rejects the exclusive use of critical argument in ideal speech situations. Instead she argues attention should be paid to a variety of ways of communicating – including the use of greeting, rhetoric and story-telling [*Young, 1995*]. This approach could create space for Maori communities to use other methods of communication (for example, *waiata* and *karakia*) in public deliberation. In turn, the introduction of a variety of methods of communication may advance ecological rationality by producing a more *flexible* and *robust* process of deliberation – one that is sensitive to the decision-making context of bicultural and multicultural communities and which enables a variety of 'ways of knowing and speaking' to inform outcomes [*Young, 1995*].

Young's theory also helps to orientate our research toward understanding real speech contexts. This is useful because it reminds us to address practical obstacles to open deliberation and ecological rationality. These practical obstacles include social pressure and lack of information. For example when public discussion occurs in small scale forums (such as New Zealand's local or regional government), participants sometimes complain that a tyranny of consensus emerges – under which people are reluctant to voice unpopular or potentially divisive viewpoints for fear of disrupting social relations [*Jaggar, 1983: 230*]. New Zealand research by Paul Harris [*1993*] suggests that conditions of intimacy such as trust, and friendship, which are important in overcoming this tyranny and maintaining open debate, are not commonly experienced, even in that small country. Furthermore, it is difficult to achieve informed deliberation when small communities lack either the skills to interpret negative environmental feedback signals, or the resources to respond to those signals.

Young's model of communicative democracy cannot address all such barriers to open, informed, ecologically rational public deliberation. But her model has reminded us of some of the practical obstacles inherent in speech situations which may inhibit citizen participation. Dryzek also recognises the importance of inclusive discussion – he notes that participants might need to be educated so that they are capable of making and challenging arguments effectively [*Dryzek, 1987: 209*]. But Young goes further and suggests that exclusive use of critical argument may itself restrict deliberation by privileging the voices of a few citizens – particularly those who are skilled in debate or whose life experiences are conveyed most effectively through the Western adversarial model of critical argument [*Young, 1995: 137*]. If ecological rationality requires a holistic approach, one that is informed by many different perspectives, then models of discursive democracy may need to be modified to include a wider range of communication methods. Modification would allow more voices to be heard in public deliberation and could enhance our social understanding of environmental problems.

Can Participatory Democracy Address Diverse Community Values?

Building on the need for more inclusive political participation, I argue that to be persuasive in an environmental context, theories of participatory democracy also need to demonstrate that they can integrate diverse community values. In New Zealand the Resource Management Act requires local and regional government to consult widely when preparing policy statements or plans, or when considering development proposals. However, arriving at a decision through a process of public consultation can be difficult. People frequently disagree, sometimes passionately, about the resource, amenity, aesthetic, historical, sense of place and/or spiritual values they attribute to an environment. They also disagree over the extent to which they are prepared to tolerate environmental degradation and natural hazards.

In developing his theory of discursive democracy, John Dryzek has acknowledged that policy discussions are 'pervaded by conflicting values' [*Dryzek, 1990: 53*]. Dryzek aims to establish understanding across different frames of reference but he recognises that over-arching consensus may be unattainable [*Dryzek, 1990: 54*]. However if agreement is not reached, Dryzek argues that 'a generalizable interest' still exists 'beneath the surface misconceptions of actors' [*Dryzek, 1990: 54*]. As noted above, Dryzek argues that environmental integrity is one such generalisable interest because large numbers of people have a stake in the environment and because we depend on the limited capacity of the environment to support human life [*Dryzek, 1987*].

Young has criticised theorists of deliberative democracy who begin with assumptions of generalisable interest on two grounds. First, she argues, it obviates the need for self transformation (an outcome valued by deliberative democrats and ecocentrics alike). Second, she argues, assumptions of unity can undermine the democratic potential of a deliberative democracy when the 'common good' is defined by dominant groups [*Young, 1995*].

There is a danger in regarding environmental integrity as a generalisable interest, as Dryzek does, in that this assumption could be used to silence dissenting voices. In New Zealand, for example, the environmental movement is largely directed towards preservation of wilderness; at times peak environmental interest groups have been very intolerant of Maori claims of ownership or use of natural resources – environmentalists complain that management 'mistakes' by Maori could jeopardise the 'common goal' of saving wilderness.

Young is concerned that less privileged groups may be required to put aside their claims of entitlement or interest for the sake of a common good [*Young, 1995*]. She has criticised deliberative models of democracy, arguing

that the assumption of common community interests neglects or minimises
the problems of community diversity [*Young, 1995: 140*]. Young argues that
we should 'understand differences of culture, social perspective, or
particularist commitment as resources to draw on rather than as divisions
which must be overcome' [*Young, 1995*].

In a specific reference to environmental issues, Young reminds us that it
is important that theorists acknowledge 'unshared meanings' in public
deliberation [*Young, 1995; 148*]. She gives the example of the way the
Black Hills of South Dakota have a particular meaning for the local Latoka
Indian community. This meaning stems from the history and spiritual
beliefs of that tribe. Similarly, the New Zealand environment often holds
meanings for the Maori community which are not shared by the Pakeha
(European) community. Iris Young does not rule out the possibility of
establishing 'shared understandings' during public deliberation however.
Young's emphasis on finding ways to understand difference in the absence
of an a priori generalisable interest leaves open the possibility that citizens
could be 'transformed' through discussion, gaining social wisdom, or an
appreciation of a wider social picture beyond their own (partial) life
experiences [*Young, 1995: 142*].

Dryzek's optimism about the possibility of uncovering common interest
and Young's celebration of diversity have both contributed, albeit in
different ways, to our understanding of why people value the chance to
participate in deliberation on environmental issues. However neither theory
fully resolves the problem of how community choices should be made in a
direct democracy when deep divisions or animosities exist. In such
situations, it may not be appropriate to apply models of participatory
democracy. Bhikhu Parekh [*1993*] cautions us about universalising any
form of democracy, suggesting that deep-seated tensions can be inflamed by
the inappropriate application of a model of democracy.[10] Communities may
prefer to use models of participatory democracy to inform some broad
policy directions while leaving other issues to be settled by elected
representatives or relevant bureaucracies.

The problem of accommodating diverse community values is related to
the question of whether constitutional mechanisms should be used to protect
the rights of citizens and minority groups. The question of whether
constitutional limits are necessary has become particularly urgent in an
environmental context in New Zealand.

Should There be Limits to Participation?

In New Zealand, attempts to introduce more public participation in
environmental management have raised the wider question of whether there

should be limits to participation by the public. New Zealand's indigenous Maori community claims sovereignty over natural resources – in particular they claim rights to full and undisturbed possession of traditional fisheries, forests and lands under the Treaty of Waitangi. This treaty was signed between the British Crown and chiefs of Maori tribes in 1840. In practice, the Treaty of Waitangi has assumed a constitutional role in New Zealand political life, protecting the rights of the Maori who were devastated by British colonisation at turn of the century. For example the Resource Management Act requires that all environmental decision-making takes account of the principles of the Treaty of Waitangi (Resource Management Act 1991: Part 8). In this context, New Zealand theorists are forced to consider the limits of participation – would a more participatory democracy result in a majority culture determining the affairs of a minority community?

David Held has argued that theorists of democracy must consider the question of constitutional limits [Held, 1987: 281]. Held is concerned that this fundamental question has been left unresolved. In the 'rush' to provide for more public participation, how are the conditions of democracy to be secured [Held, 1987: 281]? Held is cautious about any suggestion that through participation *per se*, people will become dedicated to principles of common good (which may not be identified), or will respect the rights of others. He argues that enhanced participation must take place 'within a legal framework that protects and nurtures the enactment of the principle of autonomy' [*ibid.*].

Although he is concerned with the conditions of free speech, John Dryzek does not deal with questions of constitutional protection directly in his development of discursive democracy. However, Iris Young has argued that we need constitutional measures to protect the rights of groups entering into collective deliberation [*Young, 1990; 1994; 1995*]. Constitutional protection is imperative for indigenous peoples in New Zealand. The Maori community has fought for a century for recognition of the Treaty of Waitangi and their right to make claims over traditional environmental resources. If Maori were required to constantly reassert these arguments every time an environmental issue came up for public discussion, their already unequal position could be further undermined.

In practice New Zealand has evolved its own particular approach to the problem of how group rights might be protected during public deliberation about environmental issues. Maori can ask that their claims or grievances be heard in a separate public forum established to deal with claims made under the Treaty of Waitangi. This forum (known as the Waitangi Tribunal) is a semi-judicial body which tours the country to hear disputes. It aims to facilitate discussion in a forum sensitive to cultural difference. A variety of methods of communication are used and hearings are less formal than a court of law. The Tribunal's powers are limited – it can only recommend action to government, but the Waitangi Tribunal has been an effective forum for public deliberation while protecting the rights of Maori.

New Zealand's Waitangi Tribunal illustrates one pragmatic approach to protecting the rights of groups, but the wider question of whether there should be limits to participation remains. This debate often arises in an environmental context because decisions about resource use can have serious implications at both the local level and at a wider regional, national, or international level. For example, debate about the limits of participation have erupted repeatedly along the West Coast of the South Island of New Zealand, where a World Heritage Order, national parks and mediated agreements have all been used to protect native forests from logging. Local West Coast communities have complained that environmentalists are 'poking their noses into local affairs' – logging has been an important source of local employment in an economically depressed area. Similar problems arise in all countries, and the question of 'who should have a say about what' remains a challenging issue for theorists of participatory democracy [*Mulgan, 1984*].

Representing Future Generations and Intrinsic Values

The practice of environmental policy development in New Zealand has raised questions about the need for limits to participation and constitutional protection of minority rights. It has also raised questions about the constitutional recognition of ecological concerns such as the needs of future generations and intrinsic values. The purpose of the Resource Management Act is to promote 'sustainable environmental management' – which is defined as:

> managing the use, development and protection of natural and physical resources, in a way or at a rate which enables people and communities to provide for their social, physical, economic, and cultural wellbeing, and for their health and safety while sustaining the potential of natural and physical resources ... to meet the reasonably foreseeable needs of *future* generations' (Resource Management Act 1991: Section 5).

The Act also requires that decision-making take into account the '*intrinsic values* of ecosystems' where intrinsic values are defined as: ' ... those aspects of ecosystems and their constituent parts which have value in their own right, including their biological and genetic diversity and the essential characteristics that determine an ecosystem's integrity, form, functioning, and resilience' (Resource Management Act 1991: Section 1.8). This legislative reform has assumed that these ecological interests ought to be protected. This raises fascinating normative questions but it also poses an immediate, practical representational problem for participatory democrats. From an ecocentric perspective it could be argued that neither Dryzek's nor Young's theories adequately provides for representation of intrinsic values, because these theories focus on the conditions of human communities, and because Dryzek's theory in particular uses techniques involving face to face communication between humans. Robyn Eckersley, for example, criticises Dryzek's concern to preserve the human life-supporting capability of ecosystems as 'anthropocentric' [*Eckersley, 1992: 110*]. However, John Dryzek has gone to pains to point out that he is not suggesting that other reasons for valuing environment, over and above its capacity for human life support, are unimportant [*Dryzek, 1987: 35*]. When addressing the problem of representing intrinsic values, he also notes that while non-human elements of ecosystems can not speak for themselves, ecosystems can send signals to human communities through the process of environmental degradation [*Dryzek, 1987: 218-219*].[11]

Nevertheless, until greater attention is paid to the question of whether there are ecological limits to participation, representation of both intrinsic value and the needs of future generations must rely on the goodwill of participatory communities and the ability of these communities to interpret environmental signals and anticipate at least some of the needs of future generations. For example, to help ensure that ecological values are represented, New Zealand has established a Commissioner for the Environment and a Department of Conservation [*Memon, 1993*]. These agencies have a responsibility to advocate for the environment. This role is particularly important in instances where economic practice tends to 'discount' the needs of future generations or to externalise the costs of production through exploitation of common natural resources. However, New Zealand is still a long way from securing effective representation of the needs of future generations or intrinsic values. Many local councils have difficulty in both identifying and operationalising these concepts. One planner put it this way: 'Councils often only pay lip service to the [Resource Management] Act's requirement that we consider intrinsic value and for that matter future generations – once we get everyone in the community talking about their own immediate problems, those questions usually get left to the end, if they are covered at all.'[12] If participatory democrats are to make a useful contribution to environmental problems, more detailed consideration needs to be given to the practical ways that the needs of future generations and claims of intrinsic value could be consistently represented in public deliberation, and the normative justification for this representation.

The Prospects for Participatory Democracy in a Market-Led Economy

If participatory democracy is to be persuasive in an environmental context, the preceding questions all require more research. However, no matter how carefully theorists address these questions, New Zealand's experience suggests that it will be almost impossible for a more participatory democracy to flourish in a market-orientated economic environment. As Dryzek has pointed out, free markets constrain democracies [*Dryzek, 1987: 67–87*]. New Zealand's present political economy is characterised by extensive deregulation and the use of market mechanisms for making many collective choices. For example, the Resource Management Act itself reflects the theories of economic liberalism. In a political economy dominated by libertarian ideology, emphasis is given to the resource values of the environment – typified in the title of New Zealand's comprehensive environmental statute – the Resource Management Act. Moreover, despite wide-spread public consultation during drafting, it would appear that the influence of environmentalists was more apparent than real in that the Resource Management Act was able to proceed only because the broad intentions of that Act fitted with dominant economic philosophies [*Memon, 1993*].

The Resource Management Act was acclaimed in New Zealand for providing new opportunities for public participation and incorporating principles of sustainable management into legislation. But given New Zealand's present economic climate, the participatory implications of the Act are ambiguous. This Act imposes few constraints on resource use. The Act 'manages environmental impacts' rather than 'regulates activities' [*Memon, 1993*]. This has been interpreted by some local councils (and the New Zealand Treasury) as providing 'very wide boundaries' within which individual property owners can 'do what they like' [*Memon, 1993: 96*]. Environmental planning in New Zealand is now essentially 'market led' and collective decisions will only be taken to cope with the effects of private decisions [*Memon, 1993: 105*].

Planning analyst Ali Memon sums up New Zealand's present environmental dilemma this way:

> Even though ... sustainable resource management is the central purpose of the (Resource Management) Act, its structure reflects a determination on the part of government for a more open and

competitive economy, a move away from state participation in promoting economic growth towards a decentralised administration of regulatory systems and the use of economic instruments to achieve good environmental outcomes [*Memon, 1993, 76*].

If Memon's analysis is correct, and current trends seems to support his assertions, the prospects for more active citizen participation on environmental issues seems bleak. In the past, citizens who stood to make a tangible financial gain from a decision were advantaged in deliberation because they had a strong motivation to participate. In contrast citizens concerned about less tangible issues (such as scenic beauty) often found it difficult to sustain active involvement in the sometimes costly and time consuming process of public deliberation [*Hayward, 1991*]. It appears that current trends in the political economy will reinforce these inequalities. Those who stand to benefit most from the new opportunities for public consultation in New Zealand are property-owning citizens who are freer than ever before to make individual decisions about natural resource use within very wide boundaries.

Conclusion

The environment poses a challenge for democracies. If governments wish to achieve sustainable development, they will have to make difficult choices about complex problems. Both Dryzek's and Young's theories of participatory democracy have served to remind us that attention to the process of public deliberation is important because it enhances our ability to reason collectively about environmental problems. However, New Zealand's experience with citizen participation in an environmental context has raised a number of questions which challenge theories of participatory democracy – in particular, theorists must address questions of ecological rationality, community diversity, sovereignty, the needs of future generations, claims of intrinsic value and the impacts of economic liberalism.

Young's model of communicative democracy seems well placed to address at least the first three of these questions and her ideas may assist in overcoming some of the practical limitations of discursive democracy. Communicative democracy could promote a more inclusive form of political participation – one appropriate to public discussion about environmental issues in a bicultural or multicultural community. However, no matter how inclusive it is, no form of participatory democracy seems likely to flourish in New Zealand's present political economy. Capitalist practice in New Zealand encourages minimal restraints in environmental management and advantages property-owning citizens. Even if theorists are able to resolve the questions that have emerged from environmental practice, it is unlikely that a participatory democracy could survive in New Zealand's present political economy.

NOTES

1. To add to this challenge, the nature of environmental goods is such that many are 'public' – that is, goods which, if supplied, must be supplied jointly to large numbers of people who cannot easily be excluded from accruing the benefits of supply if they have not paid for these [Dryzek, 1987: 32–33].
2. John Dryzek describes the market as a means of social organisation defined by free and open material exchange among its participants [Dryzek, 1987: 69]. Polyarchy is defined as a social choice mechanism which produces collective choice as the outcome of interactions between relatively large numbers of actors, where there is constitutional protection against authority [Dryzek, 1987: 110–11].
3. For a discussion of anarchism and Marxist theory as direct democracy, see Held [1987]; for a discussion of the impact these ideas have had on environmentalism, see Eckersley [1992].
4. Some of the variation between participatory authors can be quite significant. Iris Young, for example, does not emphasise face to face participation in public deliberation - indeed, Young has expressed concern that privileging face to face discussion can ignore the way power inequalities enter these speaking situations [Young, 1990].
5. For a discussion of different definitions of intrinsic value, see O'Neil [1993].
6. Robyn Eckersley notes the enthusiasm many environmental writers have for direct citizen participation in decision making. She makes the distinction between the anthropocentric ecological perspective which 'is characterised by its concern to articulate an ecopolitical theory that offers new opportunities for human emancipation and fulfilment in an ecologically sustainable society ... ' and an ecocentric approach which ... 'pursues these same goals in the context of a broader notion of emancipation that also recognises the moral standing of the non-human world and seeks to ensure that it, too, may unfold in its many diverse ways' [Eckersley, 1992: 26].
7. This expression is Young's [1994]; for discussion in an environmental context, see Paehlke and Torgerson [1990] and DeLeon [1992].
8. New Left ideals of active political participation have also re-emerged on the agenda of other international environmental organisations - although these ideals have often been reworked by ecocentric greens to try to reconcile citizen autonomy with claims of moral standing for the non-human world [Eckersley, 1992: 18].
9. For example, Sections 88 and 99 of the Resource Management Act, 1991 enable local and regional councils to initiate mediation or face to face discussion to develop local or regional plans and policy statements.
10. Parekh [1993] describes the situation in which a society, deeply divided on religious or ethnic lines, may erupt in intra-community violence if inflamed by the campaigns associated with liberal democracies, but his caution about universalising any form of democracy is timely.
11. Dryzek has elaborated on this idea in his contribution to this collection (editor's note).
12. K.M. Johnson 1994, personal communication (Palmeston North City Council, New Zealand).

REFERENCES

Arendt, Hannah (1963), On Revolution, London: Penguin.
'Back To The Future', Policy Sciences, Vol.27, pp.77–95.
Barber, Benjamin (1984), Strong Democracy: Participatory Politics for a New Age, Berkeley: University of California Press.

Bartlett, Robert V. (1986), 'Ecological Rationality: Reason and Environmental Policy' *Environmental Ethics*, Vol.8, pp.221–39.

Beetham David (1993), 'Liberal Democracy and the Limits of Democratization', in David Held (ed.), *Prospects for Democracy: North, South, East, West*, Cambridge: Polity Press.

Begon M., Harper, J., and C. Townsend (1986), *Ecologies: Individuals, Populations and Communities*, Oxford: Blackwell.

Bührs, Ton and Robert V. Bartlett, (1993), *Environmental Policy In New Zealand: The Politics of Clean and Green?*, *Oxford Readings in New Zealand Politics*. Auckland: Oxford University Press.

Cleveland, Les (1972), *The Anatomy of Influence: Pressure Groups and Politics in New Zealand*, Wellington: Hicks Smith & Sons.

Deleon, Peter (1992), 'The Democratization of the Policy Sciences', *Public Administrative Review*, Vol.52, No.2, pp.125–9.

Deleon, Peter (1994), 'Reinventing the Policy Sciences: Three Steps Back to the Future', *Policy Sciences*, Vol.27, pp.77–95.

Dryzek, John S. (1987), *Rational Ecology: Environment and Political Economy*, Oxford: Blackwell.

Dryzek, John S. (1990), *Discursive Democracy: Politics, Policy and Political Science*, Cambridge: Cambridge University Press.

Dryzek, John S. (1992 a), 'Ecology and Discursive Democracy: Beyond Liberal Capitalism and the Administrative State', *Capitalism, Nature, Socialism*, Vol.3, pp.18–42.

Dryzek, John S. (1992b), 'The Good Society Versus the State: Freedom and Necessity in Political Innovation', *The Journal of Politics*, Vol.54, No.2, pp.518–40.

Dryzek, John S. and Jeffrey Berejikian (1993), 'Reconstructive Democratic Theory', *American Political Science Review*, Vol.87, No.1, pp.48–60.

Eckersley, Robyn (1992), *Environmentalism and Political Theory: Toward an Ecocentric Approach*, Albany, NY: State University of New York Press.

Fischer, Frank (1993), 'Citizen Participation and the Democratisation of Policy Expertise', *Policy Sciences*, Vol.26, pp.165–87.

Fishkin, James S. (1991), *Democracy and Deliberation*, New Haven, CT: Yale University Press

Goodin, Robert E. (1992), *Green Political Theory*, Cambridge: Polity Press.

Handbook of Environmental Law (1992), Wellington: Royal Forest and Bird Protection Society of New Zealand Inc.

Harris, Paul (1993), 'Politics of a Small Democracy' New Zealand Political Science Association Annual Conference, Christchurch (NZ): University of Canterbury.

Hay, P.R. and M.G. Haward (1988), 'Comparative Green Politics: Beyond the European Context?', *Political Studies*, Vol.XXXVI, pp.433–48.

Hayward, Bronwyn M. (1991), 'Getting Heard in the Green Debate: Environmental Policy and Strong Democracy in New Zealand', *Sites: A Journal for Radical Perspectives on Culture*, Vol.22, pp.54–63.

Hayward, Bronwyn M. (1993), 'Participatory Democracy: Questions Raised by Feminist Involvement with Practice and Theory', *Political Science*, Vol.45, pp.27–39.

Heilbroner, Robert l. (1974), *An Inquiry into The Human Prospect*, New York: W.W.Norton.

Held, David (1987), *Models of Democracy*, Cambridge: Polity Press.

Held, David (1993), *Prospects for Democracy: North, South, East, West*, Cambridge: Polity Press.

Hillier, J. (1993), 'To Boldly Go Where No Planners Have Ever Gone Before'. *Environment and Planning D: Society and Space*, Vol.11, pp. 89–113

Ingram, Helen and Steven Rathgeb Smith (eds.), (1993), *Public Policy For Democracy*, Washington DC: The Brookings Institution.

Irwin, Kathy (1992), 'Towards Theories of Maori Feminisms', in Rosemary DuPlessis *et al.* (eds.), *Feminist Voices: Women's Studies Texts for Aotearoa/New Zealand*, Auckland: Oxford University Press.

Jaggar, Alison (1983), *Feminist Politics and Human Nature*, Brighton: Harvester.

Keane John (1988), *Democracy and Civil Society*, London: Verso.

Laird, Frank (1993), 'Participatory Analysis, Democracy, and Technological Decision Making',

Science, Technology and Human Values, Vol.18, No.3, pp.341–61.

Macpherson, C.B. (1973), Democratic Theory: Essays in Retrieval, Oxford: Clarendon Press.

Macpherson, C.B. (1977), The Life and Times of Democracy, Oxford: Oxford University Press.

Memon, P. Ali (1993), Keeping New Zealand Green: Recent Environmental Reforms, Dunedin: University of Otago Press.

Milbrath, Lester W. (1984), Environmentalists: Vanguard for A New Society, Albany, NY: State University of New York Press.

Miller, David (1992), 'Deliberative Democracy and Social Choice', Political Studies, Vol.XL (Special Issue), pp.54–67.

Mulgan, Richard (1984), 'Who Should Have How Much to Say about What? Some Problems in Pluralist Democracy', Political Science, Vol.36, No.2, pp.112–24.

Mulgan, Richard (1993), 'The Elective Dictatorship in New Zealand', in Hyam Gold (ed.), New Zealand Politics in Perspective (3rd edition), Auckland: Longman Paul.

Nelson, William (1980), On Justifying Democracy, London: Routledge & Kegan Paul.

O'Neil, John (1993), Ecology, Policy and Politics: Human Well-Being and the Natural World, London: Routledge.

Ophuls, William (1977), Ecology and the Politics of Scarcity, San Francisco, CA: Freeman.

Paehlke, Robert and Douglas Torgerson (eds.) (1990), Managing Leviathan: Environmental Politics and the Administrative State, London: Belhaven Press.

Palmer, Geoffrey (1987), Unbridled Power (2nd edition). Auckland: Oxford University Press.

Parekh, Bhikhu (1993), 'The Cultural Particularity of Liberal Democracy', in Held (ed.) [1993].

Parkin, Sara (1989), Green Parties: An International Guide, London: Heretic Books.

Pateman, Carole (1970), Participation and Democratic Theory, Cambridge: Cambridge University Press.

Pateman, Carole (1988), Sexual Contract, Cambridge: Cambridge University Press.

Pateman, Carole (1989), The Disorder of Women: Democracy, Feminism and Political Theory, Cambridge: Cambridge University Press.

Porritt, Jonathon (1984), Seeing Green: The Politics of Ecology Explained, Cambridge: Blackwell.

Rainbow, Steven (1993), Green Politics. Critical Issues in New Zealand Politics. No.5. Auckland: Oxford University Press.

Robynson, David (1993), 'Public Participation In Environmental Decision Making', Environmental and Planning Law Journal, Oct. pp.321–9.

The Ecologist (1993), Whose Common Future? Reclaiming the Commons, London: Earthscan.

Warren, Mark (1992) 'Democratic Theory and Self Transformation', American Political Science Review, Vol.6, No. 1, pp.8–23.

Wilson, Roger (1982), From Manapouri to Aramoana: The Battle for New Zealand's Environment, Auckland: Earthworks Press.

World Commission on Environment and Development (1987), Our Common Future, Oxford: Oxford University Press.

Young, Iris Marion (1986), 'The Ideal of Community and the Politics of Difference', Social Theory and Practice, Vol.12, No.1, pp.1–27.

Young, Iris Marion (1990), Justice and the Politics of Difference, Princeton, N.J.: Princeton University Press.

Young, Iris Marion (1992), 'Recent Theories of Justice' Social Theory and Practice, Vol.18, No.1, pp.63–79.

Young, Iris Marion (1994), 'Communication and the Other', manuscript; a later version of this manuscript appears below in Young [1995].

Young, Iris Marion (1995), 'Communication and the Other: Beyond Deliberative Democracy', in Margaret Wilson and Anna Yeatman (eds.), Justice and Identity: Antipodean Practices, Wellington: Bridget Williams Books.

Printed in Great Britain
by Amazon

25620145R00137